SAS GREAT ESCAPES THREE

Damien Lewis

SAS

GREAT ESCAPES THREE

**GRIPPING TRUE ESCAPE STORIES
EXECUTED BY WORLD WAR TWO HEROES**

QUERCUS

First published in Great Britain in 2024 by

QUERCUS

Quercus Editions Ltd
Carmelite House
50 Victoria Embankment
London EC4Y 0DZ

An Hachette UK company

A CIP catalogue record for this book is available
from the British Library

HB ISBN 978 1 52942 943 5
TPB ISBN 978 1 52942 944 2
Ebook ISBN 978 1 52942 945 9

10 9 8 7 6 5 4 3 2 1

Typeset by CC Book Production
Printed and bound in Great Britain by Clays Ltd, Elcograf S.p.A.

Papers used by Quercus Editions Ltd are from well-managed forests and other responsible sources.

For:

Teän Roberts, for doing so much to truly bring
the Great Escapes series to life.

And for the Great Escapees
as depicted in these pages.

Picture Credits

Picture credits (in order of appearance): 1, 3, 16, 20, 21 – Imperial War Museum; 2 – National Army Museum/Crown; 4, 22 – Author's collection; 5 – *Western Morning News*, 17 February 1941; 6 – *Evening Despatch*, 17 February 1941; 7 – Paradata.org; 8, 9, 10, 11 – Gerald Hough; 12, 13, 15 – *SAS and the Met*, Challenor & Draper, Leo Cooper, 1990; 14 – Wikipedia Commons; 17, 18, 19 – Catherine and Gerald Cary-Elwes.

'Let us go forward together'

Winston Churchill

Contents

Author's Note

There are sadly few survivors from the Second World War operations depicted in these pages. Throughout the writing of this book I have endeavoured to be in contact with as many as possible, plus surviving family members. If there are further witnesses to the stories told here who are inclined to come forward, please do get in touch, as I will endeavour to include further recollections in future editions.

The time spent by Allied servicemen and women as Special Forces was often traumatic and wreathed in layers of secrecy, and many chose to take their stories to their graves. Memories tend to differ and apparently none more so than those concerning operations behind enemy lines. The written accounts that do exist can tend to differ in their detail and timescale, and locations and chronologies are sometimes contradictory. That being said, I have endeavoured to provide an accurate sense of place, timescale and narrative to the stories depicted here. Where various accounts appear particularly confused, the methodology I have used is the 'most likely' scenario: if two or more testimonies or sources point to a particular time or place or sequence of events, I have treated that account as most likely.

The above notwithstanding, any mistakes herein are entirely of my own making and I would be happy to correct them in future editions.

My website – www.damienlewis.com – is the best means by which to make contact with me.

Chapter One

A COLOSSUS GETAWAY

Italy, 10 February 1941

With a distinctive crack the canopy of the 'chute snapped open. The night was clear, a full moon casting a soft glow over the Italian countryside. Suspended beneath the billowing expanse of silk was twenty-one-year-old Alfred Parker, until not long ago serving with 238 Field Company, Royal Engineers. Having recently volunteered for 'Special Service' and 'hazardous duties', Parker was now a sapper – an explosives and demolitions expert – embedded within 11 Special Air Service Brigade (11 SAS). And that unit was now engaged in the first ever airborne operation mounted by British forces anywhere in the world.

Above him, the Whitley Mark V – a twin-engine medium bomber more affectionately known as 'The Flying Barn Door', this one converted for airborne operations – executed a ponderous turn, as it headed away southwards. It had just completed what had been a decidedly perilous flight. One of eight such warplanes that had set off from Malta earlier that evening, the pilot, Sub-Lieutenant Hoad, was more than a little relieved to have finally managed to drop his charges.

As he drifted beneath his 'chute, Parker eyed the rocky hill-side below. It was rushing up to meet him at what seemed like perilous speed. He braced himself for landfall. A few moments later he hit, rolling to one side to break the impact, and just as he had been taught to do at the Central Landing Establishment (CLE), at Ringway, near Manchester, the base at which parachut-ists were being trained. As no one had ever executed airborne operations in the history of British warfare, Ringway had proved something of a Heath Robinson affair – employing circus acro-bats, stuntmen, First World War pilot veterans and anyone else with the remotest idea of how to leap from great heights without getting injured or killed.

Tonight, over these moon-washed Italian mountains, was to be their first great test. Could such a means of waging-warfare really deliver? Could parachutists really cross hundreds of miles of enemy territory, and drop over a pinpoint target, as Parker and his cohorts were tasked to do, striking hard and fast deep behind enemy lines? Would such unexpected deep-penetration missions really strike fear and consternation into the hearts of the enemy, as Britain's airborne planners intended? And would such airborne operations – something that Winston Churchill had demanded be used against the Nazi and Fascist enemy at every opportunity – really deliver the edge that Britain's wartime leader hungered for?

Getting to his feet, Parker hit the quick release catch on his parachute harness and gathered in the expanse of silk. Just yards away, the other four members of his stick – a group of para-troopers dropped from a single aircraft – were doing likewise.

Tonight, Parker and his cohort were supposed to be making military history. Codenamed Operation Colossus, theirs was the first such mission to be conducted by British paratroopers, so the stakes were inordinately high. But it was immediately obvious to Parker that something was wrong.

Apart from the five of them, there was not a soul visible across the entire expanse of the deep valley into which they had been dropped. By rights, there should have been dozens of fellow paratroopers – their comrades on Operation Colossus – on all sides. But the entire expanse of terrain seemed deserted. Equally, the massive, blocky form of the Tragino Aqueduct, their target, was nowhere to be seen. And in a final blow, there was zero sign of the canisters that should have been dropped alongside them, each of which was stuffed full of the explosives that were the tools of the trade for Parker and his comrades. In short, they had been 'tipped out into the wrong gorge', as Parker concluded, and with none of the kit to hand with which to blast that aqueduct all to hell.

Their five-man squad was commanded by Captain Gerrard Daly, 'a quiet, studious pipe-smoking officer', as Parker described him. Typically, Daly seemed remarkably calm and unperturbed by the present turn of events. After a quick study of his map, he worked out that they'd landed some six miles from where they needed to be – the Drogena Gorge, the site of the target. There, he hoped the other thirty-odd men of 'X Troop', as this team of raiders had become known, would be waiting for them. But where their explosives might have landed was anyone's guess.

The plan had been to use six warplanes to drop three-dozen parachutists directly into the Drogena Gorge, while two further aircraft would carry out a diversionary raid on the railyard at the nearby city of Foggia – the hope being that the enemy would presume that all of the British planes were engaged upon that bombing mission. The aim was to conceal the real nature of the target – the Tragino Aqueduct, which Britain's planners believed could only be destroyed by a force of men-at-arms, striking swiftly and decisively on the ground.

Three days earlier the eight aircraft had set out from RAF Mildenhall, in Suffolk, executing an epic flight to the besieged island of Malta, the jumping off point for the raid. Reflecting the massive duration those lumbering bombers had spent traversing the skies of Nazi-occupied Europe, the official report recorded that 'the force left Mildenhall about 2200 hours' and 'arrived at Malta about 0900 hours the next day'. With Malta being under constant attack from German warplanes, two of the eight Whitleys had been damaged on the runway, flying bricks and blasted debris being thrown up by falling bombs. Even so, they had been patched up by the RAF ground crews and deemed good to go.

The Whitley carrying Daly, Parker and their crew had been scheduled to take off at 1800 hours, forming one of the third wave of warplanes. It alone had been delayed. One of their party, a Corporal Chapman, had fallen sick and needed to be removed from the aircraft just as it was being readied for take-off. Due to this 'defect', as the official mission report recorded it, their aircraft, codenamed 'J for Juliet', had finally taken to the skies seventeen minutes late, and was unable to catch up with the rest of the formation.

From that point onwards their problems had snowballed. Trying to make up for lost time, the pilot had lost his way, making 'a bad landfall on the Italian coast', after which he'd flown along the path of a 'river partially obscured by mist until the Adriatic coast was reached', meaning he'd overshot the target by several dozen kilometres. He'd then made an about-turn, retraced his steps to the west coast of Italy, picked up the route of the distinctive Sele river, and had used that to fly back again towards their objective. As a result, he hadn't arrived over the target 'until 2315', meaning it was well over an hour after the main force were supposed to have been dropped. As a final blow, somehow the canisters packed with explosives had failed to arrive, which cut against the entire purpose of the mission.

Even so, Captain Daly reasoned only one option remained open to him and his men. They would need to scale the high ridge that separated them from the neighbouring Drogena Gorge, joining the main force of raiders at the target. Once there, they could take a view on how on earth the aqueduct was to be brought down. Other aircraft had carried reserve supplies of explosives; hopefully some of that at least had been dropped in the right place and would be to hand.

As a concept, Operation Colossus was bold and daring in the extreme. The idea was to employ a group of fledgling parachutists, dropping them virtually on top of the intended target, which they would proceed to destroy, before being rescued by a British submarine waiting off Italy's west coast. That escape and evasion would entail a forced march of around a hundred kilometres across Italy's snowbound Apennine mountains, in the depths of winter.

An undertaking of immense audacity, Operation Colossus had been masterminded by the head of Combined Operations, Sir Roger Keyes, a distinguished Royal Navy commander from the First World War, whose flagship had been the dreadnought battleship HMS *Colossus* (surely no coincidence). Keyes was no stranger to high stakes and daredevil missions, having commanded the Zeebrugge Raid in 1918, an attack on the German-held Belgian port of that name, which had resulted in no less than eight Victoria Crosses being awarded to those who had taken part. Following the June 1940 defeat of France, Churchill had called for the raising of seaborn and airborne 'commandos', to execute 'butcher and bolt raids' on the enemy, Keyes becoming one of his most ardent supporters.

The Tragino Aqueduct had first been mooted as a possible target by the planners at what had become known as the 'Fourth Armed Service' – the Special Operations Executive (SOE). Formed at Churchill's behest and charged to break all the known rules of war, SOE would earn the entirely fitting nickname of the 'Ministry for Ungentlemanly Warfare'. Operation Colossus would typify what that name espoused. The target had been chosen as it was 'almost the only source of pure water to the Province of Apulia . . . an area comprising two million inhabitants, many engaged in important industries'. If the mission was successful, the whole province 'including Taranto, Brindisi, Bari and Foggia' – some of Italy's key naval ports – would have their fresh water supplies cut 'for at least a month, by destroying the bridge carrying the Apulian Aqueduct over the stream at Tragino'.

In a 'Most Secret' planning document, it was ruled that a successful attack could force a decisive change in direction of the Italian war machine, especially as the area was 'full of military, naval and air force' bases. 'Mussolini and the Italian High Command may . . . be dubious of the advisability of continuing an unsuccessful campaign on two fronts (Albania and Greece),' the report advised, 'and the complete stoppage of drinking water to their main ports of shipment may be the deciding factor and cause immediate plans for withdrawal on one or two fronts.' It was the tantalising chance of striking such a decisive blow, while risking only a few dozen men-at-arms, that had made the risks associated with an undertaking like Colossus acceptable.

After all, desperate times called for desperate measures, and in the winter of 1940/41, times were indeed dark, Great Britain being the only dog in the fight, facing the might of Nazi Germany and Fascist Italy largely alone.

Of course, for Parker, and the rest of the patrol, commencing their trek over that rocky Italian hillside, all of that was immaterial right now. They had been sent in to do a job of vital importance, but the chances of them completing their task appeared to have been all but snuffed out from the moment that Chapman had taken ill and their plane delayed. Or so they imagined. Yet as luck would have it, all of that was about to change.

As the five men wound their way higher into the mountains, the roar of a massive explosion cut through the night. Though distant, and muffled by the ridgeline towering above them, immediately they recognised those sounds that echoed through the gorge for what they were: it had to be their brothers in arms detonating their charges on the far side of the ridge. Whether they had succeeded in bringing down the Tragino Aqueduct remained to be seen, but the very fact that the attackers had struck a blow raised their spirits immensely.

At the Drogena Gorge their comrades had been busy as hell. An hour or so earlier, thirty figures had drifted down by parachute towards the target. Led by Major Trevor Alan Gordon 'Tag' Pritchard, the main body of the raiders had been released almost on top of the aqueduct itself. The first Whitley to unload its contingent of paratroopers had dropped Lieutenant Anthony Deane-Drummond, Pritchard's second-in-command, plus his stick, a mere fifty yards away from their target.

'The aqueduct stretched below and in front . . . across the steep little ravine of the Torrente Tragino, the bottom of which was covered with scrub and small trees . . . the mountainside rose steeply with a group of farm buildings fifty feet above . . .' as Deane-Drummond would describe the scene. Immediately upon touchdown he'd got to work, dispatching 'two men to search the farm building above . . . and the other three to go to the farm across the ravine, with orders to bring back all the occupants'. A few minutes later, a group of two-dozen men, women and children had been rounded up and brought to the aqueduct.

By this time Major Pritchard and the other raiders had linked up with Deane-Drummond. Realising that Daly and the demolition team were nowhere to be found, Pritchard gave the job of blowing the aqueduct to Lieutenant George Paterson, a Canadian, and one of the only sappers remaining. Deprived of Daly's force and their explosives, Pritchard had around a third of what they'd counted on to blast apart the aqueduct. With the watercourse raised up on three pillars to cross the deep gorge, Paterson hoped he still had enough explosives to try to blow just one column, not all three as they had originally intended. But it would be touch and go.

The Italian captives – all civilians – were taken to a nearby farmhouse and put under guard. Fearing for their lives, they did as they were told. But when Pritchard learned that some of the canisters containing the explosives had been dropped three-quarters of a mile away, he decided to use the male prisoners to go and collect them. That would 'free the sappers for their skilled work of preparing the demolition', while the rest of his men fanned out and stood guard. Deane-Drummond took command of that 'work party', as Italian villagers, laden with their loads, hurried back and forth through the darkness, ferrying the charges to the place of their intended detonation.

Just short of midnight Paterson declared himself ready. The raiders pulled back to positions set in a semi-circle around the target, while Pritchard sent a runner to Deane-Drummond to call off the carrying parties. But as Deane-Drummond settled into cover 'on the track by the farm buildings where the Italians were', he spotted another, smaller bridge, which was wide enough to carry a truck to the aqueduct. Realising this could be used by Italian repair parties, if and when the aqueduct was destroyed, he set about planting any charges that were left over on that. This wasn't simply a good tactical idea but, as he admitted later, it was also 'for the fun of the thing'.

By 0015 hours all the charges were set. The Italian porters were returned to their families, as everyone took cover.

At precisely 0029 hours on 11 February 1941, the charges were detonated.

A massive, roaring explosion ripped apart the night, reverberating around the gorge and far beyond – which was the blast that Daly, Parker and their team had heard in the neighbouring valley. A storm of blasted debris tore across the rocky terrain, raining down in every direction, as all was engulfed in a thick cloud of dust and smoke. Gradually the air cleared, to reveal a wonderful sight. The western column holding up the aqueduct had buckled and collapsed, bringing down the waterway, the precious liquid cascading down in wild abandon, and draining into the stream that ran through the valley's depths.

A ragged cheer erupted from all who had been watching.

Against all odds, Operation Colossus had struck a blow for the Allies. Airborne operations had just come of age.

Some thirty seconds later, a further explosion rang out, catching most by utter surprise. Not having had time to warn everyone, Pritchard was taken aback as much as anyone as to the ferocity of the blast. 'Large lumps of concrete and rail . . . fell all around,' he would recount, as the bridge was torn into utter oblivion. Where Deane-Drummond was holed up, they were assailed by a barrage of debris, as chunks of blasted concrete smashed onto the roof of the farm buildings where the civilians had taken shelter. Fortunately, the roof held up, although those inside were scared out of their skin. Deane-Drummond confessed later that 'he had forgotten all about them' when he had decided that bridge should be blown.

With a torrent of water cascading down the ravine in a very satisfying manner, Pritchard examined the devastation he and his small band of raiders had wrought. The supporting column had completely collapsed. As a result, 'the waterway had broken in two where it had been supported. The two halves were sloping up to the abutment and the central pier, with the broken ends in the bed of the torrent.' In short, despite the limited explosives they'd had to hand, it was mission well and truly accomplished.

Gathering his men, Pritchard split them into three parties. With the objective taken care of, now was the time to get as far away as possible, and before the Italian army flooded the area with troops. This was now the escape and evasion phase of the mission. Reluctantly, Pritchard was forced to leave one man behind. Lance Corporal Harry Boulter had broken his ankle upon landing and was unable to move. Leaving Boulter with his trusty Tommy gun plus a supply of tinned food, the three groups set out towards Italy's distant western coastline, and the rendezvous with that British submarine which should be poised to pluck them all to safety.

In the neighbouring valley, Daly, Parker and their patrol reasoned there was little point in making for the target any more. As they fully appreciated, even now their brother raiders would be heading for the hills, with escape firmly in mind. Similarly, for them the driving imperative now was to make their getaway – which meant heading for that distant rendezvous. At the mouth of the River Sele – the same feature that their pilot had used as his handrail to guide him into the target – a submarine, HMS *Triumph*, was due to pick them up in six days' time.

Captain Daly ordered his men to dispose of 'all unnecessary equipment.' Parker, plus Lance Corporal Tomlin, and Sappers Davidson and Prior, began to dump all excess weight. They would need to travel light and fast, as they had a great distance to cover over high, rough and often snow-bound terrain. Once they had their kit pared down to the bare minimum, Daly indicated the course they would follow, before they set off towards the coast.

They pressed on all through that first night, conscious they had to make good progress if they were to make the pick-up in time. But conditions from the outset proved arduous. The steep hillsides, thick with mud, and snow in the higher reaches, made the going extremely tough. Deep ravines and gullies had to be circumvented, and freezing mountain streams forded, each involving an icy soaking.

After some time they came across tracks in the snow. Daly, convinced that it was another party of X Troop, decided to change course and follow, hoping to link up with them. 'After negotiating more deep mud and snow ... [we] succeeded in finding a more solid path,' Parker noted, one that looked as if it might have been forged by their fellow raiders. But still the way ahead appeared utterly deserted and woebegone. By dawn, they had covered some considerable distance, but hadn't come across another living soul. If the track they were following had been made by their comrades, there was no sign of them anywhere.

Tired and freezing cold, they needed to find somewhere to rest up for the day. Discovering an abandoned hut on the hillside, they entered, threw down their kitbags and weapons, and broke out their sleeping bags. They settled down to well-earned rest, as they tried to recuperate and recharge their batteries, before continuing on their way come dusk.

The following night they made similar progress, despite the harshness of the weather and mountainous terrain, but still there wasn't the barest sign of any of their fellow raiders. Yet they were acutely aware that they weren't alone on those mountain heights. At one point they 'heard sounds of pursuit and of dogs' echoing through the freezing night air. Having shaken off the hunters in the darkness, they resolved to 'lay up in a ravine' and to move on only come nightfall.

On the third night the weather truly turned. They stumbled into a terrifying blizzard. At first they trudged slowly ahead, hoping to press onwards and break through the worst. But the weather was so bad – the conditions a swirling, blinding whiteout – that they found they'd lost all direction and were 'travelling in a circle'. Finally the five fugitives came across 'a very isolated farmhouse'. In desperation, they approached 'in the hope of getting some food off the owners', plus maybe finding a little shelter. But the occupants appeared so terrified at spying these strangers who had emerged from the storm that they locked and barred their doors. Daly, Parker and the others had no option but to press on into the howling darkness.

When the morning of 15 February dawned, Daly realised how dire was their predicament. The majority of the food carried by the men of X Troop was 'pemmican' – a type of ration made from ground-up tallow (beef or mutton fat), dried meat and berries. In theory of very high calorific value, in practice it had proved repulsive, and those who had tried to eat it had ended up vomiting. They'd fallen back on the few reserves they had – mostly chocolate, biscuits and raisins. But there was nowhere near enough of that, and especially in conditions such as these.

Daly reckoned they were still some thirty kilometres short of their rendezvous with HMS *Triumph*, which was set for the following night. They were never going to make it if they stuck to their rule of moving only during the hours of darkness. So it was that the decision was made to travel during daylight hours, in a last-ditch effort to make their 2200 hours deadline the following evening. Pressing ahead through that morning, the five men stumbled onwards, until exhaustion and fatigue seemed to have them beaten. Hungry, cold and terribly fatigued, 'it was clear they could not go much further.'

Spotting a café on the edge of the small town of Palomonte, Captain Daly had an idea. If they could masquerade as German troops, perhaps they could bluff their way inside, order a taxi for Naples, and then commandeer the vehicle to speed them to their real destination – that coastal rendezvous with the submarine. Deciding upon a cover story, the five SAS fugitives approached the door to the café, knowing that they were taking their fate in their hands.

Adopting a confidence none of them were feeling, they entered. Finding a free table, they sat down. All eyes were fixed on these bedraggled soldiers in their strange looking uniforms. Leaving Captain Daly to do the talking, the others took out their cigarettes for a much-needed smoke. Daly began explaining to those inside that they were a Luftwaffe aircrew, and that their plane had crashed in the mountains. Having outlined their need for a taxi, for they were urgently awaited in Naples, he 'ordered coffee, and a few cigarettes were lit'. All they had to do now was man it out and await their ride.

As the British soldiers puffed away, someone spotted that the matches they had used were of a British variety. Unbeknown to them, the authorities were alerted, and it wasn't long before a group of Italian soldiers had the café surrounded. An officer entered and for a while Captain Daly 'persisted with the bluff that they were Luftwaffe airmen'. But he was fooling no one, least of all the Italian officer, who could clearly see by their uniforms that they were British. Finally, 'the local mayor arrived' and 'asked for papers'. With none being forthcoming, it was at this point that Parker and the rest knew the game was up. Being in no position to make a fight of it, the five men surrendered.

They had come so close, yet had fallen at the last hurdle.

In his escape report, written in November 1943, Parker would note simply: 'at 1100 hours we were captured by a mixture of soldiers, carabinieri and civilians.' The moment was one of intense drama, which those few terse words failed to reflect. Being so close to the coast and to rescue, their capture had had a devastating effect on the morale of the men. But while they were not to know it, their arduous trek had all been in vain, and equally so for all of the Operation Colossus parties. It was Daly and Parker's patrol that

14

had got the furthest, and they were the last to be caught. But even had they made the rendezvous, no submarine would have emerged to pluck them off the Italian coast and spirit them to safety.

Long before that moment, HMS *Triumph* been turned around and ordered back to her base, effectively abandoning the men of X Troop to their fate. The reasons behind this decision were complex, but it boiled down to two unfortunate twists of fate. In the first, one of the two Whitleys tasked with the diversionary raid over Foggia had developed engine trouble. Codenamed 'S for Sugar' and piloted by Pilot Officer Jack Wotherspoon, the aircraft was unable to make it back to Malta. Realising this, Wotherspoon had sent out a 'Mayday' call, advising that he would try to ditch the stricken aircraft near the Sele Estuary. By a cruel twist of fate, that happened to be the exact same spot as where X Troop were supposed to rendezvous with the *Triumph*.

Wotherspoon's choice was one of pure coincidence. He had absolutely no knowledge of X Troop's pick-up point. That information was known only to the submarine captain, X Troop's officers, and senior command. What had made matters worse was that the Mayday transmission had been made using the *Syko* code, a cypher that the Admiralty knew the Italians could break. In a second unfortunate twist of fate, a British reconnaissance flight had been made over the area of the Tragino Aqueduct, and photos had been taken. But as they were shot from directly above, and as the aqueduct had collapsed vertically downwards, they seemed to show that the target remained undamaged. That, at least, was the conclusion drawn by those who had studied the photos back at Malta. So it was that the decision was reached that Colossus had failed, and that very likely all the raiders had been killed or captured before they had reached their target.

As various messages had winged back and forth from Malta to London, an unholy row had broken out. On the morning of 11 February, so just hours after the aqueduct had been blown, a 'Hush Most Secret' signal had been dispatched from the Vice Admiral, Malta, Sir Wilbraham Ford, to the Admiralty, London, advising of S for Sugar's *Syko* Mayday call, and that the submarine pick-up point might have been blown. 'Compromise of this signal is possible,' the Vice Admiral warned. 'Am sailing HMS TRIUMPH as previously arranged and have instructed him to proceed with utmost care. I am asking AOC [Air Officer Commanding] Mediterranean to reconnoitre bay concerned near date of withdrawal to see if there is enemy patrol activity.'

While Sir Wilbraham Ford hadn't called off X Troop's pick-up, he was counselling caution. In London, the First Sea Lord, Sir Dudley Pound, baulked. At a War Cabinet Chiefs of Staff Committee meeting on the morning of 13 February, he argued, 'the enemy would now probably be aware of the rendezvous . . .' and he 'considered it wrong to risk the probable loss of a valuable submarine and its crew against the possibility of bringing off a few survivors.' At the same meeting Sir Charles Portal, Chief of the Air Staff, reported that reconnaissance photographs appeared to show the aqueduct still intact and 'it was probable that most, if not all, of the personnel had been killed or rounded up.' (Of course, the photographs had been misinterpreted.) The committee then 'agreed with the Admiralty proposal to cancel the submarine and instructed the Secretary to inform the Prime Minister of this decision'.

That afternoon, a 'Hush Most Secret' signal was sent from the Admiralty to Ford, in Malta, ordering him to recall the submarine. The message simply said, 'Investigations show that it is most probable that Syko message made by the aircraft has compromised the withdrawal orders. HMS TRIUMPH is to be recalled forthwith and the withdrawal operation cancelled.'

Unsurprisingly, that order did not sit well with Sir Roger Keyes, head of Combined Operations, who had personally seen off the men of X Troop on the evening of their departure. He felt a deep sense of responsibility to each of them. He drafted a message to the Prime Minister imploring him to intervene: 'In view of the fact that there is 100 fathoms of water within seven miles of the rescue position . . . I consider our failure to make any effort to carry out the salvage arrangements, promised to the parachutists, amounts to a clear breach of faith. I do beg of you to instruct the decision whether the rescue is to be attempted or not be left to the Vice Admiral Malta who . . . is the authority on the spot.'

But despite Keyes' best efforts, and his personal appeal to Churchill, HMS *Triumph* had already been recalled and X Troop had been left to fend for themselves. And unaware of the arguments that were raging at the very highest levels of British command, Daly, Parker and their comrades were now in the custody of the Italians.

Handcuffed, they were rushed by car to a civilian jail in Naples, a good forty-five miles to the north-west of where they had been captured. Once there, one by one the captives were separated, Parker being placed in solitary confinement for three long days. From time to time, he was brought before Italian officers and interrogated about the mission that he and his fellow raiders had undertaken. After giving his name, rank and army number, Parker answered all subsequent questions with the simple words: 'I can't say.' Though he was repeatedly threatened with being shot, no such haranguing would persuade him to give his interrogators a jot more.

Alfred Parker had been born and raised in Sheffield, South

Yorkshire, known as the 'Steel City' due to the predominance of the steel industry in shaping the city's fortunes. Leaving school at the age of fourteen, he'd managed to get a job at 'a small motor repair garage'. Over the next four years he'd become a highly skilled motor mechanic, nurturing a burning interest in motorcycles and racing. At the age of eighteen he'd started his own motorcycle-repair business, using some of the money he made to create innovative designs for 'incorporating under-slung petrol tanks in pannier fashion' on racing bikes. He'd gone on to take up a job at Hatfields, a motorcycle agents in Sheffield. His natural aptitude for engineering and mechanics were to play a huge part in the months following Parker's capture in Italy.

When war broke out in September 1939, Parker was eager to enlist in the armed forces. But on arrival at a Sheffield recruiting centre, he was greeted with a sign declaring that 'only those over the age of 21 would be accepted.' Being just nineteen, Parker was two years too young – in theory. In practice, much leeway was being shown. Parker was given the wink that the recruiters weren't asking to see birth certificates. So he straightened his shoulders, gave his date of birth as 21 March 1918 and was duly signed up. That false date-of-birth would be on all Parker's army records for the rest of his life.

With his gift for mechanics, Parker was posted to 238 Field Company, Royal Engineers, following basic training. The following summer he'd found himself in France and Belgium with the British Expeditionary Force. His skills with the tools of his trade saw him, and his good friend George Mays – the unit's two mechanics – exempted from the more mundane duties the other soldiers had to endure. But like thousands of other British soldiers, he found himself back in England in June 1940, following the fall of France, part of a vanquished army and a nation that appeared to be staring defeat in the face.

But that summer, at Winston Churchill's behest, the fightback had begun. Churchill called for the formation of 'troops of the hunter class' to foment 'a reign of terror down the enemy coast', asking for volunteers to join 'Special Service' units – groups of commandos tasked to take the fight back to the Nazi enemy wherever he may be. Churchill sought to 'raise a force of 10,000 parachutists', having seen how efficiently the Germans had used their *Fallschirmjäger* (airborne) units in France and Belgium. Sensing this was the chance to join a new outfit that promised adventure, and the chance to strike back hard, Parker had volunteered. After a highly demanding selection process, he was duly accepted. This was some achievement for the youthful Parker, especially since of the thousands who had stepped forward to answer Churchill's call, less than five per cent had made it through to the commandos and associated outfits.

After further intense training, Parker had joined No. 2 Commando. In November 1940 this unit was redesignated the '11th Special Air Service Battalion', and it had began parachute training at Ringway, Manchester. The word 'Air' had been inserted into the 'Special Service' designation, to reflect the fact that they would be dropped into action by parachute. The '11th' was supposed to suggest to the enemy that there were at least ten more units of the same ilk, in a deliciously simple deception.

When 11 SAS Brigade had been tasked with Operation Colossus – the very first airborne operation by British forces – all 450 men making up the unit had volunteered, even though they'd been warned that capture could mean being shot as spies. This had meant that 11 SAS's Commanding Officer, Lieutenant

19

Colonel Jackson, had been able to select thirty-six of his best men to form X Troop, Parker, of course, being one.

By mid-February 1941 all of that seemed in the long-distant past. Sitting in his cell in Italy, Parker contemplated a fate that appeared unrelentingly dark.

On 22 February, a week after their capture, the Operation Colossus captives were taken to the military prison in Naples. On arrival Parker realised the worst: 'The prison was bounded by a 25 foot high stone wall with patrol posts,' making escape all-but impossible. A thorough search was made of his person, numerous hidden escape and evasion devices being discovered, including 'maps, money and saws' – that last being a mini-hacksaw-like blade secreted in his uniform. To Parker, it seemed as if the 'searchers . . . know where to look', which he found highly disturbing. He consoled himself with the knowledge that 'the compass collar stud and needle were not discovered' – the tiny escape compass disguised as a button on his uniform.

Needless to say, that was a crucial piece of escape equipment.

All that summer the Operation Colossus prisoners languished in that Naples prison. Finally, on 2 October 1941, they were transferred to a bona fide POW camp – Prigione di Guerra 78 (PG78) at Sulmona, seventy-five miles to the east of Rome. They'd faced repeated threats that they were to be shot as spies. A tug-of-war seemed to have taken place between Italy's various high commands, as to whether Rome should recognise the parachutists as bona fide combatants, who should therefore be afforded all the protections due under the laws of war, or whether they should be deemed as 'captured spies', at which point trial and likely execution would follow.

The atmosphere was highly charged, following the success of their daring airborne operation. In addition to the damage they had caused to that aqueduct, those thirty-six paratroopers had struck real fear and alarm into the heart of the Italian nation and its military machine. If three-dozen such raiders might drop from the sky and strike seemingly at will, where in all of Italy was safe from such attacks? And where would Churchill's airborne fiends – those that he had charged to be his 'butcher and bolt' raiders – strike next? And how was Italy to defend herself against such a new and alarming form of warfare?

Such fears were fanned by reports in the press, as Operation Colossus had hit the news worldwide. The audacious feat had captured the imaginations of Britain and her would-be allies, even as the war itself seemed to be dogged by ill-fortune. In this Churchill had been shown to be a true visionary. He had understood, innately, that the British people needed such stories of derring-do to raise their spirits and give them the belief that the nation had the will and the wherewithal to fight; to dig deep for victory. And as with most things he did during the early months of the war, in everything he had one eye to the United States and how the news might play with President Roosevelt, and whether it might help draw the Americans into the war.

While the military high command might have written off Colossus as being a failure, there was little of that reflected in the news coverage. Just days after the parachutists had dropped in, the story broke. The venerable *Western Daily News*, founded in 1860, and covering the English West Country, ran with the headline: 'BRITAIN ADOPTS PARATROOPS. Dropped in Italy. FASCISTS SHAKEN BY DARING BLOW.' Reflecting the fear that had gripped Italy in the direct aftermath of the raid, the report continued, 'ITALY TRIES TO ALLAY ALARM. This latest daring blow at Italy obviously shook the Fascist Government, writes "The Western Morning News" Air Correspondent.'

Taking up the hue and cry, the *Evening Despatch* heralded how 'Bull-dog breed' comes out in our paratroops, as 'NAZIS ADMIT BRITISH DARING AND RESOLUTION'. Quoting from a German newspaper, the *Völkischer Beobachter*, the *Evening Despatch* reported 'admiration, not untinged with envy . . . for the British paratroops' attack on Italy . . . "The British," the German paper said, "were trying to imitate German parachutists . . . daring and resolute men have never been lacking in Britain."'

At the same time, Colossus had made headlines further afield. The American newspapers produced some of the most revealing coverage, trumpeting how 'BRITISH 'CHUTISTS SCARE DUCE PEOPLE'. That report, in the *Waco Times Herald*, then a Texas regional newspaper, was published just three days after the explosion had ripped apart the Tragino Aqueduct. It revealed how 'British parachute troops armed with machine-guns, hand-grenades and dynamite,' sought to 'blow up communications and vital water supply facilities in lower Italy'. Playing on Italian fears, London fed the newspapers hints that 'more parachute troops are at large in Italy,' as reported in the *Detroit Evening Times* on 15 February 1941.

Eventually, the very notoriety of the Colossus raiders seemed to have played in their favour, as the news reports concluded that 'the captured men are being treated as prisoners-of-war, not subject to execution as spies'. A full week after the raider's capture, the *Daily Record and Mail*, a Scottish newspaper, caught the triumphant mood of the nation, under the headline 'PRISON FOR

BRITISH PARATROOPERS'. Reporting how the captives were to be treated as bona fide POWs, it heralded how 'the work of this handful of courageous British soldiers will . . . be just as valuable as that of a full scale clash of arms between two opposing armies. The full extent of the damage inflicted . . . is not yet known, but the moral effect on the highly excitable temperament of the Italians will be considerable . . .'

For Alfred Parker, languishing in an Italian POW camp, the furore the raid had caused and the celebration of its daring at home, had largely passed him by, as would the gradual turning of the Allies' fortunes in this war. It wasn't until the first days of September 1943 – two-and-a-half long years after his capture – that Parker and his fellow POWs would witness for themselves the might of the Allied war machine that was now being turned upon Nazi-occupied and Fascist Europe.

It had just turned September 1943 when the rumbling of distant aircraft engines filled the air above their camp. Parker, busy preparing a concoction of melted cheese and breadcrumbs on a small tin stove, courtesy of the Red Cross food parcels, was intrigued enough to break off from his preparations. He'd been rustling up the feast together with his good friend, Lance Corporal George Dent, of the Royal Signals. Turning aside from the mouthwatering aroma they had created, they scanned the skies. Other prisoners claimed it was a swarm of bees, but Parker, an airborne trooper, wasn't so sure. Moments later someone spied 'the planes!'

Jostling to get a better view, Parker and Dent looked up in wonder. These were certainly no bees. And not just a few; the sky was full of mighty warplanes. The massive, gleaming forms of American B17 Flying Fortresses and Liberators – heavy four-engine bombers – seemed to fill the skies. To Parker, it seemed there were hundreds of them all in tight formation, and seemingly headed directly for Sulmona Prisoner-of-War camp – the very place where he and Dent had been incarcerated for the best part of two years.

As Parker watched, the warplanes continued to thunder ever onwards, drawing closer to the camp, and not for one moment breaking formation, even when an Italian fighter 'swept down from the right firing its guns'. A few sustained blasts from the heavily armed bombers sent it on its way. Suddenly, the air seemed to darken as it was filled with falling bombs. Suffused with relief, Parker and Dent realised the target wasn't their camp. It was the nearby town of Sulmona itself. But even from the relatively safe distance of the POW camp, they winced and ducked, as the pounding percussions of massive explosions ripped through the air. The guards in the central watchtower, scared out of their wits, scrambled down the ladder as they sought to get into cover. Unsure of what to do, one hesitated for a moment, poised on the ladder, before 'he finally deserted his post completely to the wild cheers of the prisoners', as Parker would describe the moment.

From what Parker could make out, the target was Sulmona's railway yard, but equally, it was clear that such an intense bombardment was bound to cause civilian casualties. After no more than three utterly intense minutes, and with all their ordnance dispatched, the vast airborne armada turned around and headed back towards its home base, leaving a scene of destruction in its wake. A thick pall of smoke and fire plumed above the town. Finally, Parker turned back to his makeshift feast, and let out a long sigh. While he and Dent had been transfixed by the aerial show, so their cheesy breadcrumbs had been burned to a crisp.

Life in the camp over the past two years had been far from easy. Things had not been so bad in the summer months, when the weather was fine and the Red Cross could get their food and care parcels through. The camp commandant had even allowed football and baseball pitches to be built, to give the men something to do with all the time they had to kill. Yet in the winter things had been terrible. Blaming a 'lack of transport' for the sudden absence of Red Cross parcels, food became scarce, the camp guards and commanders appearing indifferent to the hunger of those in their charge. Things had got so desperate that Parker was driven wild by hunger, confessing that 'once I ate a cat'.

While the POWs had survived in any way they could, the guards had seemed determined to do 'everything possible to foster quarrels amongst the prisoners', which fuelled suspicions that 'there were informers'. That had dampened down any plans of trying to escape. Parker also noticed that whenever the war went especially in favour of the Axis powers, 'the prisoners suffered' the most, but that in recent months their treatment had seemed to improve. On one level, he had sensed that 'the Italians never really expected to win' the war. That massive air-bombardment by American warplanes had simply underlined their fears.

A few days later, another mass air-raid took place over Sulmona, further tearing apart the town's rail yard. There was a palpable sense that change was in the air. The word on every prisoner's lips was that the Italians had had it. The end was surely near for them. Then, on 8 September 1943, it was finally announced that the Italians had surrendered unconditionally to the Allies. The following day, at noon, Parker and the rest of the prisoners were ordered to assemble on the camp's football pitch, to be addressed by the Senior British Officer (SBO) in the camp, and to be briefed on what it might all mean for them.

The SBO, a South African, proceeded to issue a very odd directive. Rather than telling the assembled POWs to break out and make for British lines, for their Italian captors were certainly not about to stop them, he had a very different set of instructions in mind. Parker, and those around him, listened in disbelief, as the SBO ordered them, in no uncertain terms, to remain exactly where they were. Under no circumstances were any of them to break out. 'He [the SBO] followed this up with a warning that in the event of anyone escaping and getting back to British lines, they would be charged with disobeying orders and court-martialled,' Parker observed. He could not believe his ears, labelling the man 'a traitor'.

This would become known as the notorious 'Stay Put Order'. Though Parker was not to know it, similar sets of instructions were being issued by SBOs in camps across Italy. Now that the Italians had surrendered, POWs were no longer classed as prisoners-of-war, and were instead viewed as serving soldiers, the Sulmona SBO explained. As he was their commanding officer, his orders were to be obeyed to the letter. Parker might well have heard the SBO's words and his warnings, but he was convinced that the man was totally wrong, and his sentiments totally misguided.

What Parker and his fellows couldn't know was that the SBO was acting on the orders of MI9 – Military Intelligence Section 9, Britain's Escape & Evasion specialists. Fearing chaos, should upwards of 80,000 British POWs suddenly find themselves roaming the Italian countryside, the Stay Put Order had been issued, wherein all POWs were to stay exactly where they were, and wait for the Allied ground forces to liberate their camps. That instruction – MI9 Order P/W 87190 – had been dispatched via coded radio signals, which were received on the clandestine wireless sets operated in most POW camps. Transmitted throughout early June and July 1943, the order stated: 'officers commanding prison camps will ensure that prisoners-of-war remain within the camp. Authority is granted to all officers . . . to take necessary disciplinary action to prevent individual prisoners-of-war attempting to rejoin their own units.'

The Stay Put Order had been overseen by MI9 chief, Brigadier Norman Crockatt, a highly decorated veteran of the First World War. Predicting that Italy would be liberated by the Allies in a matter of days, MI9 ensured that 'almost every camp's SBO received the message,' as Crockatt declared himself 'happy at what was being done'. Not all of MI9's officers agreed with the order. Some had argued vehemently against it. Worse still, it had been issued without the approval of the War Office, or the knowledge of Churchill himself.

Churchill had made it a priority for the immediate release of all POWs, once the Armistice was signed. Writing to US President Roosevelt, he'd stressed the 'highest importance' of the issue, something 'about which there will be passionate feeling in this country . . . I regard it as a matter of honour and humanity to get our own flesh and blood back as soon as possible and spare them the measureless horrors of incarceration in Germany.' Indeed, the 3rd Article of the Armistice stated that all POWs were to be 'immediately turned over to the Allied commander-in-chief and none of these may . . . be evacuated to Germany'.

Later, when it was realised what a catastrophic blunder the Stay Put Order constituted, MI9 tried to divert the blame for its origin onto Field Marshal Montgomery, at that time the commander of British forces in Italy, claiming that 'Monty . . . probably gave his directive in late May or early June.' In truth, the Stay Put Order would have the devastating effect of leaving some 30,000 Allied troops at the mercy of the forces of Nazi Germany, whose troops quickly took over the camps, shipping the prisoners north to captivity in Germany and Poland.

For Parker, and his good pal, George Dent, the order seemed utterly insane; treasonous almost. A good deal of vitriol and spite was directed at the Sulmona camp's SBO. More to the point, both men, along with scores of others in the camp, realised this was one order that only deserved one response – to be disobeyed. If they saw a chance to breakout then that was exactly what they would do, Parker and Dent being at the forefront of the would-be escapees. 'If an opportunity to escape arose, then we would not hesitate to grasp it,' Parker later wrote of this moment.

That opportunity was to come more quickly than either man had expected.

Just hours after the SBO's announcement, security at the Sulmona camp began to fall apart. While the Italians were still holding the camp perimeter, they were doing so in a slapdash manner, as they pondered just what on earth they were to do. The now-former POWs were granted 'permission for the men from one compound at a time to have a walk outside the high wall and inside the barbed wire defence system'. Sensing an opportunity, Parker and Dent took up the offer, but were surprised to see that so few others had any interest in 'seeing what lay beyond the walls'. Doubtless the threat of court martial made by the SBO had dampened any ideas they might have of getting away.

Upon reaching the camp in October of 1941, Parker had

concluded that escape was impossible. Sulmona Camp stood at the foot of the imposing Apennine mountains, with a high stone wall engirdling it, and a series of barbed-wire fences lying beyond that. Even had he managed to get outside, Parker had reasoned, where would he have sought sanctuary? But with Allied forces now advancing up the Italian peninsula, surely that changed everything.

Together with Dent, Parker proceeded to head towards the gates, as if taking a much-needed stroll to stretch their legs. Once outside the solid wall, their intention was to walk the entire length of the twenty-foot-high barbed-wire perimeter fencing, to see if they could spot 'any weak places in the defence system'. Was there any way that he and Dent could spot a weakness and effect a getaway? A gap somewhere that could be exploited?

The main entrance to the camp remained heavily guarded, with more sentries dotted along the line of the fence. As they pushed ahead, they came to a point where the ground sloped upwards. Once over this rise and strolling around the next corner, they caught sight of 'a wide farm-type gate set diagonally across the corner'. That in turn led to 'a semblance of a roadway . . . completely overgrown and obviously never used'. The gate was slightly ajar and it was guarded by a lone sentry, one who struck Parker and Dent as looking exceedingly bored.

Parker took a breath and approached the guard. Using the 'broken Italian' he'd picked up during his long years of captivity, he started chatting to the sentry, with Dent at his side. The Italian seemed 'only too pleased to break the monotony by talking with us'. Thinking on his feet, Parker spied a bright flower beyond the open gate and pointed it out. Wasn't it glorious, he suggested. Such beauty! Might he and Dent be allowed to go and pick it? At first the sentry was sceptical, but after a little cajoling he finally relented. Putting his finger to his lips in a conspiratorial manner, he gave the two men permission to go and pick their chosen bloom.

Realising they may not get another chance, Parker and Dent strolled through the gate, trying to keep as casual and relaxed looking as possible. As they bent to the flower, acting as if they were enraptured with this particularly stunning specimen of Italian flora, and tugging at the stem as if trying to uproot it, they exchanged glances.

'We're out!' hissed Parker.

Sensing this was their chance, almost in unison they whispered, 'Shall we make a run for it?'

Moments later, the decision was made.

Turning away from the sentry, they broke into a sprint, dashing down that overgrown track as if their lives depended upon it, and refusing to stop until they 'could run no further'. Dropping to the ground completely out of breath, they lay for a while, hidden in the undergrowth, but growing increasingly convinced that there were no signs of pursuit. Lying in that cover, they tried to take stock of their situation. They'd just executed an unplanned break for freedom and as such were ill prepared for the journey that lay before them. The beckoning form of the Sulmona Valley stretched out below. But all they had was what they stood up in – 'no maps, no food' and 'few escape aids of any sort'. But still they felt positive, Parker especially. This was the first time that he had been a free man, since being picked up with Captain Daly and the others on his patrol, two-and-a-half years earlier.

Parker and Dent decided to head south. It was the obvious way to go. That direction was where they would find the Allies. But how far they would have to walk they had absolutely no way of knowing. As they moved into the valley, they spotted a column of military vehicles, 'and surmised that it was a military convoy and German'. This was doubtless true, for no sooner had the Italians surrendered, than the German military began sending troops to take over the POW camps. Of course, the Stay Put Order was going to make their job a whole lot easier.

For the rest of that day the two escapees marched south, sticking to the high ground as much as they could. The weather was in their favour, being warm and dry. Eventually, after walking seven-and-a-half miles, they came to a spot which overlooked the large village of Cansano. Not being confident enough to go down and ask for help – would the locals be friendly, now that Italy and the Allies were supposedly all on the same side? – they found a small hollow and 'simply lay down together as close as possible and fell asleep'.

They awoke at around 0430, cold and damp. It was the distinctive sound of a motor vehicle that had dragged them out of their slumber. Looking out from their hideaway, they spied a German military transport passing through the village. From what they could see, Cansano was 'a collection of poverty-stricken buildings spread out in an untidy way', complete with chickens, dogs, cows and goats roaming the streets. As Parker and Dent were famished – they'd fled the camp without a scrap of food between them – they decided they had no option but to take their chances, and ask the locals for some food. If they turned out to be hostile, they figured they had enough strength to outrun any would-be pursuers.

As soon as they left their place of hiding and ventured onto the road leading into the village, they bumped into an old man, who was also heading into Cansano. Reasoning the best option was to be totally honest with him, Parker explained their predicament – they were escaped British prisoners in need of food. The elderly man turned out to speak decent English, and he quickly explained that he was no friend of the Fascists, and 'would be only too happy to help us', as Parker would describe it. He led them to his home, where his wife went about preparing them a feast. To Parker, this was 'the best meal we had had for over two-and-a-half years'. Not only that, but more food was parcelled up to sustain them on their journey.

And so, with their bodies replenished and their spirits raised to new heights, the two escapees continued on their way. As the road ahead looked deserted, they decided to take to it, to speed them southwards. Should any vehicles come their way, they reasoned they'd have ample time to dive into some cover before they were seen. They set off at a fierce pace, but as the sun rose higher in the September sky, so the hours proved taxing, for neither had a water bottle. There was no easy way to quench their thirst. Eventually they took a break in some shade. As they rested, they heard noises. It sounded as if someone might be following them.

Quick as they could, they 'hid behind a large rocky mound and waited'. Two young Italian men came into view. Figuring they could overpower them if it came to a fight, Parker and Dent stepped into view. It turned out that the men were deserters from the military, making their way home to their families, in Taranto, a city lying some 225 miles to the south, on the 'heel' of Italy. Best of all, they had water, and were happy to let Parker and Dent drink their fill.

The four men – former enemies, turned allies – decided to join forces. It was a partnership forged in mutual interest. The

Italians agreed that whenever a town or village lay before them, they would move ahead and scout for German forces. For their part, Parker and Dent would 'vouch for them if we came on the British forces', who, as all understood, were advancing up the leg of Italy. Pushing on, the partnership seemed to work well. Over the next few days the two Italians did their best to find food and shelter from friendly locals, all of whom seemed to share the same attitude – that they just wanted the war to be over. With their assistance, Parker and Dent managed to scrounge some civilian clothes, changing out of their British Army uniforms, for that way all four of them could pose as Italian civilians.

Like that, progress proved swift, but things were about to change.

By the time they reached the city of Foggia – the same place that the two Whitley bombers had targeted, while flying their diversionary raid as part of Operation Colossus – they'd covered more than 200 kilometres of their journey south. By now they could clearly hear the sounds of war. The further south they had pushed, the more common had become German troop concentrations. Parker sensed they had to proceed with extreme caution. The enemy, and the Allied, frontlines had to be close now.

It was the 22 September 1943, and they'd been on the road for two weeks. German troops were everywhere, and the four fugitives decided to keep away from the highways. In the late afternoon they scuttled across a road, heading towards some fields and a distant hilltop village. But then 'a sudden burst of machine-gun fire' erupted from the end of the village nearest them. The four froze in their tracks, as they tried to work out if the bullets were directed at them. But it seemed as if the gunners were targeting something lying to the south, in the direction of what had to be Allied lines. More guns opened up, the firing growing in a deafening crescendo, as Parker and his companions dived for cover. It seemed that they were right on the fringes of the German frontline.

Freedom was just a short distance away.

As they lay there in cover the evening shadows deepened. A latticework of tracer lit up the sky, like a crazed firework display. Though it was beautiful in a macabre sort of way, any one of those bursts of fire could kill. They had no option but to lie where they'd gone to ground, as the battle ranged all around. At first light the following day they set out once more, keeping to any thick trees and underbrush, while trying to skirt around German artillery positions that seemed to be there at every turn. After a while the inevitable happened, and they 'broke into a clearing which was occupied by a big gun and its attendant crew'. Luckily, the German gunners were too focussed on their task, and Parker and the others managed to execute an about-turn without being spotted, burrowing back into cover.

Things were now quite desperate. With so many German troops in such close proximity, the chances of discovery and capture were extremely high. But likewise, the Allied positions had to be almost within earshot, and the prize of making it across to friendly lines had to be there for the taking. It just required one last effort, or so Parker and the others told themselves.

For the next few hours they tried every path that seemed to offer the vaguest promised of safe passage. Eventually, they reached an isolated farmhouse. One of the Italians ventured over 'to investigate the situation'. Some twenty minutes later he returned, 'looking very pleased'. The farmer had revealed that German troops had been stationed at his farm, but had just withdrawn. Parker was overjoyed. The way ahead seemed open and clear. Quite by chance, they seemed to have made it through the lines for, if the Germans had fallen back, then surely Allied troops would be moving forward to take their positions.

With spirits stiffened and hearts full of hope, Parker, Dent and the two Italians set off once more, taking to a track which they assumed would lead them to Allied forces. Ahead of them, across a clear field dotted here and there with a few trees, there lay another farmhouse. Parker and Dent decided to head for it. Surely, Allied troops had to be there. But having made only a few yards further, a sudden 'volley of small arms fire' came from the farmstead, which didn't seem exactly friendly.

As the four escapees ducked down, Dent let out an exclamation: 'Christ! There's a Jerry observation post up that tree, ahead and to our left!'

Sure enough Parker spied the same, detecting 'the glint of . . . field glasses at the same time'.

Their elation at having made it across the enemy lines was now replaced with bolts of nervousness and fear. They'd clearly been spotted by the German troops positioned in that tree, the fire aimed at them. But they couldn't simply stay where they were. Instead, and trying to act as if they were a group of Italians who 'hadn't a care in the world', they proceeded to 'casually' stroll across the open field, as though that was the most natural thing to be doing right here and now. Ahead of them, about half a mile away, there lay a forested area, and it was towards that cover that they were headed.

But they'd made precious little progress when the ground erupted all around them, throwing soil and dirt into the air on all sides. Bullets cut past their heads, as the distinctive sounds of Bren light machine guns – British weapons – echoed from across the valley, as the four desperate fugitives became the focus of the British gunner's fire. This was sheer madness, Parker told himself. They had come so far, and come so close, only to find themselves a stone's throw from safety, and now their own troops were trying to gun them down. Even so, they could do nothing but run for their lives.

Spotting a natural fault line lying to their left, one which ran from the farmhouse they'd just visited towards the safety of the trees, all four sprinted for it, as bursts of fire lifted up thick clods of earth at their heels. Somehow they made it unscathed, diving down into the guts of a narrow farm track. It proved to be a good five feet deep, and offered them great protection from fire.

Hardly able to draw breath, they began to crawl towards the British lines, keeping well below the lips of the track.

Then, a guttural challenge rang out from behind: 'Achtung!'

Parker whipped his head around, and was horrified to see a patrol of German troops heading their way, machine guns raised. But when they unleashed the first bursts of fire, Parker could tell that the range was too far – their bullets were falling short. If they could only outrun the German soldiers, while remaining hidden from their own side, they might yet make it. Shouting for the others to follow, Parker sprinted ahead, as they threw caution to the wind.

Like that they careered around a corner and practically ran into a group of Italian civilians, emerging from the nearest trees. Parker noticed immediately that they were 'all young men' stretched out 'in a long line with their hands held above their heads'. Clearly they had to be prisoners, which meant that German soldiers had to be at the far end of their column, holding them at gunpoint. Which meant that Parker and his fellow fugitives were sandwiched between two groups of enemy. There was no way forward or back. If they tried to break away to either side, they'd be out in the open and get cut down.

Turning to Dent, Parker cried: 'Dump everything British and try to pass off as an Italian!'

They were dressed like Italian villagers, and if they were found to be British soldiers, they were likely to get shot as spies. This was the same fate as Parker and the other Colossus raiders had faced, during their earliest days of captivity. Having dumped all incriminating documents, Parker and Dent decided to split up and mingle with the Italian captives. With no other option they raised their hands and together with the group of Italians, they were marched back towards the farm building from which they had only recently fled.

It was a bitter turnaround to their fortunes.

For a while they were held outside, at gunpoint, before a German officer emerged from the farmhouse. He proceeded to question them all, using 'a very poor interpreter'. His Italian was so bad, few seemed able to understand the German officer's questions. Bored and frustrated, he changed tack, ordering the prisoners to form up in line. They were marched to one of the farm's rickety outbuildings, which resembled a ramshackle chicken house. Once inside, the door was rammed closed.

Through a gap in the building's wall, Parker was able to see out. He spied a squad of German troops hitching up a large gun to a farm tractor. Hoping for the best, he reasoned they had to be preparing to pull out and would 'leave us locked in'. However, a few minutes later the door was flung open, and a tall German officer was silhouetted in the entrance. Standing before them, he made a show of counting them all.

They were thirteen. 'Ah, the Thirteen Apostles,' he announced, menacingly. Pointing to Dent, plus one of the Italians, he signalled them to head outside: '*Prima due* – first two.'

Maintaining the pretence that he was Italian, Dent obediently did as he was ordered.

What happened next made Parker sick to his stomach. 'Two minutes later four shots were heard,' as he would report. Peeping through a crack in the door, Parker could only imagine the worst. His best friend, Lance Corporal George Dent, Royal Signals, and the young Italian civilian who had been with him, looked to have been murdered in cold blood.

Fearing they were all about to face the same treatment, the Italians fell into a frenzy, some sinking to their knees in prayer, while others cried out '*Mamma mia*', as tears streamed down their faces. Frantically, Parker searched about for any means of escape. He had only minutes, maybe seconds, to live and he needed to find a way out of there. However, there was nothing. There was no way he could get out, without being cut down by the Nazi murderers massed outside.

The door was flung open again, as the tall German officer came for the next two. Figuring he had absolutely nothing to lose, Parker stepped forward.

'You can't shoot me – I'm English,' he declared.

The officer looked him up and down, frowning doubtfully. 'Eine Englander?'

'Yes, I'm an Englishman,' Parker confirmed.

'Eine Tommy?'

'Yes, I'm a Tommy.'

With that Parker was grabbed by the arm and marched outside, where he was handed over to another German officer. In short order that man proceeded to question Parker in flawless

English with 'a strong Oxford accent', as Parker later described it. How had an Englishman come to be with the Italians, the German demanded. In response, Parker gave his name, rank and serial number, and related how he was an escaped POW from Sulmona Camp. No more.

Even as Parker was being questioned, the German troops continued to empty the outbuilding, two men at a time. Each pair was led to a 'large walled enclosure with a gateway', Parker observed, where some thirty German soldiers were formed up in a semi-circle. As they got to the entrance, each was shot in the back, their bodies falling in untidy heaps on the ground.

Parker felt shocked and nauseous having to witness such brutal butchery. As far as he could tell, these young Italian men were innocent civilians, caught in the crossfire of war. They had been causing no harm to anyone, as far as he knew it, yet here they were being slaughtered for no reason that he could comprehend. Worse still, he could just make out that one of those bodies lying before him had to be that of his fellow escapee, George Dent.

'Oh God, you've shot my best friend,' Parker blurted out, at the sight of Dent's bloodied form. He'd feared Dent had to be among the dead – now he knew it for sure.

His remark seemed to agitate the tall German officer, the author of all the callous murders. He pointed to the pile of bodies. 'Eine Englander?'

Parker had to think fast. He figured he was in a very delicate position. When he had voiced his claim to be British, he'd been separated from the rest of the captives, and up to this point his life had been spared. But should his captors realise they had murdered one British soldier already, then what was to stop them shooting another – especially as Parker was an eyewitness to that war crime?

'No,' replied Parker, 'an Italiano.'

This seemed to appease the tall German officer, who to Parker's eyes 'looked very relieved'.

When all of the prisoners – barring Parker – had been executed, the enemy's focus fell entirely on him, as they demanded to know just how he had come to be where he was. Some of those who had been murdering unarmed civilians only moments before, now began to address Parker in an apparently friendly manner. There were some who seemed strangely keen to talk, so as 'to give their English language an airing', as they expressed it to Parker. From cold blooded killers to being full of chatty bonhomie – it was all so surreal.

Eventually, the entire unit prepared to move out. Parker was placed in the sidecar of a motorcycle combination. No sooner had the German vehicles broken out of the cover of the farm buildings, than they were fired upon by British forces sited across the valley. It struck Parker that these were very likely the very same soldiers who had shot at Parker and his fellow escapees earlier, so forcing them into the arms of their German captors.

The motorcycle-sidecar combo sped away. Motoring some eight kilometres north, Parker was taken to the town of Cerignola, which lay forty kilometres south of Foggia. There, the driver made his way to a large building surrounded by a 'very high wire mesh fence', as Parker would later describe it. The motorcycle combination pulled to a halt and Parker was ordered to scramble out. A high-ranking German officer approached him.

'Ah, the Englishman,' he announced, in perfect English. 'I suppose you realise that you are in a very dangerous position, being in civilian clothes.'

It was now that the effects of the past few hours truly hit

home. Overcome with grief that his best friend, Dent, had been murdered, and filled with guilt at what he considered his 'denunciation of George at the murder site', Parker had reached the end of his tether. He simply didn't care any more. 'At that moment I was almost wishing to die,' he would later write.

Disregarding what the consequences might be, the rage within exploded, as he blurted out: 'You've killed my best friend, you bastards! You may as well finish me off as well!'

Almost immediately the German officer's attitude appeared to change. From one of arrogance and scorn, it seemed to have shifted to one of visible concern.

'How long is it since you had a square meal?' he asked.

'I've forgotten,' Parker snapped, exhaustedly.

'Just give me your name, rank and number, then come with me.'

Parker did as he was asked, after which he was led inside the wired-in building. There he was treated to a hot bath, followed by a change of clothes and an excellent meal. On noting the German officer's parachute emblem on his uniform, Parker told him that he too was a parachutist. The officer's response was to confide in Parker that he was 'in charge of a parachute regiment that had been pulled out of the frontline for a rest'. Oddly, he then revealed to Parker that he feared the war was not going in the Germans' favour. Astonishingly, the officer proved to be well aware of Operation Colossus, which, by this time was over two and a half years old, and he seemed to know more about the raid than Parker did himself.

Parker was told that as soon as was practicable, he would be sent to a POW camp in Germany. He was asked to sign a declaration that he would not try to escape. He refused, telling the parachute officer that 'to do so would be unthinkable'.

At that point Parker was handed back to the soldiers who had brought him to this building, and driven to a Headquarters tent lying at the edge of a nearby forest. There began what could only be described as a pass-the-parcel situation, as no one seemed to know quite what to do with their British captive. For days on end he was driven around to various German units, each of which refused to take him. Finally, he was placed in the back of a truck as a unit was moving out. It was on this night that Parker would once again witness the cruelty that some Germans at least were very much capable of. Having taken a wrong turn, the vehicle he was travelling in pulled into a farmyard on a steep track. When the driver reversed into a haystack, as he endeavoured to turn around, he knocked it over the edge of an incline.

The farmer came storming out, livid at the driver's clumsiness, and 'calling the Germans "bastardoes"'. The sergeant in charge, clearly not happy with the man's choice of words, 'calmly took out his revolver and, at point blank range, pulled the trigger', killing the farmer instantly, and in front of his wife's very eyes. When Parker tried to object, he was 'told that he was lucky not to have been shot also'.

Further attempts were made to offload Parker on to other units, but each seemed to shirk the trouble of looking after this troublesome prisoner. It was getting to the point when Parker feared they were bound to 'cut their losses and shoot me', when a German general intervened. Seemingly on a whim, he asked Parker to join him in his staff car, as the unit made its way towards its next destination. En route a large Allied air raid took place. Bombs rained from the skies, pulverising everything below. Huge fires broke out, sending massive columns of smoke billowing into the night sky, as buildings collapsed on all sides.

The raid seemed to go on for ever. By the morning, hundreds of dead littered the area, the corpses being assembled into heaps at the sides of the roads. To Parker, it seemed like hell on earth.

Eventually, the German general also seemed to tire of Parker's company. He was handed over to a unit comprising of just twelve men, occupying a farmhouse. They seemed to be a friendly-enough bunch, and they allowed him to sleep for most of the morning. He was eventually woken by one of the soldiers holding a glass of wine under his nose. While he had been sleeping they had apparently raided the wine cellar and were proceeding to drink the contents dry. Now they wanted Parker to join them. Not wanting to appear rude, or to do anything to upset them, he drank the odd glass but poured most away when no one was looking.

He did not want to get drunk, for obvious reasons. Having got so close to escaping, and seen his best friend murdered, Parker was more determined than ever to break away.

In the kitchen there was a large, angry-looking Alsatian dog chained to a wall. Each time one of the soldiers walked past, it strained at the chain, its teeth bared. When it came time to leave, the sergeant in charge approached the dog. Picking up a rusty old bucket he brought it down brutally onto the animal's nose. Blood sprayed from the gash he'd created. This only angered the dog more and it strained further trying to get at its attacker. Again the bucket was brought down onto the dog's head; and again: and again. Eventually, the dog stopped barking and began to whimper, too weakened by the savage beating to react any further. Even this didn't stop the sergeant from continuing to beat the defenceless animal, 'striking the dog until it lay in a pool of its own blood and died', as Parker later described it.

43

This show of wanton cruelty against a chained animal only made Parker even more determined to escape his captors. He vowed there and then that whatever might follow, he would make another break for freedom. Though not yet twenty-one years old, Parker showed the unbreakable spirit and fortitude that had distinguished him as a Special Service volunteer in the first place, and led to his selection for 11 SAS and X Troop.

The following day, Parker was joined in captivity by another POW, an American flying officer who had been shot down just recently. He introduced himself as 1st Lieutenant Williams and he told Parker that he was also keen to escape. This was music to Parker's ears.

A contingent of the German Field Police Corps – a military police unit – arrived the very next morning. Enough Allied captives had been rounded up to justify dispatching a batch to a POW camp in Germany. Parker and Williams were to join them. They were taken to an improvised prison, which ominously-enough, bearing in mind what Parker had witnessed in terms of executions, lay next to a graveyard. The two captives were marched into a large room, where around twenty regular British soldiers were gathered. There was also a lone US marine who was nursing a broken arm. Oddly to Parker's way of thinking, few of the captives seemed keen on trying to escape. One told Parker that 'they were all quite happy as prisoners and were not going to allow anyone to spoil their privileges' by trying to get away. But then Parker was different. He was 11 SAS and X Troop. Trying to escape was built into his DNA.

After a decent meal the prisoners were herded onto trucks, to be taken by convoy to the nearest large town, from where they were to be sent by train north to Germany. If Parker were to try to escape, then he sensed he would have to do it very soon. The further away from the frontline they were taken, the less the chance of anyone making it safely back to Allied forces. He'd been so close once before, within a stone's throw of friendly lines. He had to try again.

The route ahead snaked around a series of hairpin bends, which required careful driving for vehicles as large as these. It was hardly surprising when one of the drivers, while trying to negotiate a tight curve above a steep embankment, misjudged it, leaving one of the vehicle's rear wheels hanging over the edge. The vehicle had ground to a sudden halt, and the prisoners riding in the rear were told to get off. As the entire convoy pulled to a standstill, the dismounted prisoners were ordered to form up on the road above their truck.

The Field Police Corps asked for volunteers to help manhandle the lorry back onto the roadway. The incentive was the promise that if they all lent a hand, they would get to rest in a warm train station that evening. Conversely, if they didn't free the truck, they would have to wait for a recovery vehicle, which could take all night to arrive, and it looked as if it was going to rain.

To Parker's amazement, the British POWs stepped forward to help. In a show of bloody-minded obstinacy, he and the two Americans placed themselves at the opposite end of the vehicle, and did all they could to resist their fellows' efforts to push it free. Surprisingly, 'the Germans didn't lose their cool' on seeing such a display of barefaced defiance. They 'merely shrugged their shoulders as much to say "what else could we expect", at least from some of you'. After much pushing and shoving, all finally gave up. For the time being, the truck was going nowhere. Parker and his two American buddies had won.

By now, the light was fading. As the prisoners stood in the gathering darkness, watched over by their escort, a huge recovery vehicle appeared. Laden with 'every conceivable piece of equipment needed to get motor vehicles, even tanks, out of a rut', as Parker noted, it came to a halt adjacent to the lorry. The prisoners were lined up in threes, and a searchlight set up, so it illuminated their ranks. While the recovery mechanics and engineers got to work, Parker sensed this was very likely the only chance he would get at making a break for it.

Slowly, moving with infinite care so as not to get noticed, he slipped back in line, creeping rearwards until he was in the final rank. Beside him were the two Americans. If Parker stepped back one more pace, he would slip out of the beam of the searchlight and be enveloped in darkness. However, one thing gave him pause for thought.

'I wonder where those blokes are that were in the car and truck which was following us?' he whispered to his American comrades.

Travelling at the rear of the convoy had been two vehicles that formed part of the Field Police escort. Parker had no idea where those riding in that car and truck had got to.

Realising Parker's intentions, Williams replied, 'Go on, boy. Take a chance!'

Those few words of encouragement were enough to stiffen Parker's resolve.

Slowly, he stepped back into the shadows.

This was it – the chance he had been waiting for. He turned to the right and simply slipped away into the darkness. When he had made about twenty yards he came across the car that had been following them. Luckily, those inside had fallen asleep and so he managed to slip past.

On his right lay the dark silhouette of a hedgerow. By the light of the crescent moon he searched for a gap which he could sneak through. Just then he spied a group of people on the road up ahead. In the darkness he could not make out who they were, but it didn't bode well. But then, just ahead of him, he spotted a break in the hedge. He darted towards it, dived through, and was out of anyone's line of view on the road.

Parker found himself on the edge of a large ploughed field. He noticed that a further hedgerow ran at right angles to the road. If he followed that, it would give him great cover, his silhouette blending in perfectly with its dark form. He glanced behind, noticing that his captors and the POWs remained bathed in the pool of illumination from the searchlight. There wasn't the slightest sign that anything was amiss, so he had to presume his escape had gone unnoticed.

Parker set off, slipping along the edge of that hedgerow. The surface beneath his feet was soft and wet, the clogging mud making for difficult going. Once he'd moved far enough to figure he could not be heard, he began to run for all he was worth, pumping his arms and legs as he went, the clods of earth flying from his heels. Parker had made maybe about a hundred yards moving at pace, when the night was torn asunder by bursts of gunfire. Redoubling his efforts, Parker sensed that none of the fire was coming his way – there was none of the whine of bullets cutting through the air, or the thud of rounds tearing into the earth. He could only imagine that the two American captives had made a break for it and had been spotted.

Plagued by his jangling nerves, Parker continued to run until he was quite out of breath. He twice mistook a goat bell for a German field telephone ringing in the darkness, changing his course dramatically to avoid an imagined enemy. Finally, he reached the sanctuary of a large tract of woodland. Slipping into its cover – it was pitch dark – he slowed his progress to walking pace. Eventually he came to a track leading to some farm buildings. Seeing no light whatsoever, he went to move past, when suddenly a dog came bounding towards him from out of the darkness, snarling viciously. To his horror he noted that it was 'a very big dog indeed'. Parker instantly 'had visions of . . . being torn to shreds'. Realising he couldn't outrun the animal, he decided to stand his ground. Squaring his shoulders, he braced himself to fight. Seeing this young, fit-looking human readying itself to take him on, the dog came to a halt a few feet away. Deciding that discretion was the better part of valour, it turned and fled from whence it had come.

With renewed vigour, Parker pressed on.

He ventured into the farm buildings. They were empty, but far too filthy to sleep in. Near by, he discovered a store of dry hay. It was perfect. Forming a makeshift bed, he lay down and, totally exhausted, fell instantly asleep.

At first, Parker imagined the thing poking him in the ribs had to be the muzzle of a rifle. For a few brief moments he rubbed the sleep from his eyes, believing his luck had run out and that once again the Germans had found him. However, on sitting up he realised the object digging into his side was nothing more than the end of a shepherd's crook. The owner of it was an old man who was staring down at him curiously.

He babbled a little in Italian, but spoke too fast for Parker to understand.

'*I Inglesi escaparto priginary de guerra*,' Parker announced, using his best pidgin Italian to explain he was an escaped POW.

Clambering to his feet, he explained as best he could that he was trying to find his way back to British lines. Despite the fact that he was wearing a German army tunic – one that his captors had given him a few days ago – this seemed to convince the old shepherd. He led Parker to the bottom of a large hill. Indicating the far summit, he gestured that that was the way Parker needed to head, and that safety lay over the hilltop. Thanking him, Parker set off.

The sun was on the rise and despite the loose scree underfoot, Parker soon found his way to the top. In the valley beyond he could see large areas of tall grass. Making his way towards it, he decided to lie down in the morning sunshine and rest. Having run for half of the previous night, and then being awoken from his slumber by the shepherd, he was dog tired. Craving rest. The moment he put his head down in that field of tall grass he fell asleep.

What awoke Parker this time was not a gentle prodding with a shepherd's crook, but something infinitely more dramatic and ear-splitting. Flying at only a few dozen feet above the ground, a squadron of American fighter planes roared overhead, guns blazing at what had to be enemy positions lying in a forest just across the valley. The gun-blasts were so close that empty shell casings rained down all around where Parker was hiding.

For Parker, the sight proved an absolute 'tonic'. The US war-planes raked the trees relentlessly with machine-gun fire and salvoes of bombs. Soon the forest was ablaze, burning furiously, as secondary explosions revealed where enemy gun-positions had been blasted to smithereens. As one flight of planes turned away, their work done, another swooped in to continue the ferocious attack, and Parker had a ringside seat for the entire show.

49

This went on for well over an hour. By the time the last of the planes disappeared over the horizon, Parker figured it had to be approaching midday. His thoughts turned once again to getting back to Allied lines. He was still in among the German positions – that much the air-assault had confirmed. How far beyond lay friendly forces there was no way of telling. Parker's chief issue now was food – with all the physical exertion of the last twenty-four hours, he was famished, and he needed fuel for the journey that lay ahead.

Moving carefully through that field of grass, he crested the nearby rise, a valley rolling out below. Nestled in its folds was a lone house. An Italian man was making his way through the fields, and on the spur of the moment Parker decided to trust him. His gut instinct proved good. Upon learning of Parker's predicament, he insisted the Englishman visit his home, a place that was so isolated the Germans never visited. There, the man's wife rustled up a real feast, after which the couple insisted that he stay with them, to get some proper rest. While he was desperate to reach Allied lines, Parker was touched by their hospitality, and he decided to sleep the one night there, secure that no enemy troops would come searching.

The next morning, he set out once more, pressing ever southwards. He no longer needed a map or the guiding hand of helpful Italians. 'The noise of war was a reliable guide,' as Parker would describe it, the sound of the guns drawing him onwards. Keeping away from the main roads wherever possible, he simply headed in the direction of the booming artillery and the crump of exploding bombs.

As he crested a rise later that day, Parker saw something that 'cheered me no end'. A train laden with German military equipment was heading north – moving into territory through which Parker had already passed. German forces looked to be pulling out, taking as much hardware with them as they could carry. The train tracks ran along a road. That too was heavy with military traffic. To continue his journey, Parker would need to cross it. With infinite care he slipped up to it, keeping to cover, and dashed over when the coast appeared clear. As there were no cries of alarm or bursts of fire, he figured he'd not been seen.

Pressing on, he came across another isolated farmstead, just as the sun was setting. Again, Parker decided to chance his arm. It turned out to be a repeat of the kind of welcome he'd enjoyed from the previous villager. He was invited in, fed and persuaded to stop the night in the stables. From the farmer he learned that German forces were indeed in the process of pulling out, falling back to their next defensive lines, which lay further north in Italy.

With 'the noise of war getting very close', Parker found himself unable to sleep. He got up and was treated to a light show to rival the aurora borealis. Tracer fire scorched across the valley in both directions, as Allied and German forces traded blows. With countless bullets howling through the heavens, Parker realised he was sandwiched pretty much slap-bang between the opposing lines. He became gripped by excitement, as he contemplated 'the possibility of getting back to England and home'. He had been away for well over two-and-a-half years. The prospect of freedom had never seemed so close, barring that fateful moment when he and his good friend Dent had made a dash for Allied lines, only for it all to end in recapture and Dent's awful murder.

After devouring a hearty breakfast, Parker bade farewell to his hosts and set out. The sound of war was all around him now.

Ahead lay a deep valley thick with trees. Plunging into a thicket, he headed towards what looked to be a road on the far side, all the while stopping whenever he heard the sound of German voices near by. Crouching in the shadows, he waited until they fell quiet, before creeping onwards. This went on for what seemed like an age, but eventually Parker could hear no further German voices, nor detect any signs of their presence.

Finally, he reached the edge of the road. It stood to reason that this could be the German defence line, the very vanguard of their positions. Keeping to the security of the dense undergrowth, he resolved not to risk breaking cover until he was sure it was safe to do so.

And then he detected it. It was a sound that he had not heard for such a long time that, at first, he feared he might be dreaming. But being an expert in all types of motorcycles, he just knew in his heart that this was the sound of a Norton engine. A Norton motorcyle was heading in his direction, of that he was certain. Inching his way through the thick vegetation, he spied it zipping past. And then, coming along the road was a second Norton, and seated upon it was a British soldier.

In an instant Parker had scrambled onto the roadway and he began to wave wildly. The Norton rider slowed to a halt. Explaining to the incredulous soldier that he was an escaped POW, Parker was duly invited to climb aboard, riding on the pillion seat. And so, turning the motorcycle around, the rider took him back the way he had come, towards the local Allied headquarters.

A couple of minutes later, the motorcyclist pulled up at a house. Parker was led inside. There he discovered a British Army officer and eight further soldiers. They were a signals unit that had just that morning taken over the building. It lay no more than 300 yards from where Parker had emerged onto the road.

As Parker sat down and explained who he was, and told his story, he was given the most 'wonderful welcome'. He was fed and 'plied with a good collection of wine'. It transpired that the officer was, like Parker, a native of the Steel City, Sheffield.

In more ways than one, it was like coming home.

For the first time in what felt like an eternity, Parker could truly relax, the threat of capture and death no longer hanging over him. He had come so close to being killed on so many occasions, but his spirit had prevailed. However, his freedom had come at a price. There was someone missing from his side, who by rights should have completed this journey with him – his good friend Dent, murdered by the Nazis only a few weeks previously.

Parker's epic journey of escape didn't end there. Getting back to England would prove less simple than he may have imagined. After a tortuous journey involving first being sent to Foggia, for 'interrogation' – to prove he was who he claimed to be, and not some kind of enemy plant – he was moved on to Taranto, in southern Italy. His escape report, given to MI9 on his return to Britain, chronicles his onward journey. 'On 18 October I sailed for Bizerta [in Tunisia], arriving there on 22 October. As there was going to be a considerable delay before I got a train, I hitch-hiked to Tunis on 25 October and there got a plane for Algiers. I left Algiers by boat on 27 October . . .'

It was 6 November 1943 when Parker finally reached British shores. He'd deployed on Operation Colossus on 11 February 1941. It was just short of three years in the interim, the majority of which he had spent in captivity, or on the run from the enemy.

*

For a short time, Parker wondered if his war was over. It occurred to him 'that after being a prisoner-of-war, I may have been excused from further service'. But it was not to be. After being debriefed by MI9 in London, he was ordered to report to the Royal Engineers (his parent unit), at their Training Unit at Kitchener Barracks, Chatham. On arrival, he spoke to the commanding officer (CO), telling him his real unit was 11 Special Air Service Battalion. However, 11 SAS no longer existed, as it had been absorbed into the 1st Parachute Battalion in September 1941. Of course, David Stirling's Special Air Service had been formed in the desert of North Africa in the summer of that year, taking on the name and the mantle of 11 SAS, and it had gone on to achieve great things.

Parker was told by his CO that he had merely been 'on loan' to 11 SAS, and that he had 'never been officially transferred'. Hence he was to rejoin his parent unit. Parker baulked. He complained that a return to the Royal Engineers would mean a drop in pay – parachutists were paid at a higher rate. Using that as his excuse, he asked to be transferred back to airborne forces, and on a permanent basis. His request was finally acceded to, and not long after Parker joined the Glider-Pilot Regiment, to train as a glider pilot.

For his part in Operation Colossus and his epic escape, Parker was Mentioned in Despatches, his citation reading:

Captured 16 February 1941 in Italy, six days after being dropped by parachute with one officer and three other sappers on a special operation. Imprisoned in Campo 78 (Sulmona). Released 12 September 1943. With Lance Corporal George Dent, Royal Corps of Signals, became detached from the main party and on 23 September was captured by Germans near Cerignola. Dent and an Italian were taken out and shot by the Germans. Parker escaped shooting by declaring himself British, but ten other Italians were shot. Parker escaped from the German Field Police on 5 October when the lorry in which he was travelling was ditched. He made his way to the British lines which he reached on 11 October.

In his official escape report, Parker wrote the following: 'On 12 September the camp evacuated to the foothills. L/Cpl G. Dent, Royal Sigs, and I were together and we got separated from the main body.' This differs from what he would write regarding his escape, after the war was over. No doubt this was due to his having disobeyed the Stay Put Order, which he'd been warned would lead to court martial were it wilfully disobeyed.

After executing such an extraordinary escape, Parker might have been forgiven for imagining that one such episode was quite enough for any young man's war. But in truth, some four years after he'd first found himself marooned far behind enemy lines, he would end up in an equally daunting situation, only this time on the very borders of Nazi Germany. It was March 1945, and Parker was one of the thousands of airborne troops who had deployed into Germany as part of Operation Varsity, the largest airborne landings of the Second World War.

Piloting a glider over the Rhine, Parker and his co-pilot were unable to find their landing zone, due to heavy anti-aircraft fire. Putting down near a village crawling with enemy troops, for the best part of a day they had put up stiff resistance, even though the house in which they had taken cover was surrounded by German forces. They killed many, but eventually, heavily outnumbered and with their defences severely damaged by fire, they were forced to surrender.

For two days Parker and his fellow captives were marched east, away from the fighting, eventually arriving at a railway station where they were herded onto goods wagons. Unsurprisingly, Parker's thoughts once again turned to escape. Having spent so long in an Italian POW camp, he had no desire to spend the rest of the war in a German one. Breaking away some planks from the wagon's sidewall, and fixing a small mirror to a stick, he was able to check along the train's length for guards.

At first, all those within the carriage were up for trying to escape. But when the chance came, just outside the city of Osnabrück in north-western Germany, some sixty kilometres the wrong side of the border, he found that he was the only one willing to give it a go. After a halt, the train pulled ahead at a very slow and ponderous pace. Parker was able to force open the door and edge out onto a step-board. From there he managed to lower himself, until he was suspended beneath the train, waiting until it came to a dead stop. At that point he dropped to the ground. Slowly the train began to move again, leaving him lying between the rails, with the train's undercarriage flashing past inches above his head.

The train passed over him, leaving him unscathed, but his predicament was far from over. He discovered that it had pulled to a halt at a railway station. It had departed leaving him 'bathed in full light', so he quickly climbed onto the nearest platform and headed for the exit. On seeing a large group of people near the entrance, Parker decided to brazen it out, walking right past them. Astonishingly none challenged him, his British airborne overalls very possibly giving the impression that he was a German rail worker with every right to be there.

For several days he followed the railway line back the way he had come, occasionally having to pass through sentry points. By posing as an Italian railway worker who was unable to speak any German, he managed to bluff his way through. At one point a German officer, suspecting he was a deserter from the German military, thrust a pistol into his midriff and threatened to shoot him. Maintaining the pretence of being an Italian working on the rail lines, Parker was again able to bluff his way out, though he was left mightily shaken at coming so close to being shot.

Eventually, after scrounging food wherever he could, he found his way to the frontline. For a whole day he lay hidden near a tree, covered in dense foliage, while German soldiers dug foxholes all around him. A huge aerial bombardment ensued, as the German troops traded fire with attacking Allied warplanes, from positions just a few yards away from him. At one stage Parker lost consciousness – whether from lack of sleep and sustenance, or injury, he didn't know. Sometime later he was awoken by a British soldier standing over him.

The Germans had retreated.

Parker had just pulled off his second miraculous escape.

Operation Colossus had put the Tragino Aqueduct out of action for several weeks. But perhaps the greatest achievement of the mission was to prove that using airborne troops on missions deep behind enemy lines could prove extremely effective. This was 'rubber-stamped' a year later, in February 1942, with the success of Operation Biting, wherein a few score British paratroopers were dropped near Bruneval, on the Normandy coast, to steal a state-of-the-art German 'Würzburg' radar dish – something that would have a very significant impact on the prosecution of the war by the Allies.

Alfred Parker was not the only soldier of X Troop to escape captivity. Lieutenant Anthony Deane-Drummond, the mission's second in command, who blew up the small bridge near the farm buildings, escaped to Britain sixteen months after his capture. He was able to provide a detailed account of the mission's success, despite official reports to the contrary. Lieutenant George Paterson, who had taken over the job of planting the explosives on the aqueduct, when Daly and Parker's patrol had failed to materialise, also pulled off a daring escape.

Captain Daly himself would make three escape attempts while in captivity, the first taking place the day of his capture, on 15 February 1941. However, each time he was rounded up by the enemy. He was finally liberated near Mulhouse, in eastern France, on 10 March 1945. During his time in captivity Daly was to send 'valuable information to the War Office by secret means', for which he was Mentioned in Despatches.

At the time of the Italian Armistice, Sulmona POW camp held around 3,000 Allied prisoners-of-war. Despite the Stay Put Order, and the SBO's threat of court martial to any who might disobey it, two-thirds of the prisoners in the camp broke out when the Italians guarding them downed their weapons and deserted their positions. On 14 September 1943 German troops arrived and took over the camp, rounding up many of the POWs who had taken to the hills.

As a result of the notorious Stay Put Order, some 30,000 Allied POWs were seized by the German military in Italy. Of those, some 2,500 are believed to have perished in captivity. After the war, some of the families were intent on suing MI9 for issuing such a misguided order in the first place. Somehow, the original Stay Put Order has disappeared from the official War Office records, which are held at the National Archives in Kew, London. The original creator of the order, and the author of one of the greatest untold scandals of the Second World War, may never be known.

Even as Alfred Parker and George Dent had been languishing in Sulmona POW camp, so another SAS unit was pressing far into North Africa, intent on spreading mayhem deep behind enemy lines. Driving several thousand kilometres across sun-blasted desert in their heavily armed Willys jeeps, their incredible mission was to be one of the most daring SAS sabotage operations of the war. But it would also prove to be costly, triggering another series of breathtaking getaways.

For so many, the epic escape back to Allied lines would prove testing in the extreme.

Chapter Two

FROM DESERT FIRE TO FROZEN SNOWS

Libya, December 1942

Twenty-four-year-old Lieutenant Anthony Hough grabbed his field glasses and scanned the coast road to the north. He and his group of five troopers from B Squadron, 1 SAS, had been placing mines along the section of road that stretched from Khoms in the west to Leptis Magna in the east, their area of operations for what was codenamed Operation Palmyra. For the moment they were cloaked in darkness, the near-full moon hidden behind cloud. They would be impossible to spot from the roadway, which lay half a mile away, their jeeps hidden behind a small sandy rise.

Three days earlier they had blocked a section of the road by blowing down trees with explosive charges. The trunks had fallen across the highway. Their intention was to stop any enemy convoy that might come along, so they could shoot it all to hell using the firepower of their heavily armed Willys jeeps. But after waiting all that night no vehicles had shown, and they had been forced back to their hideaway. The mines were there to add an extra dimension to the mayhem they hoped to cause, but Hough remained concerned. He reckoned they had only enough fuel left to execute this one ambush, before they would be forced to head for their deep-desert base, at Bir Fascia, to refuel and pick up supplies from the cache they'd left there.

Hough's six-man patrol had been allocated a sector on one of the most westerly points of B Squadron's operational area. Only two more patrols were positioned further west, one of which was led by his good friend, Lieutenant Carol Mather. They were the most-advanced SAS troops then fighting in North Africa, operating the very furthest distance from friendly lines. Hundreds of kilometres of inhospitable desert lay between their present position and any semblance of safety.

Hough had deep reservations about being so far behind enemy lines, and especially as they had deployed into an area in which the SAS had never operated before. He felt the whole mission had been rushed; that their newly formed B Squadron was seen as being somewhat 'expendable'. His chief hope was that they could do their job and get out again alive.

Eventually, their patience was rewarded. Hough spied an approaching convoy. Away to the west the twin beams of head-lamps lanced through the darkness. A line of vehicles was approaching, moving directly to where they had laid their mines. Onwards the convoy came, motoring ever closer, and without a hint of any vehicles slowing or showing any signs that they had spotted the impending danger. Scrambling down the slope, Hough gave the order for his men to mount up their three Willys jeeps and get ready. This was it. After spending weeks braving horrendous desert terrain, they were finally about to see some action.

Placing his sand-goggles over his eyes and pulling up his she-magh – his Arabic headscarf – to cover his mouth and nose, he jumped into the driver's seat. Beside him, his gunner took hold of the twin Vickers machine guns and prepared to open fire. He had already checked the ammo and made the pivot-mounted weapon ready. Hough glanced across at the other two jeeps. Getting a confident thumbs-up from his men, he gunned his engine and set out in the direction of the oncoming convoy. Swiftly the other jeeps fell in line behind. They followed Hough's lead as he motored out of their place of hiding, after which they moved into positions line-abreast – attack formation.

Their wheels began to throw up clouds of dust and sand as they accelerated away, heading towards the target. All of a sudden, a blinding white flash lit up the night sky as the lead vehicle in the enemy convoy hit one of the mines. The explosion blasted it into the air, doubtless killing those riding in the cab outright, before the vehicle came to a rest on its side, burning ferociously. As the trucks behind came to a juddering halt, so the three SAS jeeps sped out of the darkness, like ghosts of the night, hell-bent on causing havoc and mayhem.

The vehicle-mounted machine guns opened up, concentrating their fearsome firepower on the second truck in the line. Long bursts of tracer lit up the night, as streams of bullets tore across the desert sand. The effect of those three sets of twin Vickers was murderous, the concentrated onslaught tearing into the second truck, bullets raking along the exposed flank of the vehicle as the gunners let rip. Almost instantly, it too had burst into flames. A few seconds later a deafening roar rent the night, a massive explosion engulfing the truck, blasting chunks of hot metal and debris in all directions. That vehicle had to have been carrying a load of explosives. Triggered by the bursts of fiery tracer the cargo had ignited, throwing up a huge mushroom cloud of thick, dark smoke, that punched high into the air.

The heat from the almighty explosion was so intense it scorched over those riding in the jeeps, like the breath of some fiery dragon. Ignoring the searing blast, Hough turned his attentions on the remainder of the convoy. There was a long line of trucks backed up behind the two heaps of twisted, burning wreckage – all that remained of the leading vehicles. Hough sensed some busy manoeuvring, as enemy vehicles prepared to mount a pursuit. Knowing that they didn't have the fuel for a long, drawn-out fire-fight, let alone an extended hunt across the desert, he unleashed a few final bursts, before giving the order for the jeeps to turn about and execute their getaway.

Their work here was done. The front of the convoy had been transformed into a blasted heap of fiery death and ruin. Striking this far behind enemy lines, they would have put the fear of God into those enemy troops riding in the trucks. Word would quickly spread: nowhere was safe while the SAS were marauding across the open expanse of the desert. Turning as one, the three SAS jeeps sped away, leaving behind them a deadly inferno.

As the jeeps raced across the open desert, making for the sanctuary of the night, Hough noticed that a number of the trucks seemed to be giving pursuit. Whoever was manning that convoy, they didn't seem inclined to give up the chase so easily. These were Italian vehicles and would be packed with their troops – soldiers who had just witnessed the death and destruction that the British raiders had wrought. Hough knew that they to get away and fast. They had to find some place in which to hide up, for sunrise was not so far away. If they were caught in the open come first light, their chances would be dire indeed, especially since they didn't have the petrol to execute a high-speed escape and evasion across such terrain.

As the enemy trucks snorted and grunted their way across the desert, moving in the wake of the more nimble, lighter jeeps, sod's law came into play. The sky, which had been dark and overcast, cleared. The moon's eerie, silvery-blue wash lit up the desert from end to end. Hough glanced behind, his eyes straining to see through the thick cloud of dust thrown up by the speeding vehicles. A few hundred yards to their rear was that phalanx of Italian Army trucks, sticking resolutely to their tail. Washed in the moonlight as they were, it would be a tough job to lose their pursuers.

Hough had been soldiering in North Africa for well over two years, and he knew the desert intimately. He knew its vagaries and its beguiling beauty, but mostly its predations. Being no stranger to the desert's ways, he was acutely aware of how quickly fortunes could change here. He'd experienced at first hand the toing and froing of the desert war, as each side had sought to gain an advantage, some means to drive the other into defeat and oblivion. But above all, Hough did not want to be captured by the enemy and to spend the rest of the war rotting in a POW camp. He had many reasons to hunger to fight, all anchored in the long years that he had spent at the harsh end of war.

Hailing from Epping, Essex, Hough's family owned a paper mill at Victoria Wharf, in East London. Educated at Uppingham boarding school, Hough had proved a keen sportsman, excelling at rugby, hockey and tennis as well as becoming a fine equestrian. During his latter years at Uppingham he was made house captain, and he'd gone on to command the school's Combined

Cadet Force, something that he'd loved. In 1936, with his time at Uppingham over, he'd joined the family firm. But he'd found 'the drudgery of the daily commute to Limehouse, the boredom of learning about cardboard production and most of all, the inactivity' soul destroying. He'd considered applying for officer training at the Royal Military Academy, Sandhurst, but was put off by his father, who was a veteran of the Great War.

Still hungering for excitement and action, he'd joined the 1st Battalion Tower Hamlets Rifles, where he was commissioned as an officer. A keen skier, he'd organised a trip to Zermatt in the Swiss Alps, along with some fellow officers. His proficiency at skiing would lead, a year later, to his first great wartime adventure. With hostilities declared, Hough had found himself serving as an officer in the Rifle Brigade, 'a motorised unit expected at times to be at the vanguard of the army, and even to operate behind enemy lines'. This was his kind of thing. Training was intense for the anticipated fighting to come.

As 1939 drew to a close, a notice in the officer's mess caught his eye. The War Office were looking for soldiers who had experience of skiing, to form a new winter warfare battalion and to train for operations in Finland. The Finns were engaged in conflict with the Soviet Union, in what would become known as the Winter War. That summer, Stalin had overseen the signing of the Nazi–Soviet Non-aggression Pact, which meant that Moscow was aligned firmly with Berlin. Acting on the premise that 'the enemy of my enemy is my friend', Britain sought to aid the Finns in their David-and-Goliath battle with their eastern neighbour.

Hough volunteered, finding himself in Chamonix, in the French Alps, training for winter warfare. Among those who had stepped forwards were some future notable characters in the SAS, including Carol Mather and the SAS's founder, David Stirling. Four weeks later the Finns and the Soviets had signed an armistice, ending hostilities. The Soviets had suffered punishing losses, and their reputation as a military force had been badly tarnished. But Finland had also been hit hard, losing eleven per cent of its territory. The peace deal was a compromise, as both sides licked their wounds and prepared for the next stages of the coming war.

With that conflict over, Hough was returned to his parent unit, the 9th Battalion, Rifle Brigade. They were dispatched to North Africa, and after spending weeks undergoing intensive desert training, the battalion was finally deployed. But during his preparations for desert operations Hough received some shattering news. Though just forty-five years of age, his mother had died suddenly of a brain haemorrhage. The 9th Battalion was moved into the frontline, near Benghazi, in modern day Libya. Hough saw action at Mersa Brega and Agedabia, where the fighting was particularly brutal, involving fierce hand-to-hand combat.

En route to the port city of Derna, the battalion was thrust into its most desperate battle yet, being ambushed by a 'well-armed force of enemy tanks and infantry'. A ferocious firefight had ensued, as the 9th Battalion called on the anti-tank skills of the Royal Horse Artillery, whose guns knocked out 'a large number of [the enemy's] armoured vehicles . . . eventually clearing the road, but at great cost'. Four officers of the battalion had been killed, all of whom were close friends of Hough's, along with a large number of their men. Worse still on a personal level, during eight days of bloody combat Hough had lost half of his platoon, either wounded or killed in action. The transitory nature of life in wartime was to affect him deeply, Hough writing later that 'it is shocking, deeply so, and the trauma of it lives long in the heart.'

Withdrawn from the lines, what remained of the battalion was evacuated by destroyer, and a period of rest, recuperation and training followed. Promoted to captain, Hough soon found himself back in the thick of it, as the 9th Battalion relieved the 2nd at Maaten Gerawla, in Egypt. It was now that he and his men were called upon to carry out reconnaissance patrols, penetrating behind enemy lines and moving in close proximity to German and Italian positions, as they sought out intelligence. This would give him a good grounding for what was to come when, a year later, he joined the SAS.

The predatory nature of war in the desert hit him again that October, when one of his closest friends, Tommy Meyer, failed to return from one of those probing patrols. Meyer and his sergeant had been spotted by the enemy and killed in the resulting firefight. Hough had to blank out the trauma that he was feeling. 'I knew I was going to have to find a way of locking that part of me away,' he would write, 'otherwise it would dominate me and I would not survive it mentally.' Although he forced himself to do this, he still believed 'it was inevitable that my turn would come,' such was the ferocity of the war in the desert.

North Africa – the Sahara – was a hugely challenging environment in which to conduct a war. During the day the heat would become unbearable, contrasting sharply with the bitter cold of the night. What the men dreaded most was the *khamseen*, an extremely hot and heavy wind that gusted up from the south. It would flatten tents, fill every nook and cranny with hot, clogging sand, and leave any exposed skin raw and irritated. It also cut visibility to a few yards, ruined food supplies and clogged up air filters, rendering vehicles temporarily undrivable. It meant that the men had to be constantly on guard, ready to clean their weapons and equipment, and shield their most sensitive kit.

On 18 November 1941 the battalion was again on the move, this time as part of the force sent to relieve Tobruk. After the RAF had conducted a bombing run on advancing German tanks, Hough was horrified to see around fifty Ju 87 'Stuka' dive-bombers circling overhead. Expecting a pasting, he and his troops dug themselves in. Astonishingly, the German planes proceeded to bomb their own tanks, giving them an almighty battering, leaving many as burning hulks. What remained of the German forces, their spirits shattered, turned and headed back to their lines, leaving Hough and his men to issue a collective sigh of relief.

By December 1941, Hough found himself back at Mersa Brega again. The irony was not lost on him. British forces were back in roughly the same positions as they had been some seven months earlier – 'right where we had started at the beginning of the year, making one wonder at the stupidity of it all,' Hough reflected. Hough had witnessed the killing and wounding of combatants, which was to be expected during times of war. But then, on 19 January 1942, he was to experience something that he would find 'hard to forget and even harder to forgive'. Adjacent to the British positions at Mersa Brega there was a large camp of Bedouin – semi-nomadic desert people – their tents flying white flags to indicate their neutrality.

That evening a large group of Italian and German dive-bombers thundered over. Hough assumed they were coming in for another aerial attack and dashed for the shelters. However, the target for the aircraft was not the British positions. Instead, they swooped upon the Bedouin encampment. Those watching could hear the screams of the women and children, as the bombs exploded among them, killing and maiming many. Hough saw this as 'a deliberate act of savagery against defenceless people caught in the unwelcome clutch of a war they had no part in'. It was something that defined for him the barbarism of the enemy.

As the Afrika Korps attacked, Hough endured an entire month in the frontline, constantly under fire from ground forces and suffering under repeated Luftwaffe bombing raids. By now, he'd spent the best part of twenty months waging war in North Africa, losing so many good friends – killed, captured, or fate unknown. So far, he had been lucky. After so long in combat, he and his fellows had learned to depend on each other absolutely. As he would later reflect, 'we had become a close-knit group who had learnt to rely totally on each other, learnt to make level-headed decisions under severe duress, learnt to lead with compassion and fortitude and above all, to keep fighting, even when it seemed as if the gates of Hell were open and welcoming.'

The battered and bloodied remnants of the 9th Battalion were pulled out of the line, and the unit was sadly disbanded. The surviving men were to be assimilated into other units or returned to the UK. But Hough was determined to see the battle for North Africa through to the bitter end. He'd been there for so long and had given so much to the cause of victory. He felt he still had a mission to fulfil – to defeat the Italian and German enemy. He felt he owed it to those of his brothers in arms who had lost their lives so valiantly. Despite the emotional impact of seeing so many good men die, he was convinced he remained 'capable of taking the fight to the enemy . . . There was an anger in me that burned intensely and drove me on.'

As fortune would have it, at this moment Hough was asked if he would consider volunteering for the SAS. The unit's founder, David Stirling, remembered Hough well, from the time they'd spent at Chamonix undergoing ski training. He was desperate to recruit officers with combat experience for a new unit he was then raising. It was to be known as the SAS's B Squadron, the long-serving A Squadron being commanded by Sterling's right-hand-man, the legendary Captain Blair 'Paddy' Mayne.

Hough viewed a move to the SAS as 'a natural step for me . . . as much of what it did was what we had been doing already'. Two of Hough's stalwarts from the 9th Battalion were keen to go with him. He headed for Kabrit, the SAS's training base, together with those two men, Alfred Handscombe and Mick Levy, having warned them that for the SAS, 'you have to volunteer'.

While Handscombe had turned into a peerless soldier, things had not started well for him. A year or so earlier, Hough had witnessed the man crumbling when first finding himself thrust into the heat of combat. He'd cowered in a slit trench, as the enemy had attacked their position. But after receiving a stiff talking-to, and upon seeing some of his friends killed, there was a change within Handscombe. He began taking the fight to the enemy and was soon putting himself in grave danger to help his comrades, becoming a courageous and 'resourceful soldier'. Hough could not have asked for 'anyone braver to stand alongside' him as a fellow volunteer for the SAS.

B Squadron training began in Kabrit that September 1942, under the command of Major Vivien Street. It proved intense and arduous in the extreme. Many of those who had volunteered fell victim to the relentless pace and were rejected. Only the very best could endure. Curiously, those who came across as arrogant and brash were the ones who tended to fail first. David Stirling and Paddy Mayne were looking for men of a very particular calibre and spirit. Strength of character coupled with an urge to succeed, despite all the odds, and the mindset to never give in – those were key attributes. So too was being able to think on your feet and act quickly and decisively, plus being able to work as part of a small team under intense and brutal conditions.

Hough proved to have those qualities in abundance.

Even as B Squadron was undergoing its relentless training, so British forces won a major victory at El Alamein, and gradually they began to push the enemy back, reversing their most recent gains. Then came Operation Torch, the landing of US-led forces along the west coast of North Africa, in a move designed to crush the German and Italian armies in a pincer movement. With Torch, the enemy were trapped between the British Eighth Army in the east and the American-led First Army in the west. The war in North Africa was tipping decisively in the Allies' favour.

The SAS's forthcoming mission, codenamed Operation Palmyra, had been devised as a spur to that push. Fresh out of training, the men of B Squadron were to play a vital part in it.

On 18 November, Major Street called his officers together to outline the mission. Operation Palmyra would involve B Squadron crossing over 3,000 kilometres of desert to reach their operational area. In the process, they were to pass beyond A Squadron, currently camped at a remote outpost called Bir Zalten, under the command of Paddy Mayne. They would roll through Mayne's area of operations, so as to hit Rommel's supply lines beyond, pushing further west than they had ever gone before. Once in position they were to be split into patrols of three jeeps, with two men to each vehicle, to execute hit-and-run attacks on the enemy's supply columns plying the coastal road. The raids were to take place at night, so forcing the enemy to move by day, making them vulnerable to strikes by the Royal Air Force.

As Handscombe and Levy had made it through B Squadron training, Hough requested they be assigned to his patrol. He had little doubt that their means of insertion – the Willys jeeps – packed a real punch. Each was armed with a pair of rapid-firing Vickers K machine guns, and carried several thousand rounds of ammunition, plus a hundred pounds of plastic explosives and around a dozen landmines. Each vehicle also carried seventy-two gallons of fuel and enough rations to last twenty days. Hough didn't doubt he had the means, and the men, with which to fight. It was the mission itself – Operation Palmyra – that had left him feeling distinctly edgy.

Their area of operations lay along a 300-kilometre stretch of coastal road, leading from Bouerat to Tripoli (in modern-day Libya). As yet this was largely 'unknown territory for the SAS'. Hough hadn't been impressed with the plan. Knowing the desert as he did, he feared it would be nigh-on impossible to make it back to Allied lines once their supplies were exhausted. Fuel was a particularly vexing issue. There just wasn't the capacity to carry enough in each of the jeeps to cover the distance required. This being the case, the fallback plan seemed to involve stealing fuel from the enemy when the squadron's own supplies ran dry. With many believing that the Allied advance would be swift now, there was also a sense that B Squadron would have no problems linking up with their forces. But Hough was experienced-enough to know that the war in North Africa didn't always go the way the Allies intended.

In the SAS War Diary, B Squadron is noted as setting out from Kabrit just before midnight on 20 November 1942. After driving through the night, they reached an area that Hough knew intimately, for he'd spent many months fighting over this very stretch of territory. They were joined by David Stirling, and upon reaching Benghazi they turned south, heading for the open desert. After motoring for over 300 kilometres they arrived at Bir Zalten, where A Squadron was encamped. Called to an officer's meeting, Hough met that unit's commander, Captain Paddy Mayne, for the first time. He found the legendary desert warrior to be 'charming, friendly and relaxed'. Indeed, Mayne 'gave the air of a man completely at one with the war,' Hough noted. 'His reputation as a ferocious fighter without fear for his own safety was well known to all of us.'

His impression of David Stirling was somewhat different. 'David was filled to the brim with energy and with a recklessness that while enervating, also suggested the welfare of his men was not a priority when it came to attacking the enemy,' Hough observed. On studying the plans for Operation Palmyra, his misgivings redoubled. He seriously doubted if his three-jeep patrol would be able to make it out of the area, 'given the depth of our incursion into enemy territory'. He had a bad feeling that 'B Squadron was the expendable one,' and that he and his men were now some of the expendables. His old friend Carol Mather was also at Bir Zalten. Mather had joined the SAS a few months before Hough and had already seen action. Worryingly, Mather too 'expressed grave doubts that we would make it back' from what was coming.

In fact, Hough and Mather were far from being alone in entertaining such misgivings. Lieutenant Brian Dillon, another patrol leader, had been given the job of attacking the railway lines lying to the west of Tripoli. Having calculated the mileage he could cover on the fuel the jeeps carried, he posted the obvious question to David Stirling, asking 'how he was supposed to get back'. Stirling merely shrugged his shoulders, before confessing to Lieutenant Dillon that he had asked Montgomery the very same thing. No one seemed to have a concrete plan of how to withdraw, except to pilfer fuel from the enemy's own supplies.

Either way, the die was cast.

A few days later, B Squadron had set off, heading deeper into enemy territory. They had arrived at their forward base on 2 December 1942. There they left their convoy of three-tonne lorries, laden with supplies, and pushed further west with just the jeeps. The journey was fraught, the terrain being all-but impassable and causing damage to many of the jeeps. Stirling, who was travelling in their midst, ordered parts to be cannibalised from disabled vehicles, so those that remained could keep pushing on.

At one point they were ambushed by an Italian Army armoured car patrol. Two jeeps were shot up and their occupants killed. More vehicles were hit and put out of action. Answering fire with fire, the SAS gunners poured a barrage of Vickers rounds into the enemy armoured vehicles, forcing them into a retreat. A small group paused to bury their dead, while the remainder of the B Squadron convoy pushed ever west towards their objective.

By 11 December the Squadron had reached Bir Fascia, its final rallying point. There, each of the patrols was to split off, making directly for its target. So it was that Hough and his patrol had set out, travelling in convoy with Carol Mather's unit. Finally, Mather and his jeeps peeled away further to the west, for that was where their objective lay. Hough, meanwhile, had settled down to study the stretch of road that was his to deal with. In short order he and his men had felled the trees that were used to block it, and laid their mines.

That in turn had snared the enemy convoy, the two lead trucks getting blasted into fiery ruin. But those that had survived had come speeding after the raiders in a hot pursuit, as the hunt across the desert had begun.

As the night-dark desert chase continued, Hough kept glancing behind him, trying to gauge the progress of the enemy. The Italians were showing no sign of letting up and Hough was worried. The terrain thereabouts was mostly soft sand, which prevented them from driving at the jeep's maximum speed, so hampering their progress. Normally, they could outrun such heavy trucks as these. Their jeeps were far more nimble. But hampered as they were, it was crucial they found somewhere to go to ground. A place to hide.

Hough figured he needed to do something to slow down the hunters. Signalling to the other two drivers, he gestured for them to turn around, following his lead. In one smooth move the three jeeps swung around into line abreast and came to a halt. Allowing the leading trucks to get within 300 yards, the gunners opened up with their Vickers Ks, spraying a blaze of fire into them. Tracer rounds ricocheted off the metal cabs and shot up into the night sky, while the glass windows and headlamps shattered and imploded. Without waiting to see exactly what damage they had wrought, Hough executed an about-turn as the three vehicles endeavoured to slip into the cover of the night.

But bad luck and trouble were to dog their every step now. Even as the jeeps were speeding for sanctuary, one began to splutter and stutter, before eventually it juddered to a halt. The thing Hough had most feared had finally happened. One of their vehicles was all out of fuel. Grabbing their small arms and ammunition, the soldiers riding in the stricken vehicle jumped aboard the remaining jeeps and they got under way once more, leaving an explosive charge in the abandoned jeep to destroy it before it could fall into enemy hands. Hough was acutely aware how dire was their predicament now. The two remaining vehicles were running on fumes, and soon both started to judder and cough due to the lack of fuel.

It was then that he saw it.

Ahead, that wide open desert devoid of cover was cut by a wadi – a dry, sunken riverbed. Finding an area where it sloped down gently enough to allow the jeeps to enter, they descended into its depths. Nosing into cover, they pulled to a halt as the six men leapt down and grabbed their camouflaged netting. As fast as they could they threw it over the vehicles, hiding them as best they were able. They prayed the hasty camouflage job would be enough to conceal the jeeps from the hunters.

Shortly, the rumble of approaching vehicles filled their ears. It sounded as if the enemy's trucks were coming from both sides, effectively surrounding them. Pressing themselves into the side of the wadi, Hough and his men held their breath and waited. Soon enough, they heard voices close by. Italian officers were shouting orders to their men. It had to be fairly obvious where the British raiders were hidden. In open desert such as this, the wadi was the only place where they could have gone to ground.

It was not long before Hough saw the first enemy troops. A group of Italian soldiers were moving cautiously along the wadi floor, approaching from one direction. With the sun not yet fully up, they appeared as shadowy figures, hunched low, searching any patches of cover for signs of their prey. Their weapons at the ready, Hough and his men steeled themselves for combat. There was no way they could avoid being seen. They would have to fight it out.

Shortly, the six fugitives were spotted. With shouts of alarm, the Italians raised their guns. Hough and his men were quicker. They opened up, spewing Sten sub-machine gun and rifle fire into the midst of their adversaries, knocking enemy fighters to the ground. Having cut down that first enemy patrol, they rushed to another patch of cover, even as further Italian soldiers poured into the wadi. There were groups of enemy on all sides now. Hough and his men were hemmed in.

Slowly, the Italians advanced. The cornered SAS men opened fire, forcing them back, before moving again, for their muzzle flashes would have betrayed their position. Hough remained hopeful that 'the darkness would ... work in our favour and give us a chance to get away'. By firing at the Italians on all sides, he was gambling that they could get the enemy to open fire on each other, which might allow the six of them to slip away in the confusion.

Hough sent two of his men to see if they could spot any gaps in the enemy cordon. But they returned with warnings that they were surrounded. Still the firefight raged, bullets ripping through the air on all sides. Hough and his men kept blasting away at the Italians each time they came within range. But the enemy were likewise returning fire, bullets smashing into the rocks all around Hough and his men, who were heavily outnumbered.

Hough knew this couldn't go on for much longer. They were surrounded by a far superior force, and would soon be out of ammo. Even if they could make it out into the desert, they couldn't drive anywhere, for their jeeps were all out of fuel. Being on foot would almost certainly result in their capture, and especially as dawn was but a short time away.

As the first rays of the sun began to show over the distant horizon, Hough knew he had to make a decision. In hurried tones he spoke to the others. If he could create a diversion, it might force a gap in the Italian lines. At that point his men were to break out and try to make it back to Bir Fascia on foot, he told them, Bir Fascia being their final rallying point before the patrols had gone their separate ways.

'You get going,' he urged. 'I'll hold them up.'

With that, Hough made his move. Crouching low he sprinted along the wadi and climbed up to a point where he could reach the rim. Once there he spied a boulder that would give good cover, even as he opened fire upon the enemy from a flanking position. He could see the nearest Italian troops around a hundred yards away, shooting at his comrades where he'd left them in the wadi. Using his rifle, Hough opened up. Instantly, the enemy's attention was drawn to him, just as he'd intended. They opened fire, bullets pinging off the rock with such intensity that he was forced to dive for cover.

Hough slid back down the wadi wall, scurried twenty yards further along, before rising up to engage the enemy again. By now, they seemed to be firing at him from all directions. It was a miracle that he hadn't been hit. He checked his ammunition; it was virtually exhausted. With no other options, he decided to make a run for it. Sliding down into the wadi again, he put his head down and sprinted for his life. But he'd not made it that far when he stumbled into a group of enemy troops, their weapons raised menacingly. This was it. The game was up. He just hoped his diversion had been enough for Handscombe, Levy and the others to have slipped away.

Throwing down his rifle, Hough raised his arms.

After two and a half years of waging war in North Africa, he had finally been captured.

The enemy troops approached, looking distinctly confused. They obviously knew there should be more than one lone man. Where was the rest of Hough's patrol? Where was the force that had wreaked so much havoc and harm? Hough could see none of his SAS comrades anywhere thereabouts, so he had to assume his diversionary attack had worked. He just hoped they could make it safely back to Bir Fascia, and from there to British lines.

The commander of the enemy patrol was a captain. He looked livid, his face contorted in a mask of fury. Snatching a rifle from one of his soldiers, he rammed into Hough's guts. Hough held his breath. Was this it? Was this how it would end for him? Gunned down while unarmed and a prisoner? The enraged captain pulled the trigger. There was an audible click as the firing pin hit home, but it struck on an empty chamber. The rifle wasn't loaded.

The captain stepped back, 'an expression of disbelief on his face', as Hough would later describe it. With trembling hands he handed the rifle back to the trooper from whom he'd grabbed it, before ordering his men to search for the remaining British soldiers. There had to be more, he urged. With three men assigned to guard him, Hough was manhandled towards one of the trucks and ordered to clamber inside.

As the search continued for his comrades, Hough pondered what had just taken place. He began to doubt his own decisions. Had the others really managed to slip away? Surely, if one man could be shot out of hand, as the Italian officer had attempted, then they all could? He had always entertained misgivings about their ability to avoid capture, operating so far behind enemy lines with so little fuel. Now, his worst fears had come to pass. As he would reflect later: 'This was a dire moment for me, and I began to feel utterly dejected.'

With no sign of the rest of his patrol, finally Hough was driven to Misrata town, on the Mediterranean coast, under close guard. The following morning he was joined in his cell by someone claiming to be an RAF gunner, and to have been shot down a few days earlier. From the outset Hough was suspicious of the man. There was something about him that didn't ring true. It was as if he was putting on an act about how bad he felt at being in captivity, but it was simply too forced. Whenever Hough asked about his RAF service, the supposed 'airman' turned the conversation back to Hough. Hough smelled a rat, and began to mock him. Eventually, he warned the newcomer that he was going to sleep, and he 'might like to bugger off'.

When Hough awoke the 'RAF airman' was gone. Hough was left in no doubt that the man was a stool pigeon – one of the most ancient and nastiest species of traitor. The term 'stool pigeon' derives from the habit of hunters tying a pigeon to a stool, to lure other birds in. In military and espionage parlance a stool pigeon is an informer, one who inveigles himself into the confidence of prisoners-of-war by posing as one of them. Simply by listening in on the prisoners' chat, and posing the odd, seemingly innocent question, the stool pigeon could garner useful intelligence. That at least was the theory. But Hough – a seasoned desert warrior – had given this one very short shrift.

A day or two later, Hough was put in a truck and driven to

Tripoli, around ninety miles away. During the journey he noted the nervousness of the Axis forces. Passing through checkpoint after checkpoint, he was pleased to see how busy the roads were. They were crammed with lorries loaded with troops and supplies, despite its being broad daylight. This had been one of the key objectives of Operation Palmyra – to force the enemy to move during daylight hours, when they could be preyed upon by the RAF. It seems B Squadron's raids had borne fruit after all.

On arrival at Tripoli, Hough was taken directly to a wharf where he was bundled onto a waiting submarine. As he was shoved into the cramped confines of the forward torpedo compartment, he noticed someone he instantly recognised. Sitting forlornly on the metal deck was his close friend and fellow B Squadron officer, Carol Mather. Hough settled beside Mather as they exchanged stories. Mather's patrol had been spotted by Italian forces as they were driving through a small village. The hunt had begun and they were run to earth the next day. After a fierce skirmish they were surrounded and had been forced to give themselves up.

By the time the submarine weighed anchor, more prisoners had been loaded aboard. All were officers, around fifteen in all. After a horrendous journey, in which they were rarely allowed out of the compartment, and during which they feared a horrible death when depth charges were dropped by an Allied destroyer, they eventually arrived at Taranto, the port city lying on the heel of Italy. From there they were taken to a prison camp in Bari on the Adriatic coast.

After spending two months in squalid conditions, Hough and Mather were moved to a camp further north in late February 1943.

Prigione di Guerra 21, or Campo 21, at Chieti, in the Abruzzo region of Italy, was notorious. Housing around 1,300 officers and men, it lay 150 kilometres to the east of Rome, and adjacent to the coastal city of Pescara. Conditions at Campo 21 were horrendous. Life was unbearable for those unfortunate enough to be incarcerated there. Cells were crammed with many more men than they were designed to hold, there was an absence of clean sanitation, food was scarce, and what little they did get was barely edible.

It was winter when they arrived, so conditions were that much worse. With no real heating or hot water, and with the POWs wearing clothes designed for warmer, North African climes, the threadbare blankets they were issued with did little to ward off the cold. Many fell ill, suffering from jaundice and dysentery. Due to the terrible conditions, 'fights would break out over the smallest of things and resentments would fester for days,' as Hough noted.

To make matters worse, the running of the camp was little short of brutal. The camp commandant was a Colonello Massi, but the real authority lay with his notorious adjutant, Captain Mario Croce. Croce was a diehard Fascist and as Hough soon realized, he nursed a burning hatred of British POWs. Captain Croce was in the habit of ordering the POWs to parade multiple times a day, just to tire and frustrate them, and would carry out invasive searches, leaving rooms in chaos, and with mattresses sliced apart, plus personal possessions scattered across the floor. To make matters worse, Croce withheld the all-important Red Cross food parcels, and refused to pass on letters from home or to dispatch letters from prisoners to their families.

Unsurprisingly, escape was foremost in Hough and his friend Mather's minds. As the weather started to improve, Mather sensed an opportunity whereby maybe he could better his chances of escape. A group of prisoners were to be transported to a camp further north, at Fontanellato, near Parma. Mather argued that if he could join that party, escape would be easier from there, for it was closer to neutral Switzerland. Swapping places and identities with another prisoner, Mather was taken to the waiting trucks and he set out for the new camp. 'It was a sad moment when he left the camp, as he had become a good friend,' Hough would write of their parting.

With Mather gone, Hough tried to adjust to camp life but he had too much time to dwell on what had happened over the past two years. Faced with the very real danger of falling into a deep depression, he was fortunate to be befriended by a lieutenant from the Rifle Brigade, Peter Gunn, who'd been taken prisoner in 1941. In a short space of time they became firm friends. Gunn proved to be a good listener, one to whom Hough could confide. He offered Hough practical advice and encouraged him to talk openly about how he was feeling. 'After a while I felt myself begin to mend,' Hough would observe of this time.

Hough began to think about escape again, sensing that Gunn would be the ideal travelling companion. He was aware that there were several tunnels being dug under the camp, but the escape teams were full, and in any case he was too tall to suit a tunnel-based getaway. If he was going to breakout he would have to find another means entirely. Hough's spirits really lifted, as news reached the camp that the Axis powers had been defeated in North Africa. This buoyed up the morale of the entire camp, especially when their Italian captors increased the distribution of Red Cross parcels, as they began to sense that they might lose the entire war.

Then, on 8 September 1943, there was further fabulous news: the Italians had surrendered. On hearing this, the camp commandant, Colonello Massi, handed the running of the place to the Senior British Officer, Lieutenant Colonel William Marshall. Some of the Italian guards remained, although many more discarded their weapons and headed for home. The joy this gave the POWs was tempered greatly when Lieutenant Colonel Marshall, learning of MI9's Stay Put Order, proceeded to enforce it to the letter. To prevent anyone from trying to slip away, he 'put British patrols on the perimeter of the camp with an order that any man found attempting to escape would be court-martialled for desertion'.

Like many in the camp, Hough fumed at such a misguided attitude. There was no way Allied forces could reach Campo 21 before the Germans did. To stay could mean only one thing – falling into German captivity, with all that would follow. There was talk of simply disobeying Marshall's orders and walking out of the camp en masse. But when Marshall got wind of what the officers were discussing, many, including Hough, were given a severe dressing down. He was the senior officer, the men were under his command, and they would do as ordered, Marshall warned. Hough was furious, but he managed to keep his thoughts to himself. There was no way that he was going to stay and be made a prisoner of the Germans.

Casting around for a means to break free, Hough noticed that the door to the camp's water tower, a tall brick building, was ajar. Each day an Italian worker visited, to turn on the water, before returning a while later to turn it off again. Hough watched how that man killed time in the interim, having a smoke out the back of the building. His curiosity getting the better of him, Hough pushed open the door and slipped inside. In front of him rose a ladder, leading up to the water tank above. Just below the tank was another level, and when he clambered up to inspect it, he found a large dusty area containing various tools. It was big enough to house a number of people, and just two small windows looked down on the camp below.

Immediately, a plan started to form in his head. With Marshall insisting that they 'stay put', and with German Army convoys passing the camp on a daily basis, the situation was looking desperate. The Stay Put Order was now surely invalid – not that it should ever have been issued – for the situation on the ground had changed. The Allies were nowhere near Chieti, while the Germans were building up their forces in the area. Surely it made sense for the men to leave while they could and to try and make their way south. Even those few Italian guards who had stayed were deserting their posts, for they were unwilling to face the conflict they knew was coming – against a German army of occupation.

Hough could sense that the Germans were only days away from taking over the camp. He feared they would spirit the POWs to Germany, moving them ever further away from the advancing Allied forces. In light of that impending danger and inspired by his visit to the water tower, he presented his idea for escape to Peter Gunn. As Gunn backed his plan, they sought out two fellow officers who were keen to join them, Captain 'Mac' MacDermott of the Royal Engineers, and Lieutenant 'Ricky' Rickett of the Royal Northamptonshire Regiment.

MacDermott and Rickett proved of immense help. They knew of a prisoner who was said to be something of a locksmith. If they could get a mould of the key to the water tower door made, then he could very likely make a copy. Waiting until the Italian worker had done his thing and left again, Hough saw the key left in the lock. The four would-be escapees hustled their locksmith to the door. As they shielded him from view, he was able to make a perfect imprint. A few hours later he handed them a metal replica, and all for the princely sum of 'our ration of cigarettes and some additional food', as Hough noted.

The four escapees collected together as much in the way of supplies as they could. On 13 September, German officers were seen visiting the camp. But it wasn't until a week later that, just as all had feared, the Germans made their move in force. A large number of military trucks pulled up at the camp, unloading squads of well-armed German troops. Shortly, they started to fill the trucks with prisoners. Convoys began to pull out, their ultimate destination being POW camps in Germany.

It was now that Hough and his fellow escapees needed to make their move. Under the cover of darkness, the four grabbed their provisions and crept over to the water tower. Thankfully, the key worked and they slipped inside. But the door failed to lock from the inside, no matter how hard they tried. They had no choice but to leave it like that and hope. Quickly, they climbed up the ladder to the level below the water tank and settled down on that dusty platform.

Come sunrise, conditions there were grim. The heat became oppressive, the stench from the bucket they were using as a toilet, overpowering. Flies and mosquitoes buzzed about and they found it hard to keep still on the bare wooden floor, as the dust clogged up their nostrils. But with the camp crawling with German soldiers, they would have to remain still and silent, or risk giving themselves away. At one point, the Italian worker came to turn on the water, before leaving and locking the door behind him, which meant they were now trapped.

Keeping away from the windows for fear of being seen, they could hear trucks coming and going. It sounded as if the camp were being evacuated of the last of the prisoners, just as they had feared it would be. They had been proved a hundred per cent right: Lieutenant Colonel Marshall's insistence on sticking to the Stay Put Order had been completely misguided. Any number of Allied prisoners were now heading towards an uncertain fate in Germany, when they could have taken to the hills and struck out for Allied lines.

All through the following two days the camp was emptied, before finally it fell silent. That morning the four fugitives heard a noise of a quite different kind. It was a group of Italian children playing just outside the tower. MacDermott chanced a look through the window, but he was spotted by one of the kids. With no other option, the four men were forced to make their move. They descended the ladder to the ground floor. Again, no matter how hard they tried the key would not open the lock. Some tools were brought down from their former hiding place, and with those they managed to smash a hole through the door. It was clear that the Germans had left, as nobody came to see what all the noise was about.

Once they had slipped outside to the camp perimeter, they headed for a building that the camp's escape committee had told them about. It was supposedly a safe-house operated by the Italian resistance. They reached it, to be greeted by an elderly Italian couple who took them in. But after a brief handshake, MacDermott and Rickett announced that they were off, for they were keen to get to Allied lines. Hough was eager to go with them.

Gunn demurred. He figured they should lie low and await the arrival of Allied forces. As Gunn had been such a fine friend to Hough, he decided to stay with him. The elderly Italians warned them that Chieti was occupied by a German battalion, who conducted regular patrols. Their place could serve only as a brief stopover, after which they would have to move on to somewhere safer.

The following morning Hough and Gunn were offered fresh clothes, but declined. They knew that to be caught in civilian attire could mean being shot as spies. That was a risk they didn't want to take. Shortly, they were visited by a young man from the Italian resistance, more usually known as the partisans. He warned them that they were to be moved that very evening. Although they were far from safe yet, Hough felt positive and buoyant: 'we felt the exhilaration of being in charge of our future,' he would later remark.

That evening they were led to a small house lying deep in the woods. They were warned that German troops were making regular house-to-house searches, so they would be moved on again. Their aim was to get to the village of Pretoro, which lay on the fringes of the Maiella mountains, part of the Central Apennine range. The towering hills around Pretoro, with their high plateaus and knife-cut gorges, were remote and inaccessible. The place was a hotbed of partisan activity, and the people there had 'little regard for the Germans and the Fascists', Hough and Gunn were told.

A few days later, in the early evening of 30 September 1943, a small band of partisans arrived to escort them on the next stage of their journey. Not long after they had set out, Hough heard something that gave his morale another major boost. It was the unmistakable sound of Rolls-Royce Merlin engines. Glancing to the sky, he saw three Supermarine Spitfires flying low over their heads. No doubt about it, the forces of the Allies were on the march.

A young Italian woman named Frieda was in charge of their group. She spoke excellent English. As they walked that first night, Frieda was able to give Hough and Gunn an update on the wider fortunes of the war. She herself was a widow, her husband having been conscripted into the army and killed in North Africa. This had given her a deep hatred for both the Italian Fascists and now their German occupiers. She shared the news that Italy's former dictator, Benito Mussolini, had been imprisoned on a high plateau, on the Gran Sasso massif, which includes Italy's highest peak. But two weeks earlier Mussolini had been rescued by German paratroopers, in what sounded to Hough like a daring, SAS-style mission. She also told him that partisan groups were getting organised across Italy, but were holding off from engaging with the enemy after being warned that, for every German killed, the Nazi powers would execute ten Italian civilians.

For hours they walked and they talked. Hough found himself captivated by Frieda's bravery and her single-minded tenacity. Their conversation ranged over many subjects, including life before the war and their aspirations for when it was over. As they talked, the terrain became ever more taxing, the hills growing steeper, the valleys deeper and the streams and rivers more ferocious. While the scenery was breathtaking, the going proved hard, and especially for men who had endured a regime like that at Campo 21 for so long.

Their route skirted around the village of Roccamontepiano,

after which they rested on the terrace of a mountainside convent. They pressed on through dense woodland and over many steep ridges, until, eventually, at nightfall on the second day, they reached their destination. After descending into a valley, Hough looked up to spy the 'village of Pretoro perched above us, seemingly glued to the side of a steep hill'. The brave people of this mountainside settlement were to provide the two SAS fugitives with sanctuary for the next few months.

It was a time that Hough would remember for the rest of his life.

Gino Francioni had lived in Pretoro ever since the day of his birth. He hated the Fascists with a passion, believing they had 'destroyed the whole fabric of Italy'. When approached by the partisans to help with escaped Allied POWs, he had jumped at the chance. It was dusk by the time Frieda knocked on his door. Once she had introduced Hough and Gunn, Francioni told her he was only too willing to offer them shelter and assistance.

Hough was impressed with his tanned, open-faced appearance. He was possessed of 'a resourcefulness and inner strength that we found very reassuring ... the sort of chap you would like on your shoulder in a tight spot,' Hough observed. Indeed, Francioni would go on to be their saviour many times over in the coming weeks. Showing them to a bedroom on the upper floor, he advised them to keep away from the windows. Although most in the village were united in their views of the Germans and Fascists, there were a few who would give them away at a moment's notice.

With those thoughts foremost in their minds, Francioni led them downstairs to show them the cellar, and a hidden passageway that reached out to a narrow alleyway running beside the house. They were to use this as an escape route, he warned, should the Germans come knocking. With no running water in the village, a bucket in the cellar was there for their ablutions, fresh water being collected from the valley each day. It was a somewhat primitive set up, but at least they were safe and hosted by someone they were confident would look out for them.

Three nights later, Francioni moved them to another location – a house 'tucked away in one of the many narrow streets rising steeply up the hillside'. It was owned by Titino and Maria Santurbano, who lived there with their eighteen-year-old daughter, Juliana. As the village possessed no street lighting, Hough and Gunn would be able to move in relative safety during the hours of darkness. Even so, they reasoned it was worth scoping out possible escape routes that would take them to the valley below, should they need to make a quick getaway.

At the Santurbanos' they were given a comfortable bedroom on the top floor of the house. As they settled into their new routine, they did their best to improve their Italian, something Gunn was to pick up easier than Hough. They also learned of the state of the Allied advance. British forces had taken the city of Foggia, and were about to push on towards Termoli. Hearing of this was welcome news, but it meant that the frontline was still around a hundred kilometres south of where they were hiding out.

They also heard news from the Santurbanos that was distinctly alarming. After the Armistice, some of the POW camps had simply thrown open their gates. Tens of thousands of Allied prisoners had escaped, defying the Stay Put Order en masse. However, a significant number had been recaptured or shot by the Germans. This was another good reason, Gunn argued, for

91

the two of them to lie low. They should wait for the Allied advance, and not take their chances on a difficult trek over harsh terrain, risking recapture or death at every turn.

But Hough remained unsettled. He was itching to get moving, and he envied MacDermott and Rickett their 'trek south'. Even so, his loyalty to Gunn, who had been a constant friend during his darkest times in captivity, compelled him to stay. During the days the two fugitives would stay up in their room, practising their Italian and waiting for night to fall when they could go downstairs and sit with the family by the fire. For Hough, although he enjoyed the company of their Italian hosts, especially Juliana, he hungered to be on the move.

They'd been lying low in the village for the best part of two weeks, when, at 4 a.m. on 20 October, Hough was rudely awoken by the lady of the house. She was shaking him almost violently. A large group of German soldiers had arrived outside, she warned. She was clearly terrified, and Hough could appreciate why. If they were discovered, her life and that of her family was at an end. Slowly, Hough made his way to the window and cautiously pulled the curtain to one side. Sure enough, on the street below there were a large number of German troops. Even more ominously, one was gripping a large black dog on a lead.

Hough stole a glance in the direction of their planned escape route – the one he and Gunn had scoped out, for just such an eventuality. He was horrified to see that the alleyways on all sides were blocked by more German soldiers. He turned to find the three Santurbanos standing before him – father, mother and child. They looked scared out of their wits. There was simply no way out. There was nothing they could do but wait. Eventually, they heard the harsh sound of rapping on a door. But for some reason it wasn't their own. The troops were banging on the entrance to a house two doors away. A moment later their neighbour opened up, and the search party forced its way inside, the dog to the fore, snarling viciously.

After what seemed like an age, the soldiers reappeared, their officer yelling furiously in German. Hough fully expected them to head up the street to the Santurbanos' home. But after a short while the troops began to move off. Finally the last echo of the enemy's boots died away, and they were able to breathe a sigh of relief. Shortly, they learned what had happened. Hough and Gunn had been betrayed by an informer, but the Germans had been given the wrong address.

It was too dangerous to remain where they were. Gino Francioni collected them, even as dawn was breaking, and he led them out of the village into the forest beyond. Hough felt exhilarated at being out in the open once more. Breathing in the fresh mountain air seemed to rejuvenate him. Once again, he voiced the idea of making a break for British lines, but was persuaded against it by Gunn. Gunn argued that the area was crawling with German troops, and that they had no chance of making it 'fifty or sixty miles through occupied territory without being recaptured or killed'. Reluctantly, Hough agreed. 'We decided to stick to the plan, even with my misgivings,' he reflected, later.

For the remainder of that day they waited for Francioni, hiding deep in the forest. Eventually he reappeared and led them to a ramshackle house owned by an elderly couple – shelter for the night. The following day he took them back into the village. One of his close neighbours, Angela Perseo, had offered to take them in for as long as they might need. This was despite the fact that she had five of her own children to feed and care for. The children were aged between nine and twenty-two, but it was Maria, aged eleven, who seemed the most thrilled at having the two British soldiers staying with them, being 'full of excitement and energy'.

After the near miss with the previous family that had offered them sanctuary, Hough was very conscious of putting the Perseos at risk. This was doubly so, for with winter approaching the weather would worsen, slowing the Allied advance. But he was equally reluctant to break away from his friend, Gunn. For two weeks everything remained quiet. Nobody other than their hosts, and Gino Francioni, knew where they were hiding. Occasionally, a German patrol would enter the piazza – the village square – forcing Hough and Gunn to go down to the cellar to hide. But by early November the atmosphere in the village had begun to darken.

A major German defensive line was being established just five kilometres to the south. In the process, surrounding villages were being evacuated to make way for German troops. Many villagers flooded into Pretoro. In just a few days, the population more than doubled. As Francioni warned, there was now upwards of 80,000 German troops between there and the frontline. While it was clear that the Allies were pushing ever northwards, for 'the sound of heavy guns thundering' could be heard coming from the south-east, the combat remained intense and hard fought.

Amid this pressure-cooker atmosphere, disaster threatened to strike once again. Hough and Gunn had had their spirits boosted, spying Allied warplanes flying low over the village. But they were brought down to earth with a crash, as a large group of German soldiers marched into the piazza. Before Hough and Gunn had had a chance to make it down to the cellar, a German officer had barged his way into the Perseos' house. He demanded to look around, with a view to billeting his officers there.

As he started up the stairs that led to where Hough and Gunn were hiding, he was met by one of the Perseo children, who was bringing down the fugitive's dinner tray. The German officer halted, and for some unknowable reason made his decision there and then. He would use the property to house his men, he declared. Had he carried on just a few more steps to the bedroom, he would have discovered Hough and Gunn, at which point their fate, and that of the entire family, would have been sealed.

No sooner had that officer left, than Hough and Gunn grabbed their things and hurried for the cellar. To try and get out of the village then, with the piazza thronged with German troops, would have been suicide. Instead, they had to hide in the dark cellar and hope for the best. Just a few minutes later, their former bedroom was taken over by German troops. This was the closest they had come to being discovered. Remaining in Pretoro was now untenable; to do so would be inviting a death sentence. They had to move out, and not only for their own safety.

That very night, and with German soldiers singing in the kitchen directly above them, the Perseos' daughter, Assunta, crept into the cellar. Bravely, she steered Hough and Gunn away from the house, using a narrow tunnel that led to the outside, after which they took to an alleyway leading to the outskirts of the village. From there they made for a small cave, where Francioni had left the two fugitives a pile of blankets. After telling them that someone would come in the morning with food, she left Hough and Gunn to bed down on the cave floor.

The following morning the trusty Gino Francioni appeared. After gathering up their meagre possessions, he led them to another, remoter cave, cut deep into a steep hillside. The entrance was covered by a screen of hanging vegetation, the path leading to it enshrouded by a thick mass of trees and shrubs. For anyone who did not know it was there, the cave would be nigh-on impossible to find. It was split into two parts: there was a smaller chamber lying just inside the entrance, with a large spacious area leading off that. There they would be able to light a small fire that should not be visible from the outside.

Over the next few days they were visited by young Maria Perseo, the eleven-year-old who had welcomed them to her home with such glee. She brought a basket containing food and the odd flagon of wine. As she readily confessed, it was only the younger children like her who would be able to bring them provisions now, for the Germans paid little attention to them. The streets of Pretoro were thronged with enemy troops, and any adult was under suspicion. Assunta, the eldest Perseo daughter, certainly couldn't risk the journey, Maria added.

This upset Gunn greatly, for he had formed a powerful attachment to young and beautiful Assunta. After drinking too much of their wine, he vowed that he would head back to the village to pay her a visit. Hough was furious. Gunn returned almost immediately, having practically blundered into a pair of German sentries. As Hough fully appreciated, for purely selfish – romantic – reasons, Gunn had put them both in grave danger. Once he had sobered up, Gunn offered a profuse apology. Reconciled, they discussed the chances of making a break for friendly lines. But again, Gunn argued to stay. He was convinced the Allies would break through before Christmas. Again, Hough reluctantly gave in. As he was to write later, 'My loyalty to him overcame my desire to get on with it. I knew I had more determination than him and felt protective of him, almost as if he was under my command . . .'

The Germans began sending patrols into the valleys and hills. A group of escaped Allied POWs were sheltering not so far away. They were captured and the villagers who had been helping them paid the price. To add to such dangers, the weather was growing ever more severe. Winter was kicking in, with freezing winds whistling down the mountains and snow starting to fall. The nearby river began to swell, its roar filling their cave twenty-four hours a day. The nights drew in, bringing a huge drop in temperature. It became extremely difficult for the two fugitives to sleep or to keep warm. Worse still, the screen of vegetation that had shielded them from prying eyes was starting to shed its leaves. It left the cave entrance increasingly exposed, and Hough and Gunn at ever greater risk of being seen.

As the weather worsened, the children could no longer bring them food. Instead, Gino Francioni and two of his friends took on the incredibly risky task. Even so, with so many refugees from evacuated villages now sheltering in and around Pretoro, and with the Germans looting supplies at every turn, provisions were growing scarcer. Hough and Gunn's rations dwindled. Plagued by hunger, their condition worsened, and Hough grew even more desperate to make a break for it.

Occasionally, artillery shells from Allied guns would crash down close to their cave, demonstrating just how near they must be to the frontline. Hough took to wandering up the nearby track that led out of the valley, seeking the high ground to spy out the lie of the land. Time was never wasted in reconnaissance, and this might prove especially useful if he could ever persuade Gunn to make a break for it. But eventually the enemy presence in the area was so great, that the risk of being spotted was simply too high. Forced to remain in the cave, he only ventured forth to collect water from the river, and then only when he knew it was safe to do so.

Hough and Gunn's health suffered. The lack of food, combined with the intense cold, put their natural resistance to disease at a low ebb. Both men became infested with fleas. Eventually, Gunn went down with a severe bout of dysentery, which lasted several days. Hough likewise caught it. He was able to throw off the affliction reasonably swiftly, but even so he found even simple tasks like collecting firewood had become a real physical strain.

Things in Pretoro village were also growing dire. As the Germans increased their presence, villagers were likewise taking to the caves. On 10 December 1943, Gino Francioni was able to confirm some of the worst news yet. Villagers were being rounded up and bussed out to places like Chieti – to the POW camp in which Hough and Gunn had languished for so long. Many chose to take their chances in the freezing caves. Entire families were heading into the hills, seeking shelter in the crevices and grottoes that littered the mountains.

Francioni wanted Hough and Gunn to move. They would be safer the further they moved from the village. German troops were constantly on patrol, and the chances of their being discovered were growing by the day. Reluctantly, the two weakened fugitives gathered up what few possession they had and followed him to a small cavern set higher in the hills. On arrival, they were surprised to discover that the Perseo family were to be their neighbours, for they too had taken to hiding out in a cave thereabouts.

Over the next few days Hough and Gunn were visited regularly by the children. Maria, too young to fear the hardships that lay ahead, seemed to be loving the adventure. Her excitement wasn't shared by her mother, who, after letting off steam to Hough and Gunn about how much she hated the Germans, 'walked away with drooping shoulders'. This would be the last time Hough would ever see her, 'this wonderful strong woman of the Maiella, who was as brave as a lion and enduring as an Arctic tern'.

On 22 December, Hough – having only recently overcome another bout of dysentery – gave an ultimatum to Gunn. Their health was deteriorating catastrophically. If they didn't make a break for it, they might not survive. While Gunn argued stubbornly against 'moving across the mountains in mid-winter', Hough was having none of it. The time for talking – and vacillating – was over. Seeing Hough was not about to back down, Gunn agreed that they should go. When next they saw Gino Francioni, they informed him of their decision. The brave Italian warned them that there were informers hiding out in the area, and to be extremely careful. He would get one of his friends, Enzio, to guide them to a cave higher up in the hills, and from there they could scope out the rest of their journey.

The following morning there was no sign of Enzio. Gunn, with his spirits fired up by the prospect of action, volunteered to go down into the valley to find their missing Italian guide. No sooner had he left the cave, than a cold mist descended upon the hillside, obscuring all from view. After a while Hough heard German voices, and the sound of shooting. Chillingly, it was accompanied by the screams of women and children.

Returning to the cave, there seemed no sign of Gunn anywhere. Hough figured he had no option but to wait. Then he spied something that chilled him to the bone. Just below the level of the cave entrance two German helmets came into view. Moving silently, Hough slipped deeper into the cavern and lay down in the shadows, turning his face towards the wall.

The pair of Germans entered. With his heart pounding in his ears, Hough held his breath. The enemy troopers were standing just ten feet from him, talking to each other and smoking. Should either glance down in his direction then he would surely be seen. He had never felt so vulnerable or so defenceless in all his life. But amazingly, after a few minutes chatting and puffing away, the German troopers turned and walked out of the cave, vanishing like a pair of wraiths into the mist. This was the closest Hough had yet come to being recaptured.

Shortly, Gino Francioni appeared. He'd brought food for Hough and Gunn's onward journey, together with a map he had drawn to guide them on their way. He was also there to wish them a final goodbye. Hough shook his hand. 'I thanked him . . . for all he had done for us. He looked at me with sadness in his eyes and wished me success in our venture. He knew I would not be returning. What a remarkable man he was.'

A few minutes after Francioni's departure, Gunn reappeared. Bizarrely, he had a huge grin on his features. It turned out that he had wandered off and been caught by the Germans, but had managed to slip away in the mist. Buoyed by this brush with the enemy, he now seemed as keen as Hough to get on their way. Agreeing to set out early the following morning, the two men settled down to rest.

But shortly they were assailed by the sounds of screaming from the valley below, as German troops rounded up civilians. The wailing of women and children was difficult to stomach, as their cattle and food were seized, and the rest of their possessions were torched in the caves. Wisps of smoke rose up the hillside and the crackle of flames was clearly audible. As he listened to the unfolding horrors, Hough's hatred for the Nazis intensified. 'My loathing of them increased. It was as if these poor Italians no longer had any identity.'

The following morning, an hour before dawn, they set forth. As it happened, it was Christmas Eve, but for them it was to be spent on a gruelling climb high into the mountains. Shortly, the heavens opened. The freezing rain pounded down, soaking them to the skin. As they moved out of the valley, they had to take extreme care. The ground underfoot was wet and treacherous, with steep inclines plunging to either side, jagged rocks being the only thing that might break their fall should they slip. As they climbed higher, the valleys rolled out far below, and the sound of the enemy's predations began to fade away; the screams and desperate cries of the civilians grew quieter with each step. But the more they ascended, the worse the weather became. The rain turned to sleet and snow, chilling them to the bone. With each passing minute the going grew more and more hazardous.

They reached a height of 5,000 feet, by which time they were in desperate need of shelter, for they were going down with hypothermia. The snow lay deep underfoot, transforming their feet into blocks of ice, and the wind was blowing icy gusts into their faces. By a stroke of good fortune they came across a cave, which was crammed full of villagers hiding from the enemy. Offering them shelter, and to share some food from their meagre provisions, the Italians welcomed the two fugitives in. The chance to get warm and to dry out was an utter godsend. They were told that the best way to reach Allied lines was a route lying 'north of Pennapiedimonte [a mountain top village] but . . . it was very difficult to get across and many trying had not made it.'

Despite such warnings, the two men were determined to push on.

Retiring to a shelter just outside the cave entrance – the cave itself was packed – Hough and Gunn managed to kindle a fire. But sleep did not come easily. They were undernourished and battling sickness, and despite the heat from the fire that December night was well below freezing. At some stage during that long night Gunn's mood changed. His enthusiasm for the coming trek ebbed away. By daybreak he was 'sullen and uncommunicative'. Hough tried to lift his spirits, talking animatedly about their return to England. They had come so far together and they were so near the end, as Hough kept reminding Gunn. 'He was a brave and resourceful man who had been a great friend,' Hough reflected. 'I wanted to finish this with him.'

It was Christmas Day 1943, but there was little good cheer. The fire had gone out and both men were shivering uncontrollably. For the first time, Hough began to doubt that they would make it, but he kept his worries to himself. Then Gunn's melancholy seemed to lift suddenly. He would head back into the valley, he declared, to find food and seek more accurate information. Hough tried to protest. After their epic ascent of the day before, this was madness. But Gunn was adamant. After a heated argument Gunn got to his feet, shook Hough's hand and walked away, assuring him he would be back before sundown. But Hough knew in his heart of hearts that was a lie. For whatever reason, this was the end of the line for the two of them. 'I felt a sense of doom and somehow knew I would not see him again.'

Sure enough, by that evening Gunn had not returned. Hough

drifted into a fitful sleep. Memories of all they had been through plagued his dreams. Awakening to find a foot of snow had settled around the shelter, and the storm still raging, he knew he was not about to see his friend anytime soon. The weather being so bad, and with no sign of Gunn anywhere, Hough moved into the cave, for doing so was now a matter of survival. By morning he knew that he had a decision to make. Should he accept that his friend had most likely been caught or, due to the thick snow, was benighted somewhere?

With little food and the weather worsening, to stay where he was would be foolhardy in the extreme. Most of the locals who had been sheltering in the cave had left by now – defeated by the terrible conditions. Likewise, Hough simply would not survive if he strayed put. If he was going to make it then he would have to do so on his own, and quickly.

His mind made up, he set out. He clambered up the final two hundred feet, reaching the summit of the mountain gasping for air. Having made the decision to go it alone, Hough 'felt a strong sense of exhilaration which gave me a surge of strength in my legs'. He decided to disregard the advice from the villagers to cross the lines north of Pennapiedimonte, for there he feared the route would prove too treacherous and cold. Instead, he took out the map Gino Francioni had given him and set his own course. He would try to cross at a point south of Pennapiedimonte, where he figured he would stand a better chance. He would still have to surmount at least two high ridges, but to Hough it looked the better route through.

That decided, he set forth once more. With his feet sinking deep into the snow, his will and determination seemed to be the only things that were keeping him moving. He was tired, hungry and cold beyond imagining, but the thought of finally making it to safety spurred him on. It forced him to keep putting one foot in front of the other. Upon cresting the first ridge and slipping down towards the valley below, the snow began to thin out and the going became a little easier. Finding a narrow track that snaked through the trees, Hough made it right to the valley floor. Ahead of him rose another massive ascent, up to the heights of the Campanaro ridgeline. Slowly, he trudged on, a bank of low cloud rolling downslope, and bringing with it freezing temperatures that did little to help.

As he began the ascent, he heard voices. Stepping off the track, he crouched behind some rocks. A few moments later the source of the noise came into view. Two German soldiers and an Italian. Thankfully, they had not seen him. Focusing solely on his efforts to climb, his mind had been wandering. He needed to be vigilant if he was to make it out of there.

Near the top of Campanaro ridge, he discovered yet another cave full of Italian civilians. After stopping a while to warm himself by their fire, and accepting some hot broth and bread, he continued – the food and the welcome having rekindled his determination to make it. He topped the rise, only to discover a third ridge, La Rapina, lay ahead of him. The going got tougher. As he approached the top, the ground became a mass of hard snow and ice, the treacherous going slowing him almost to a crawl. Finally, he was forced to double back, in an effort to find a safer route. Retracing his steps only added to his exhaustion. The wind picked up, the temperature dropping still further, but by now he was past the point almost of caring. There was no way that he could abandon the idea of escape and return to the life he had been leading before. The journey back would probably kill him. The journey ahead might well do the same. But either way, he had to continue the slog towards British lines. That was his only hope.

Skirting around to the south of Pennapiedimonte, which lay high on the hillside above, Hough pressed ahead. Once the sun had set, the only hint of light came from a crescent moon. He took to a path which led across open terrain. About a hundred yards to his left he spied a group of German troops. Hoping they wouldn't see him in the darkness, he trudged on, telling himself repeatedly that by now he had to be very close to the frontline.

Suddenly, right ahead of him, two German soldiers appeared from the brush. Hough stopped dead in his tracks, his heart beating furiously. Luckily, they failed to notice him and carried on walking. Taking a massive gamble, he decided to follow them, praying they would not hear him and turn around. After about two hundred yards, he broke off to the right, scaling a steep bank. It brought him alongside what had to be the German lines. Passing a small house, he could see German soldiers within, smoking and laughing. He stumbled across a communications wire and stepped over it. A few minutes later, he spotted another group of German troops, just twenty-five yards to his left. Again, for some reason they failed to see him. It was as if he were a ghost. Invisible somehow. At the same time, he was acutely conscious that one wrong move would bring his whole world crashing down around him.

Lying on the ground so as not to be seen, he crawled across a dirt track, before scuttling ahead at a crouch. The terrain became horrendous, patches of slippery clay making the going nigh-on impossible: 'I slipped and rolled in the mud trying desperately to make progress, but the effort sapped my energy.' By now, Hough was utterly drained. He felt he could continue no more. He craved rest. He knew if he were to lie down and sleep he would probably never wake up, but lack of rest would lead to his vigilance failing and him being caught. Finding a small hollow he simply dropped down into the mud. It oozed around him, offering him some protection against the fierce elements. Thoroughly drained, he dropped off to sleep.

At sunrise on 28 December, Hough was awake again and able to get his bearings. He could sense how close he was to the Allied lines. He could hear the deafening sound of artillery, as British field guns pounded the German positions. A river flowed past nearby. Hough sensed that if he was to follow its course, it should lead him home. But if he risked taking to its steep banks, he could be seen and stopped. With no other option, he did the only thing that seemed to make any sense right then: he eased himself into the river's freezing embrace.

The shock of immersion in the ice-cold torrent hit him immediately. He told himself that he had no other option but to endure it. Slowly he made his way forward, following the river downstream. On either side the banks loomed high above. They were thick with German troops. At one point he looked up and saw the barrel of a German artillery piece jutting over the water. While he seemed perilously close to the enemy, the river itself seemed to have been left unchecked. Unguarded. He prayed that no one decided to glance down into the water, for if they did he was bound to be seen.

On he went, his whole body numb with cold. Again he heard German soldiers on the bank above him. He was forced to submerge his whole body, in an effort to slip past unseen. This was arduous in the extreme. This was hell. A frozen, watery hell.

Eventually, after maybe a quarter of a mile of this, Hough spotted a small, run-down house, a thin ribbon of smoke issuing from its chimney. He couldn't see any enemy troops anywhere thereabouts. He crawled out of the water, his body shivering uncontrollably. Cautiously, he approached and stole a glance inside. It was occupied by an Italian couple. When they spied this soaked, muddied, freezing British soldier standing before them, they refused his requests for food, instead telling him he should continue downriver if he wanted to make it to safety. They appeared terrified, his presence there deeply threatening and unwelcome.

Leaving them, Hough forced himself back into the river. His entire body was numb now and shaking with cold. After another fifteen minutes of freezing immersion, he could take it no more. He crawled out onto the muddy bank. For a while his body suffered multiple spasms, as it tried in desperation to generate some warmth. Unwilling to re-enter the river, he forced himself to continue along the bank, sensing that he was physically incapable of taking another immersion. Although exposed, he would sooner run the risk of being spotted by the Germans, than freezing to death or drowning in the water.

After a while he came across a dirt track. Beyond it lay a destroyed bridge. He figured he had no option but to slip back into the water for a few instants, in order to cross to the other side. After dragging himself out onto the far bank Hough came across a group of tumbledown houses. Glancing up exhaustedly, he saw an Italian approaching. The man beckoned him over.

'*Niente Tedesche qui*,' he cried – No Germans here!

Hough needed no second urging. Moving like a wraith, he dragged himself inside the man's house. Thrusting a glass of wine into his hand, the Italian bade him drink. Next, he got Hough to remove his soaking clothes and dry them by the fire. Sitting in a fireside chair, with the warmth slowly returning to his body, Hough drifted off into a deep sleep. After some time he was shaken awake by his Italian host. The man seemed to be telling him that the Allied lines were very close by. Pointing to the east, he urged him to make a move.

Hough pulled on his clothes, which were now quite dry. Thanking the man for all his kind help, he set off. For a moment he looked back, the Maiella Massif rising high above, and his thoughts turned to his good friend, Peter Gunn. He'd hoped to finish this epic trip side by side with Gunn. They were supposed to have done this together. What had happened to him, Hough wondered? He had no way of knowing. But he hoped to God that Gunn was safe. 'For a time I stood and willed Peter to be with me,' he would later write, 'hoping he may have followed my trail over the mountains.'

Turning back to his present predicament, Hough continued on his way, the wine, the heat of the fire and the sleep having given him renewed strength. Even so, his walk was more of a stagger. Suddenly, from somewhere ahead he heard a voice crying out a challenge.

'Stop right there and raise your hands in the air!'

With immense elation, Hough did as he was ordered. Approaching him were three New Zealand soldiers – two nervous looking privates and a corporal. Each held a rifle, bayonets fixed, and they were pointed directly at him. It was then that Hough noticed a machine gun jutting from a sandbagged emplacement just behind them. As the soldiers drew closer, he became aware of what a complete mess he must look. With weeks of beard, his uniform scruffy and torn, and his body smelling utterly foul, he cut an altogether vagabond figure.

The corporal demanded to know who this strange fugitive might be. For a brief moment, Hough's mind went blank. As the soldier waited for an answer, his finger hovered over the trigger of his rifle. Pulling himself straighter, Hough finally announced: 'Captain Anthony Hough, 1 Special Air Service, escaped from Chieti POW camp in September.'

The corporal lowered his weapon, quipping that Hough had taken his time. Bringing his men to attention, they gave Hough 'a respectful salute and welcomed me back'.

It was then that he learned how he had cheated death one final time. The route he had taken had been mined. He had just staggered through a minefield. It was only due to pure luck that he hadn't trodden on one and blown himself to pieces. Regardless, he had done it. After nearly four months on the run, suffering extreme hardship and repeated brushes with death, Hough had made it back to Allied lines.

Shortly, he was fed and driven to the Brigade headquarters, at nearby Casoli town, where he was able to shave off his beard, clean himself up and get into a clean fresh uniform. After being debriefed by an intelligence officer, where he was able to give good information about German positions, he was moved to a Field Medical Centre, to be properly checked over and to get some well-earned rest.

But it would be some time before Hough would be able to return home. Suffering from attacks of jaundice and dysentery, he was forced to recuperate in a hospital in Algiers. Finally, he sailed for England, arriving in Plymouth on 8 February 1944. After reporting to the Rifle Brigade HQ in Retford, he spent the next few months 'filling in here and there and kicking my heels'. Then, he was once more struck down with dysentery and hospitalised. Eventually, that July, he was declared well enough to take some leave.

In total, it had been four years since he had last set foot in the Hough family home.

For his escape from Chieti camp and his epic trek to Allied lines, Anthony Hough was Mentioned in Despatches. His citation reads:

> Captured at Homs on 20 Dec 42. Sent via Bari to Campo 21 (Chieti). After the Armistice this camp was taken over by the Germans who moved P/W to Sulmona en route for Germany. Lt Hough hid in a water-tower with three other officers while the Germans were evacuating the camp. They then escaped over the wall and made their way south, meeting British troops at Casoli on 27 Dec 43.

It reads like a decidedly understated account, considering all that Hough had endured and overcome.

Hough did not rejoin the wartime SAS – or at least, not immediately. Instead, on 22 December 1944 he was posted to 21 Army Group in Europe, of which his old brigade was now part. After the surrender of Nazi Germany in May 1945, he became Assistant Town Major in Springe, in the far south of Germany, before taking up the role of Town Major in Bad Pyrmont in the north-west of the country. He was discharged from the regular army the following March, after reaching the rank of major.

In January 1950 Hough went on to join the newly formed 21

SAS (Artists Rifles) Regiment, for the links ran deep. This was the start of the re-formation of the Special Air Service, after it had been summarily disbanded at war's end. In 1952 he took up a position as a director of the family paperboard business. He died in 2000.

As Hough had feared at the time, Peter Gunn had been recaptured, on Christmas Day 1943, after returning to the Pretoro valley. He would spend the rest of the war in a POW camp in Germany. Afterwards, he and Hough renewed their friendship, Gunn becoming godfather to Hough's son, Gerald. Gunn died in 1986.

Carol Mather spent nine months in Fontanellato prison camp until he escaped, following the Italian Armistice. Instead of heading for Switzerland as he had intended, he trekked 600 miles down the Apennine mountains to British lines. Later, Mather would become adjutant to Field Marshal Montgomery, earning a Military Cross at Nijmegen during Operation Market Garden in September 1944. A career soldier, he left the army in 1962. He went on to become Conservative MP for Esher and was knighted in the 1987 New Year's Honours List. He died in 2006.

Captain MacDermott and Lieutenant Rickett – (Mac and Ricky) – made it safely back to Allied lines following their escape from Campo 21. MacDermott's escape report, dated 28 October 1943, states that he 'hid in water tower when the Germans began to evacuate prisoners from the camp (23/9/43). Stayed there for 2 days and went over the wall 26/9/43.' He had travelled with Rickett as far as Mafalda, sixty miles south of Chieti, last seeing him at a farmhouse with two other British officers. These were Lieutenants Hugh Gordon-Brown and 'Sandy' Hope, both of whom had escaped Chieti POW camp by hiding in tunnels after the Germans had arrived. MacDermott made it to Allied lines shortly thereafter. In his escape report Rickett confirmed he travelled with McDermott as far as Mafalda, and that he 'came into the British lines west of Guglionesi on or about 10 October 1943'.

After spending months hiding in the forests and caves near Pretoro, Gino Francioli, the Perseo family and the remainder of the Pretoro villagers returned to their homes, when the German defensive 'Gustav Line' was broken, in May 1944. The village had no strategic importance once the Germans had retreated, so the Allies did not stay there for long. The peace the Pretoro villagers craved was finally with them.

Sadly, Hough's attempts to give his SAS section a chance of escape from the desert wadi, following their attack on the Italian convoy, ultimately failed. Although the others managed to get away, they were all subsequently captured. Many of the others in B Squadron who took part in Operation Palmyra were caught or killed by the enemy. The SAS War Diary reports a number of the officers missing or killed in action. For example, in its entry dated 1 February 1943, Captains Mather and Morris-Keating, and Lieutenants Maloney and Hough, were all reported missing, with Major Oldfield reported as wounded, believed captured.

Palmyra was to be the biggest loss of personnel (killed or captured) of any SAS mission during the war. Those of B Squadron who did return were of the impression that Stirling's gamble had not paid off. But the mission had proved effective in forcing the Italians and Germans onto the roads during daylight hours, leaving them at the mercy of air-attack from the RAF. Hough's opinion that Stirling considered B Squadron as 'expendable' is debatable, but the fact remains that some of the newest members of the regiment had been given the most hazardous area of operations in which to conduct their raids.

With the war over in North Africa and British and American forces engaged in bitter fighting as they advanced up the Italian mainland, the SAS would once again be called into action. Even as Anthony Hough and Peter Gunn had made their breakout from Chieti POW camp, so another SAS patrol had headed deep into the Apennine mountains, intent on spreading mayhem far behind enemy lines. Parachuting some 600 kilometres to the north of Chieti, that unit would undertake one of the most successful SAS sabotage raids of the war, but that would lead in turn to another breathtaking escape.

Thankfully, those spearheading the mission would avoid the predations of the Stay Put Order. But their epic getaway would still prove to be one of the most extraordinary of the entire war.

Chapter Three

THE SPEEDWELL SABOTEURS

Magra Valley, Italy, 7 September 1943

The rumble of the Armstrong Whitworth Albermarle – a twin-engine RAF transport aircraft – was the only sound to break the stillness of the autumnal Mediterranean night. Heading on a northerly bearing from its base in Kairouan, Tunisia, it was now well over five hours since the aircraft had taken to the skies. The purpose of tonight's mission – SAS Operation Speedwell – was to drop parachutists deep behind the lines, charged to blow to pieces railway lines and rolling stock in northern Italy, with the aim of preventing reinforcements and heavy weaponry from reaching the enemy's frontline positions. Just four days earlier, Allied forces had landed on the shores of southern Italy, as they attempted to bludgeon open a foothold in enemy-held Europe, and Speedwell was timely in the extreme.

In the cramped fuselage sat six paratroopers, their faces blackened with camouflage paint. Underneath their highly unusual attire – blue-grey US-issue overalls – each wore the uniform and insignia of the Special Air Service. In addition, each carried German Army-issue weaponry. The inspiration for their rather odd-seeming outfit was to lend the appearance – from a distance, at least – that they were German soldiers. The hope was that thus attired they would avoid any close scrutiny by enemy patrols, or curious Italian civilians, as they went about their sabotage work. Desperate times called for desperate measures.

One of the six SAS parachutists was twenty–one-year-old Trooper Harold Challenor, known as 'Tanky' to all. Eager to do his bit, Challenor had been itching for some real action. Seemingly thwarted at every turn, he saw tonight's mission as an opportunity to do the thing he longed for most – to strike a blow against the reviled enemy. After hearing numerous stories of Nazi atrocities, he had developed an 'intense hatred of Germans', as he described it, adopting an uncompromising approach to any who came his way, vowing that, 'hands up or not, [they] would be killed'.

Just a few months earlier, Challenor believed his chance had come when he was selected to take part in the deliciously named Operation Marigold. A combined mission by the SAS and the SBS – the Special Boat Section; the water-born raiding unit – Marigold's aim was to land a force on the 'east coast of Sardinia [the island off Italy's western shores] to simulate a reconnaissance in force and to capture a prisoner'. Dropped by the submarine HMS *Safari*, Challenor and his fellow raiders had struggled ashore in their small collapsible boats. During the fraught landing, one 'member of the party dropped his Thompson SMG [sub-machine gun] on a rock'. Weighing in at some five kilograms when fully loaded, that Tommy gun had made a distinctive clatter, which had alerted the nearest German sentries to the SAS's presence.

Seconds later bursts of machine-gun fire had raked the area around the raiders, who were totally exposed as they scaled a shingle slope leading up from the shoreline. Facing withering fire, a hasty retreat back to the submarine was ordered. As Challenor and those on his boat struggled to paddle against the waves, shots flew all around, tearing into the water like swarms of 'angry hornets', as Challenor recalled. Eventually they made it to the *Safari*, and after a claustrophobic week cooped up beneath the waves, they arrived safely back at harbour, albeit empty-handed.

The experience of Operation Marigold had taught Challenor something about himself. As he had faced the enemy's machine guns for the first time, he hadn't been 'scared stiff', as he had feared he might be. Indeed, his only regret was that he hadn't had a chance to kill any of the reviled enemy.

His desire to engage with the enemy had been thwarted once more, a few weeks later, during Operation Husky, the daring Allied invasion of Sicily. Unable to locate the expected landing signal at the drop zone (DZ) and coming under heavy anti-aircraft fire, the pilot of the aircraft carrying Challenor and a patrol of fellow SAS had aborted the drop. Running low on fuel, the warplane had been forced to land at an American airbase on the Tunisian coast, the last few miles being flown on empty tanks. In fact, Challenor could consider himself doubly lucky. Not only had that aircraft made it back sipping on fumes, but many of the airborne forces deployed on Operation Husky had flown into ferocious winds and dropped into a storm-lashed Mediterranean. Hundreds had drowned.

Now, some two months later, Challenor was back aboard a British warplane as it droned northwards, deeper into enemy airspace. In the cramped confines of the Albemarle's darkened hold,

Challenor studied the other members of the stick. Led by twenty-three-year-old Captain Patrick Dudgeon, they were charged with destroying the railway lines running between Genoa, La Spezia and Bologna, three cities in northern Italy hosting vital rail links. Once on the ground, the six men were supposed to split into pairs. Challenor was to team up with Lieutenant Tom 'Tojo' Wedderburn – that teasing nickname being after the Japanese wartime leader, Hideki Tojo, and due to the short stature and distinctive glasses both men shared. Challenor and Wedderburn were to seek out and destroy the La Spezia to Bologna line, a stretch of rail track being used to bring supplies from the port city of La Spezia south to the front.

The other members of the stick, Captain Dudgeon, Sergeant William Foster, Corporal James Shortall and Parachutist Bernard Brunt, were tasked with hitting other sections of railway line. A second warplane was also airborne right then, packed with a further seven SAS, codenamed 'Group One'. Led by twenty-eight-year-old Captain Philip Pinckney, they were charged with a similar mission a little further to the south. Though deploying on the same night, the two groups were to act independently of each other.

Some five-and-a-half hours after taking off, the RAF dispatcher yelled out the first warning: 'Ten minutes to go!'

Warning issued, he lifted open the jump-hatch on the fuselage floor. Instantly there was a sharp inrush of cold air as the noise within the aircraft increased massively. Each of the six stood up and stretched the cramp out of their legs. After checking each other's straps and ensuring their kit was secure, they clipped their static lines to the hawser which ran along the aircraft's roof, and waited for the order to go. For Challenor, this would be only his fourth ever parachute jump, and his first into combat. Unsurprisingly, he felt 'distinctly uneasy'. The three previous jumps had been training exercises, dropping from just 300 feet. Tonight's jump was to be executed from over twenty times that height – some 7,000 feet. Plus, they were leaping far behind enemy lines and deep into 'hostile mountain country', as Challenor would describe it, no one having the 'vaguest idea' of what they were likely to encounter on the ground.

As they neared the jump point, Captain Dudgeon cried out a warning, having to yell to be heard above the noise in the hold. 'Watch your drift going down . . . stay as tight as possible. I'll remain where I land and you are to walk to me. Number six walking on to number five and so on, until we pick each other up.'

No sooner had he spoken than they were over the DZ. As the jump light flashed from red to green, the dispatcher gave the order to go. Dudgeon stepped forward and dropped from the Albermarle, disappearing into the howling void. With barely a moment's hesitation, the others edged forward, each falling from the aircraft in quick succession, with Challenor bringing up the rear. The shock of the icy mountain air hit him the moment he tumbled into the open, causing him to gasp for breath. But a moment later his static line caught, and above him the canopy snapped open, breaking him from the free-fall.

The roar of the Albermarle faded away, as the aircraft banked to the right to begin its long flight south to Tunisia. In its absence a deep silence descended, disturbed only by the flap of Challenor's 'chute, plus the sound of a distant air-raid siren, which he figured had to be in the direction of La Spezia. Below him Challenor could see the others spread out across the sky, oscillating gently beneath their parachutes, and strung out in 'perfect formation'. This had been a fine example of how to jump from an Albermarle, or any such aircraft for that matter. But now was coming the most dangerous part of any jump – making landfall.

A small tree broke Challenor's fall. He'd come down in a sparse copse on a barren and scrubby mountainside. Releasing himself from his harness, he grabbed his dagger and began to scrape a hole in the dirt, in which to bury his 'chute. That done, he made his way forward to find the man who had jumped ahead of him, his soon to be partner, Lieutenant Wedderburn. Once all had linked up, Captain Dudgeon took a quick roll-call. That confirmed all were present and that there had been no injuries during the drop. Dudgeon posted a sentry, before allowing the men to grab some rest. It had been a long, uncomfortable flight and they were tired. With their sleeping bags still packed in the drop-containers, which had been released just after they had jumped, they had to bed down in the open. It being relatively warm this shouldn't be a problem, and they could collect the containers once it was light enough to see.

They awoke to a magnificent dawn, a red sun rising above the mountain tops that towered to the east, and casting a warm glow over all. Rubbing the sleep from their eyes, the six men went in search of the canisters. Once gathered, they lit a fire and brewed some tea. Dudgeon decided they would remain where they were for the day. They'd lie low, checking their kit, distributing the explosives and getting their bearings. Come nightfall, they'd move out, seeking their targets under cover of darkness.

To Dudgeon, it looked as if they'd been dropped short of their intended landing zone. They were supposed to be in the Borgo Val di Taro, an area of deep, rugged valleys and forested hills.

But it looked as if they'd actually dropped some thirty kilometres away from there, near the village of Barbarasco, set in the Magra Valley. Ironically, for Challenor and Wedderburn, this supposed error put them closer to their own target, though Dudgeon and the others had further on foot to fare.

Dudgeon's determination that they would move only at night was in part due to their uncertainty of how any Italian civilians might react to their presence. Would the ruse that they were German soldiers hold good? With Allied troops even then wrestling a foothold onto mainland Italy, was a surrender of Italian forces imminent, as many seemed to believe? Even if it was, would Italian villagers in such a remote region as this welcome their country's exit from the war? Or would they remain hostile towards Allied troops marching into their lands? Dudgeon and his men just didn't know, which meant that caution was the order of the day. The golden rule was to trust absolutely no one, at least until matters were proved otherwise.

Before they split up to execute their separate sabotage tasks, Dudgeon gave a final pep talk. Pointing out a spot on his map, he confirmed that was their rendezvous point (RV). In seven days' time they were to meet at a tiny little church that served the small hamlet of Villafranca, an area not far from their present location. This was a central point for all – somewhere to retire to after they'd blown up their targets. From that 'RV' point, all six were to execute their escape and evasion together, though exactly how they were to do so remained a little uncertain. For now, Dudgeon gave strict instructions that none of them were to wait any longer than three days and three nights, before setting off on foot to reach Allied lines.

Shortly after Dudgeon was finished with that final briefing, he, Brunt, Shortall and Foster shouldered their packs, grabbed their weapons and set off. That left Challenor and Wedderburn alone on the mountainside. Once the four men had disappeared into the gathering night, so Challenor and Wedderburn checked their bearings one last time, before they too set off in search of their objective. They were heading south-east, towards their more distant target.

As they were swallowed into the gloom, this was the last time that Challenor and Wedderburn would ever see Dudgeon and the others again. Not that they knew it at the time.

The objectives of Operation Speedwell were vital to Allied fortunes at this stage of the war. Even as the fighting had raged in Sicily, thoughts turned to what would happen when Allied troops pushed ahead to land on the Italian peninsula. Even if Italy surrendered, the Italians would still be ensnared in the war, for Hitler had vowed that Italy would not fall. Berlin had charged German forces to fight for every inch of territory, and to give no quarter. As all knew full well, the German military would seek to pull in reinforcements, via southern France, to strengthen their hold on Italy. Operation Speedwell was designed to frustrate that process – to stop the flow of Nazi Germany's war materiel in its tracks.

Not only did the operation need to be done, it needed to be done quickly.

Preparations for Speedwell had begun in August 1943. As Major Eric 'Bill' Barkworth, one of the SAS's foremost intelligence officers, would declare of the mission, its objective was to target the passes through the Apennine mountains, stopping the enemy trains from being able to get through. Those were the key routes that Dudgeon and his men were setting out to sabotage right now.

Barkworth's original plan had called for the *whole of 2 SAS* – the recently formed sister regiment to 1 SAS – to be deployed, so several hundred men at arms. Due to a lack of available aircraft plus time pressures, just thirteen men had deployed – Dudgeon's six, plus Captain Pinckney's stick of seven. As Major Roy Farran, 2 SAS's soon-to-be legendary commander, appreciated, the lack of available aircraft meant they had been able to dispatch just a handful of raiders into the field.

What lay before Challenor and his comrades was some challenge. On their shoulders rested the entire success of the mission.

Challenor had been born into poverty on 16 March 1922, in Bradley, Staffordshire. The second of five children, he'd suffered under a domineering and abusive father. Due to his father's mounting debts, the family had been forced to move repeatedly, to avoid creditors, until finally they'd settled in Garston, near Watford. Singled out for regular beatings, Challenor had no feelings for his father other than a lingering contempt. The abuse only stopped when Harold grew into 'a powerfully built teenager', his father being 'astute enough to know I would take no more'.

Not only had his father abused him physically, he had also done so mentally. Upon winning a scholarship to Watford Grammar School, Challenor was warned by his father to 'forget any bloody fancy ideas about grammar school. At 14 you're going out to work . . .' He'd also sunk his son's hopes of becoming a professional footballer, stopping him from attending trials at Watford Football Club. His dreams had been 'killed in the kitchen', as

Challenor put it. Being a gifted sportsman, the young Challenor was offered a job at a local truck company, the real reason being the company needed a winger for its football team. After a while he changed jobs, joining the nursing staff at the nearby Leavesden Mental Hospital (now long-closed), something that would have long-lasting consequences for his military career.

When war broke out, Challenor – like Alfred Parker – was just seventeen. Although desperate to get involved in the fighting, he was too young to join up. As soon as he turned eighteen he'd applied to join the military, but a mild hernia prevented him from being taken on. Frustrated, he'd waited impatiently for his call-up papers, which arrived in April 1942. Due to his time at Leavesden Hospital, he was assigned to the Royal Army Medical Corps (RAMC). This left him feeling 'bitterly disappointed', for he was desperate to join a fighting unit.

After his initial training he was posted to North Africa, and it was there by chance that his fortunes would change. Engaged on a recruitment mission for the commandos, Randolph Churchill – son of the Prime Minister – paid a visit to the RAMC camp. Listening to Churchill's pitch, Challenor seized his chance for a shot at some action. Stepping forward to volunteer, once again he was told that due to his medical training, he would be taken on as a medic. Regardless, Challenor insisted on putting himself through all of the rigorous training the commandos undertook – weapons and explosives, unarmed combat, endurance tests and guerrilla tactics. Challenor would later describe himself as 'the most aggressive medical orderly the commandos ever had'.

It was at this time that he was given his distinctive nickname, 'Tanky'. Having lost his RAMC headgear, and with none of the distinctive green commando berets then available, Challenor was given an old beret from the Tank Corps that happened to be lying around. He was instantly christened 'Tanky'. The nickname was to stay with him throughout his life, despite never once having served in an armoured unit, or had much at all to do with any tanks.

After training with the commandos, Challenor was able to volunteer for the SAS, for the unit was then expanding into two regiments and hungry for recruits. Challenor joined 2 SAS, the second regiment then being raised at a remote base in Algeria. Two months after signing up he had been dropped into Italy, charged with making Operation Speedwell a reality on the ground.

Pressing onwards through the darkness, Challenor and Wedderburn sought out their target. Ideally, they needed to locate a tunnel passing through a remote area, where derailing a train would cause the enemy maximum problems and delay. 'The mountain air was cold, clean and invigorating,' Challenor remarked, and as they trekked higher into the hills he 'felt the adrenalin pumping . . . With any luck I'll be killing my first Jerry soon,' he told himself.

As Wedderburn led the way, weighed down by his huge pack, Challenor was struck by the difference between the two of them. Whereas he stood over five foot ten inches tall and was strongly built, Wedderburn was a good deal shorter, barely coming up to Challenor's chin. Even so, Challenor knew the diminutive lieutenant to be tireless and a powerhouse when marching over the hills. Wedderburn had been something of a mountaineer before the war, attributes that put him in good stead for this kind of mission.

The differences between the two men were not only those of height and stature. Wartime tended to throw together strange bedfellows, and sometimes in a quite literal sense. Challenor's working-class and troubled upbringing stood in sharp contrast to that of his Speedwell partner. Thomas McCleggan Wedderburn, at nearly thirty years of age, was almost a decade older than Challenor, who was still barely twenty, and Wedderburn hailed from a well-to-do, middle-class Edinburgh family. Studying law before the outbreak of war, a gulf separated Wedderburn's education and career prospects from that of his deputy.

Not that this mattered much to either of them right now. The SAS had been founded by David Stirling to be a 'classless' regiment. Indeed, merit mattered above rank, and officers had to earn the respect of the men they commanded. Recruits were prized for being independently minded self-starters, and a touch of the pirate and the maverick never went amiss. Challenor likewise considered himself 'stubborn, defiant' and more than a 'trifle wild', but that didn't prevent him from being 'totally loyal to anyone who commanded my respect'. And here in Italy, Wedderburn was about to earn it in bucket-loads.

They pushed onwards for several hours, advancing south-east in search of their target, climbing all the time. It was hard going, the terrain steep and rocky with scrub-filled gullies, the chill of the night air penetrating their bones. But they were buoyed up by a sense of purpose, and that drove them onwards. Eventually, at around three o'clock in the morning, visibility began to improve, the clouds clearing to reveal a waxing moon. In the eerie blue wash of its light they spotted what had to be a railway line, snaking along the base of an adjacent mountain. At one point it passed over a bridge that spanned a wide, fast-flowing stream. They didn't have enough explosives to have a go at that bridge, tempting target though it was. In any case, their orders were to stick to their objective – to sabotage trains running through tunnels. They decided to trace the line further into the hills, until they came across a suitable place to lay their charges.

For six days they trudged onwards, resting during the daylight hours in whatever remote spot they could find, before pushing on into the darkness. Sleeping rough under bushes far up the mountain slopes, the two men were forced to huddle together to share body warmth. All apparent gulfs between them – of class, of rank, of education – had been subsumed under the driving needs of survival. They'd awaken at nightfall, eat their meagre rations of bully beef, cheese and sardines, and then press on. Already, they were beginning to regret the quality and quantity of the food they had brought with them. With the cold, the altitude and the rigour, it was nowhere near sufficient.

In an after-action report written by Lieutenant Anthony Greville-Bell, who'd dropped with the second, seven-strong Speedwell force, he would remark, pithily: 'I consider the food we took to be most inappropriate and to be a bad choice on our part, consisting as it did of cheese, sardines, biscuits, sugar and compo tea.' He went on to suggest that for future SAS missions, and especially if they took place in a country where the locals were friendly, the bulk of food should be gathered on the ground.

It was seven days after their drop when Challenor and Wedderburn finally found what they had been looking for. Far ahead of them the rail track they had been following was swallowed deep into the side of a mountain. By the sheer bulk of the massif that towered above, it was clear that the tunnel had to stretch ahead for a considerable distance. In short, it was a perfect target.

Settling down at a suitable vantage point, they observed the line. From what they could see, most traffic was made up of goods trains laden with war materiel that had been unloaded at La Spezia, for onwards transport to Bologna and south to the frontline. It took a long time for any train to pass through the tunnel, noted Challenor, reflecting how great was the tunnel's length. Buoyed by their observations, they realised that if they timed it right, they could place their charges at *both* ends of the tunnel. In that way they could hit both the 'Up' and 'Down' lines – those taking rail traffic both south and north – so causing maximum mayhem. The trick would be to place the charges a considerable distance apart, so the first explosion wouldn't be spotted by a second, inbound train.

Under a moonless midnight sky – day seven of their mission – the raiders made their careful way down the slopes, inching towards the tunnel entrance shrouded in darkness. They'd had the good sense to leave their main backpacks behind in a cache, attaching tape to the odd tree or boulder they passed to act as a guide when retracing their steps. Thus unburdened, they could move lighter and faster on their feet.

As they neared the gaping arch of darkness – the tunnel entrance – they reckoned there had to be sentries on watch. Challenor volunteered to go ahead and deal with them. After his commando training, he fancied himself as 'something of a dab hand as a silent killer'. He set off with his commando knife held to the fore, eager to 'pierce from behind the heart of any sentry'. Slowly creeping forward, he stopped every few seconds to listen. But the only sound to break the stillness of the night was the gurgling of a small stream that followed the route of the railway line. Cautiously, he stepped across the water and pushed on. After a few minutes he reached the tunnel mouth, finding that no sentry had been posted, at least at this end of the line.

Feeling 'deflated' as he expressed it, he returned to Wedderburn with the news. 'All clear,' he whispered. 'Now let's go bag a train or two.' With that the two men set off into the pitch black of the tunnel.

Despite the cold inside, Challenor realised that he was sweating. They hurried ahead, following the line deeper into the bowels of the mountain, using the feel of the rails underfoot to guide them in the thick darkness. After a hundred yards they stopped. Taking the knapsack from his shoulder, Challenor placed it on the ground to one side. He glanced to his right. In the darkness he could barely make out Wedderburn. But as his eyes adjusted to the gloom, he could see what little light there was reflected off Wedderburn's – Tojo's – thick glasses. The SAS lieutenant was busy doing the same as he was – preparing his charges.

Challenor unwrapped his first parcel of plastic explosive. The distinct odour of almonds filled his nostrils, so typical of this type plastic explosives, one used extensively by the SAS and the Special Operations Executive (SOE). He taped the sticks to the rails. They'd estimated they'd need around 3lb to blow the track. Once the charges were set, they connected them to a 'fog signal' detonator, an SOE invention. A standard such device was used on the railways to warn a driver should a stop signal be obscured by fog, hence the name. As the locomotive ran over the fog signal, it would detonate, the sound warning the driver to slow down. SOE had adapted the device to trigger an explosive charge lying just ahead of the locomotive, thus causing a speeding train to derail. In the pitch dark of a tunnel like this, the driver would have no way of avoiding the trap. In the narrow confines, the derailment should cause the carriages to concertina, thereby blocking the tunnel from floor to ceiling.

With the charges set on the 'Down' – southwards – line, the two soldiers jogged deeper into the darkness to do a similar job with the 'Up' track. If they could block both ends, it would take the enemy an age to clear, which in turn should stop a mass of war materiel and reinforcements from reaching the frontlines. No sooner had they set their explosives on the Up track, than Wedderburn turned to Challenor.

'Well done, Tanky,' he announced. 'Let's get out of here.'

Neither wanted to stay a moment longer, for obvious reasons. The two men hurried back the way they had come. But suddenly Challenor brought himself to a halt. He'd sensed something untoward. He figured he'd heard something that was distinctly alarming. He listened hard, before turning to Wedderburn.

'Listen . . .' he announced. 'There's a bloody train coming.'

Wedderburn too strained his ears. There was no doubt about it: a faint hum was emanating from the tracks. It could only be the sound of an approaching train. As sod's law would have it, there was a locomotive bearing down on them, even as they were still deep in the tunnel – a tunnel they had just rigged with charges set to blow.

'Good God!' yelled Wedderburn. 'Move, man! Run like hell!'

Challenor didn't need to be told twice. Fancied as a professional footballer in his youth, Challenor could certainly run. He gave it everything he had, leaving the much shorter Wedderburn for dust. But oddly, the dim light emitting from the distant exit – the tunnel mouth – seemed to move further away the faster he ran. The sound of the locomotive grew louder by the second, as both men dashed towards the oncoming train, in a desperate race against time. Pumping his arms and legs, his lungs fit to burst, Challenor ran as fast as ever he could remember. As he dashed ahead, he was struck by the bitter irony of being caught in the blast of their own bombs.

Finally, first Challenor and then Wedderburn were vomited out of the far end of the tunnel. They dived to their right, barely moments before the snorting, fiery form of the locomotive went thundering past, and was swallowed into the tunnel entrance. Challenor and Wedderburn had leapt for cover landing in the small stream that ran beside the tracks. Soaked to the skin, at least they were alive. A few seconds after the unsuspecting train driver had taken his locomotive steaming into the tunnel's mouth, all hell let lose.

A huge explosion rippled through the night air, being magnified in sound and intensity by the narrow confines of the tunnel, like a bullet blast inside a gun barrel. There then followed the awful sound of metal twisting and buckling as the train broke from its tracks, engine and carriages colliding with the walls and roof of the tunnel, each concertinaing and slamming into the one in front as they went. The noise was utterly deafening, the train's sheer momentum ensuring that the mangled remains kept twisting and tearing themselves to pieces along a length of ruptured track, the wreckage piling up in a chaotic, macabre monument to the damage that the two SAS saboteurs had wrought.

Hardly had Challenor and Wedderburn managed to scramble to their feet to inspect their handiwork, when a second explosion pierced the night. It sounded somewhat further away and had clearly come from the far end of the tunnel – a tunnel which was already comprehensively blocked at the near end. It was followed instantaneously by another ear-splitting noise, as hundreds of tonnes of locomotive and carriages smashed into each other, rebounding off the insides of the tunnel, and ripping the rail tracks to shreds in the process.

The two men locked eyes, their expressions a picture of utter amazement. Their second charge planted on the 'Up' line had clearly also done its work. The two trains had reached the tunnel almost simultaneously, and it was fortunate indeed that the two saboteurs had slipped out of there as they had. Lady Luck had smiled on them tonight. In terms of their objectives, things could not have gone better.

After the thunderous noise of the blasts and the devastation that had followed, a taut and eerie silence descended over. Their work done, Challenor and Wedderburn needed to get as far away from the site of the attack as fast as they possibly could. Once the enemy got wind of what had happened, the area would be crawling with troops. There was no time to linger or to celebrate their success. Hurrying ahead, they retraced their route. Shortly, they arrived at the hideout where they had stowed their gear. Grabbing their packs and slinging their 'Schmeissers' – British soldier's slang for the German military MP40 sub-machine gun – over their shoulders, they set off towards their distant objective.

At that church near Villafranca, they'd seek to rendezvous with Captain Dudgeon and the rest of the SAS raiders, assuming of course that they could navigate their way to it in time. Most of their explosives had been used up on the tunnel sabotage, so this was now the 'scoot' stage of a classic SAS shot-and-scoot attack.

Challenor and Wedderburn made for the thickly forested heights, seeking to avoid all contact with civilisation. But even as they pressed onwards, they were aware that their food rations were all-but exhausted. Fortunately, the weather was holding good, but still it proved tough going. Stumbling and falling in the thick darkness, grazing knees and arms on rocks, it made for hard, bruising progress. Come daybreak they burrowed into a patch of thick undergrowth and crawled inside their sleeping bags to rest. While water wasn't an issue – mountain streams abounded – they were down to their last few handfuls of food.

After two nights' hard march they reached the rendezvous point at the stream adjacent to the church. Both men were surprised to see that they were the first to arrive. They'd expected Captain Dudgeon and the rest of his party to be there ahead of them, for Challenor and Wedderburn had been on the move for nine days, two days longer than the deadline that Dudgeon had set. As they lay in hiding, keeping a watch on the rendezvous, they realised that the nearby road was in heavy use by German military convoys. Several thundered past. It was obviously not the healthiest of places for British saboteurs to hang out, especially after the carnage they had wrought back in that rail tunnel.

Sensing that they were asking to be caught, they retired to the mountain heights. Wedderburn decided they would spend the days hiding out at altitude, coming down only at night to see if their comrades had made an appearance. The hours of waiting were horribly tense and anxious, Challenor would recall, each check proving there was still no sign of any of their SAS comrades. Dishevelled, exhausted and extremely hungry, they were really up against it now. By the third day of the stakeout, they were too fatigued to attempt the climb into the high ground again. So, the two heavily bearded raiders decided to lie-up in a ditch, not far from the church and the nearby stream.

Once they'd crawled into it, they fell into a deep sleep.

Challenor awoke to someone gently kicking his ribs. He opened his eyes, the sun shining directly into his face. Blinking, he was about to reach for his Schmeisser when he saw a wrinkled face looking down at him – an elderly 'peasant farmer', as he would later describe it. What made him hesitate in grabbing his weapon was that the man was smiling broadly.

'*Inglesi?*' the old man queried.

Challenor nodded. *So much for the uniforms which were supposed to make us look like Germans,* he thought, ruefully.

Luckily, Wedderburn spoke decent French and so did the Italian farmer. After a few exchanges of words, the lieutenant turned to Challenor. 'He's inviting us to follow him to his farmhouse,' he explained.

Although they had been warned to trust no one when preparing for the mission, Wedderburn and Challenor decided they should act on their instincts. The plans for Operation Speedwell had been very much rushed. It was up to them to adapt to what they found here on the ground, and to place their faith in their own judgement. In truth they had few other options, and if that meant trusting the word of this aged Italian farmer, so be it.

The Speedwell patrols had been dropped into Italy with no means of making long-distance communications, reasoning that radios were too heavy and cumbersome to carry. That meant that they had no means to make contact between their own raiding parties, let alone with headquarters. Lieutenant Greville-Bell would conclude of this lack of radio kit, and the resulting vacuum in terms of up-to-date information: 'It was rather depressing, and very lowering to the morale of the troops not to know where our army was.' It wasn't particularly useful for planning an escape and evasion route, either, as events were to prove.

Right now, for Challenor and Wedderburn, the lack of any means of making contact would have one major negative impact:

the two men had no idea that Italy had signed the Armistice of Cassibile, so joining forces with the Allies. Signed into law on 3 September 1943, all Italian forces had surrendered unconditionally. That was a good two weeks ago, but neither SAS man had the slightest idea that the Italians had capitulated. As far as they were concerned, they were very likely going to be viewed as enemy soldiers by all.

Still, they were desperate for a good meal and a proper rest. They liked the look of the elderly farmer. They decided to take their chances with him. They followed him to a large brick-built house not too far away. Once inside, the farmer asked his wife to rustle up a suitable feast. Not long after sitting down, Challenor and Wedderburn had their first hot meal in well over a week – spaghetti and bread, washed down with a number of glasses of wine. Instantly they felt invigorated, the strength flowing back into their veins and their spirits lifting.

The farmer gave his name as Pietro Massimo Petriccioli. He was sixty-eight years old, and most importantly was no friend of Italy's Fascists. Disregarding the immense danger it posed to him and his wife, he agreed to shelter the two soldiers for the next few days, giving them time to muster their strength as they awaited their comrades. Had the Germans found the two saboteurs, Petriccioli and his wife would have been shot on the spot, and their farmstead burned to a smouldering ruin, as Challenor well appreciated. That was what had happened to any number of locals who had been caught helping the Allies across much of Italy.

While sheltering with the Petricciolis, the two raiders finally learned about the Armistice. Rather than Italy being an enemy state, the country was now an occupied nation, much like France and the numerous other countries suffering under the yoke of Nazi oppression. For most Italians, aside from the diehard Fascists, the German occupiers were now the enemy.

Despite such a turn-around in their fortunes, there was still no sign of Captain Dudgeon or the other SAS troops. Aware of Wedderburn and Challenor's growing disquiet, Signor Petriccioli offered to venture into the local village to see if he could find out anything about the four missing men. He did as promised, but could learn nothing of their fate. As Dudgeon and his men were long overdue, Wedderburn figured it was decision time. Should they remain a little longer, thereby putting the Petricciolis in further danger? Or should they follow Dudgeon's order and move out, especially as they had lingered well beyond the deadline that the SAS captain himself had set?

It was a tough decision. Finally, Wedderburn decided that the only right thing to do was to leave. As Challenor would remark in his memoir, written after the war: 'It was a decision I was glad I had not had to make, although I agreed with the order.'

Before deploying on Operation Speedwell, each soldier had been issued with a quantity of Italian currency. It was to be used to buy food from friendly locals or to pay bribes should the need arise. The officers, including Wedderburn, also carried a number of gold coins. Wanting to show appreciation for the Petricciolis' help, Wedderburn offered them a substantial portion of the money. But the farmer and his wife refused. Instead, they accepted one gold coin. Though to them it represented a considerable sum of money, they declared that they would never cash it in or trade it, but would retain it as a keepsake of the time they had spent together.

Lieutenant Wedderburn wanted to do something more to ensure

the farmer's bravery would not go unrecognised; to show just how much his help had been appreciated. After all, when the old man had come across the two SAS soldiers sleeping in that ditch, they had been in an absolutely pitiful state. Worn down with exhaustion and hunger, they were pretty much on their last legs. He'd taken them in, fed them and given them time to regain their strength. It was down to the Petricciolis that they would be able to press on with the rest of their journey, wherever that might lead.

In that spirit, Wedderburn penned a short letter for the Petricciolis to show to any Allied soldiers passing through the area. It read: 'To all English and American Officers. The bearer of this note housed, fed and sheltered me and my companion parachutist at great risk and inconvenience to himself, for two days. If there is any way in which you can repay them, I wish that you would do it. Tom Wedderburn Lt. 2SAS Regt.'

With no real escape plan in mind, other than trying to push south to meet up with advancing Allied forces, wherever they might be, the two men bade farewell and set off once more. There was no plan for the Speedwell raiders to head for the coast to be picked up by boat or a submarine, as there had been for the Operation Colossus parties back in February 1941. In short, the Speedwell saboteurs had been dropped hundreds of kilometres behind enemy lines and left to their own devices to make it back to safety.

Not far from the Petricciolis' farmstead ran the La Spezia to Parma rail line, passing between Aulla and Pontremoli. This was another arterial route that the Germans could use to rush supplies and reinforcements to the frontline. Reinvigorated as they were, it struck Wedderburn and Challenor that this constituted a prime target. Still having sufficient explosives in their packs to blow another length of track, they decided to give it a go. Though they were still some 500 kilometres away from safety, with a long and perilous trek through rough mountain terrain lying ahead, they decided what the hell – they'd go on the offensive.

Moving quickly, they slipped into the hills, chose an appropriate stretch of line and set their explosives, listening out for any oncoming trains as they did so. Not waiting to watch the outcome of their handiwork, they set off for the high ground of the Apennine mountains, the string of peaks that run along much of the length of Italy. Once they were in among those heights, they would be in a place of relative safety. They'd only got as far as the foothills when they heard the distant whistle of a train. They didn't have to wait much longer before an ear shattering blast echoed around the hills. The two saboteurs burst into peals of laughter, slapping each other on the back in celebration. It could not have gone better. They had been sent out to destroy trains and wreck tracks. This they had done to massive effect.

All they had to do to make the whole mission perfect was to make it safely back to friendly lines.

Unbeknown to either Challenor or Wedderburn, the sound of that explosion had also been heard by two of the SAS who had dropped from the Albemarle with them. Captain Dudgeon and Gunner Brunt had finally made it to the rendezvous point at the church. There they too were treated to the hospitality of the Petricciolis. But by a cruel twist of fate they had arrived just a few hours after Wedderburn and Challenor had departed. Had Wedderburn decided to give it another day, the two groups would have been reunited, and the fate of Dudgeon and Brunt might very well have turned out very differently.

It was from the Petricciolis' house that Dudgeon and Brunt

heard the distant blast, as their fellow raiders blew up yet another stretch of railway track, and the train that had been passing along it. Even so, that offered them little help in tracking down their missing SAS comrades. Challenor and Wedderburn had been swallowed into the wilds of the Apennine mountains, and the two parties could not be reconciled.

After spending some days as guests of the Petricciolis, during which Dudgeon and Brunt kept a close watch on German troop movements, they decided to steal a vehicle. Whether this was to be used to aid their escape, or to carry out further missions, remains uncertain. At the time the area was crawling with German troops. Field Marshal Erwin Rommel himself was believed to be there, the SAS's erstwhile opponent in the war in North Africa. There were targets galore, that was for sure. Slipping down to the road leading to the village of Santissima Annunziata, Dudgeon and Brunt managed to seize a car. In the process, a German soldier was killed and another badly wounded.

But shortly, both SAS men were captured.

Dudgeon and Brunt had been seized by an enemy who were well aware of the sabotage that had been wrought in the nearby hills, as trains and their tracks had been ripped asunder. Shortly after their capture, Captain Dudgeon and Gunner Brunt would be subject to Hitler's infamous, and illegal, 'Commando Order', which decreed that all Allied special service troops were to be shot out of hand. Almost a year earlier, on 18 October 1942, the Commando Order – *das Kommandobefehl* – had been issued at Hitler's personal behest. This was a directive emanating from the Führer's legal team and bearing his personal signature. It read: 'Henceforth, all enemy troops encountered by German troops during so-called commando operations . . . though they appear to be soldiers in uniform or demolition groups, armed or unarmed, are to be exterminated to the last man . . . If such men appear to be about to surrender, no quarter should be given to them.'

Clearly illegal under the rules of war as outlined in the Geneva Convention, the Commando Order was nevertheless being adhered to by many enemy commanders. Even worse for Dudgeon and Brunt was Lieutenant-General Gustav von Ziehlberg's decision, which accompanied their death sentence. The commander of the German 65th Infantry Division, the unit then garrisoning the region, von Ziehlberg ordered the round-up of some three-dozen Italian villagers, who were to be shot alongside the British saboteurs. (In fact, von Ziehlberg's order was to be countermanded by Rommel, and the Italian hostages were eventually freed.)

On 3 October 1943, Dudgeon and Brunt would be murdered by firing squad, just outside the village of La Cisa, a short drive from the Petricciolis' farm. Their bodies were dumped together in an unmarked shallow grave. The two men had remained remarkably stoical until the very end. Even as the execution squad had prepared to open fire, Dudgeon had started to sing God Save the King, Brunt's voice joining in. Unbeknown to either man, their two other comrades – Sergeant William Foster and Corporal James Shortall – had also been captured. Though taken prisoner wearing full British uniforms, on 21 September 1943 they too had also been murdered by firing squad.

All four men were buried in unmarked graves, hidden away from prying eyes, in an attempt to cover up these heinous war crimes.

*

By early October 1943, Challenor and Wedderburn – their second, daring job of sabotage just recently executed – were the only men from the original six who were left alive. They of course knew nothing of their comrades' dire fate. Indeed, realising now that the local civilians were far less likely to be hostile, they decided to press on during the hours of daylight. Keeping to the highlands, to avoid any towns that might harbour enemy troops, their spirits remained buoyed by yet another success, in blowing up that third train.

At one stage, Challenor suggested heading into a nearby village to buy some wine, and maybe to find a bit of female company. This display of youthful vigour was shot down by Wedderburn, who was adamant that if they relaxed their vigilance they would be courting disaster. As if to underline his warnings, and the need to keep eternally watchful, they rounded a corner in a narrow mountain pass and practically stumbled into three figures heading directly towards them. Two were German soldiers, rifles slung over their shoulders, and they flanked an Italian woman carrying a large bundle of laundry. The two German troopers appeared as surprised at seeing the two SAS saboteurs as they were at seeing them.

Challenor's first instinct was to grab his Schmeisser and open fire. After all his commando and SAS training, he considered himself an intensively trained and honed professional killer. But he feared that if he opened up, he would more than likely hit the Italian woman as well. He and Wedderburn decided to brazen it out. The Germans looked as if they didn't want any kind of trouble, the sudden appearance of the SAS men seeming to cause them 'considerable unease'. To Challenor's eye, it was clear that these were no elite German troops. Very possibly, they had never seen any action. Had they opted to engage the two SAS men, there would likely have been only the one winner, and they knew it.

As they slipped past each other in a tense silence, Challenor nodded a greeting, as if to say, 'There'll be no trouble unless you want it.' On reaching a bend in the road he looked back, only to see the Germans doing the same. Once they had rounded that bend, he and Wedderburn ran as fast as they could for the high ground, not stopping until they had put some considerable distance behind them.

Once in a place of relative safety, they paused to weigh up what had just happened. Not engaging the Germans had been the right decision, they reasoned. Had they attacked, then the area would have been flooded with German troops. Their situation would have been infinitely worse. More to the point, Wedderburn reckoned the Germans were never going to report the encounter for fear of recriminations, as they had failed to take the slightest action to prevent the saboteurs' escape.

'Those Germans daren't report us,' he told Challenor. 'If they do, what are they going to say? That they let us roll past without even challenging us?'

But that close encounter did serve to remind them that they had to remain vigilant. Of course, this was something they had been trained to do. Yet the long weeks of operating behind enemy lines, with little food or proper rest, had taken their toll. If they were to make it safely back to Allied lines, they would have to redouble their vigilance, despite all.

The harsh slog through the high ground continued. For days they stuck to remote ridges and peaks, trudging ever onwards.

They had no idea just how long they had been on the move now; no exact sense as to where the frontline was, or how far Allied forces had advanced up the leg of Italy. There was just no way of knowing. Increasingly, they began to lose track of time. Finally, it reached the point where they no longer knew what day it was. To relieve the boredom of their march, they took out their Italian phrasebooks and began to practise, passing words back and forth until it reached a point where they were both reasonably proficient.

Eventually they came to a farm lying just outside a small village. A massive dog approached, snarling menacingly and baring its vicious looking fangs. Challenor brought forward his gun and pointed it at the animal, knocking off the safety catch. He was ready to pull the trigger should the animal go for either of them. A woman appeared in the doorway of the farmhouse, two farmhands to her side. After she had called off the dog, and Challenor had lowered the Schmeisser, it was established that, just like the Petricciolis, they were friendly. Challenor and Wedderburn were invited into the house for a meal. The woman informed them that she was a war widow. She looked after the farm with her brother, who just then was taking care of their sick mother in the village.

After a while Wedderburn retired to the nearby farm shed, where he fell into a deep sleep. But Challenor, deprived of female company for so long, lingered to enjoy the company of the widow. Eventually, he too retired for the evening, the first in a long time spent under decent shelter. The following morning the woman's brother returned; he confirmed there were no German troops in the immediate area. And so, after bidding farewell, they set off once more.

After another hard day's march they came across a dilapidated looking hut high in the mountains. As they neared it, an old man came out and beckoned them inside. Recognising them as British soldiers, he invited them to join him in his meal. With hunger taking its toll, they tucked into what appeared to be nothing more than fried grass, laced with olive oil. Being so desperately famished, they wolfed it down.

The old man offered an apology, explaining that he had no better food to offer, and could barely afford to buy any wine. Upon hearing this, Wedderburn pulled out a wad of lire and peeled off several notes, which he handed to the old man. Would he go down to the village and purchase as much wine as he could, Wedderburn asked. Challenor, seeing this as an opportunity to finally have some fun, added a few more notes, jokingly telling the old man that he'd be best off taking a wheelbarrow to carry the wine.

By now, they had spent weeks on the move, sleeping rough, starving hungry, never knowing for just how much longer they could go on. Winter was nigh, and the nights were starting to draw in. Each night spent in the open they huddled together in each other's arms, in an effort to stave off the cold. Right then, they figured a few glasses of wine were the least they deserved.

Shortly, the old man returned, clutching several bottles in his arms. They settled down to some serious drinking, and a night of letting their scraggy, long hair down. Both awoke the next morning to throbbing heads as the hangovers kicked in. But it had been worth it. Somehow, they felt invigorated. That had been one night where they had been able to put their trials and tribulations to one side, and had enjoyed being young men again, and almost carefree. It had done them both a world of good in terms of their morale. Challenor reflected on the survival courses he had undertaken during SAS training, and wondered why none had ever made mention of the 'therapeutic value of getting "stoned"'. Both of them agreed that they should, as they now felt better than they had done in many weeks.

Waving goodbye to the old man, they set out once more, but the weather was turning wintry. The days dragged on as they pressed southwards, sleeping wherever they could find a spot of shelter. Through rain and wind they trudged, the conditions growing ever worse, as what would become one of the harshest winters in Italian history set in. By this stage they were forced to survive on whatever they came across: mostly a few wild berries, raw chestnuts and mountain water drawn from nearby streams.

Precious little thinking had been put into exactly how they would make their getaway, were their sabotage successful. Not for one moment had they imagined being forced to escape and evade for weeks on end. Bizarrely, it had just been assumed that the Allied advance would prove so swift and sure that contact with the vanguard of British or American troops would be made in a matter of days. In truth the Allied landings had been met by fierce German resistance, as Challenor and Wedderburn were starting to realise.

They continued to stick to the high ground wherever they could, which offered a good view into the valleys below. From their vantage point they could avoid any areas where German troops were concentrated. But both men knew that to live like this was not sustainable, especially as the wintry conditions worsened. They needed quality food and proper shelter, otherwise they would fall victim to exhaustion and disease.

One morning sometime in October, they came across a group of women washing clothes in a stream. Taking their chances, they approached and asked if it was safe to proceed through the village. No sooner had they posed the question, than they heard the sound of an approaching vehicle. In a flash the women grabbed the two soldiers and forced them down and out of sight, covering them with a pile of washing. Moments later a car stopped and two men got out.

Hearing German voices, Challenor felt his 'emotions overrun my common sense'. He grabbed his weapon, and prepared to leap up and open fire. His intense hatred of the enemy drove him to engage with them and this seemed like the ideal time. His hatred had only deepened, after hearing stories of Nazi atrocities. To him, they 'seemed to take a perverse pleasure in killing innocent people as a reprisal'. As he was about to spring up and start shooting, he was grabbed by Wedderburn, who prevented him from doing so.

From the tones of their voices, the Germans had stopped to simply chat with the women. Listening from under the pile of washing, it was clear to Challenor that the women's laughter was false and very forced. Whether this was all down to the fact that they had two British soldiers hidden only feet away, or it was a genuine dislike for the Germans, he didn't know. After a few minutes the Germans finally drove away, their flirting done. They'd clearly never suspected just how close they were to two elite British soldiers, one hell-bent on killing them.

Wedderburn was not happy with what he viewed as Challenor's lack of self-discipline. He told him as much, explaining that if he had opened fire on the enemy the Italian women would almost certainly have been put to death in reprisal. Of course, there was a time and a place for the aggression and combative spirit that Challenor had displayed, but in Wedderburn's view this was not it. It was a sharp lesson for the younger soldier.

They pressed on, moving through village after village – at times being aided by friendly locals, at others having to skirt around to avoid enemy patrols. At one point an old man offered them a lift in his horse-drawn cart. It was packed full of sheep, and by lying in among them Challenor and Wedderburn managed to slip by a number of German patrols unnoticed. But there was a cost. At one point one of the animals decided to defecate on Challenor's head. At that Wedderburn burst into laughter, telling him it was a sign of good fortune.

Despite such rare moments of levity, they had little idea where exactly they were, or for how long they had been on the march. They were starving, haggard and cold. To add to their discomfort, Wedderburn's feet were beginning to swell ominously. For the first time they began to entertain very real doubts about whether they were going to make it. Upon reaching the next village, they decided to risk walking right on through it. No German troops were visible, and they were desperate.

Almost immediately, the villagers gathered around and began to make a fuss of them. The local schoolmaster warned them that, but for their beards, they would have been mistaken for German soldiers. Recognising the pressing need to tidy themselves up a little, the village barber was called. With their beards duly shorn and their hair cut short, Challenor and Wedderburn now looked slightly less like the vagabonds they feared themselves to be, and they continued on their journey.

But things were getting desperate. Wedderburn was finding it almost impossible to walk. Each time he put a foot to the ground, it was met with an intense stab of pain. Challenor was also beginning to feel unwell. At first, he'd reckoned it had to be a dose of flu, brought on by the worsening weather and the lack of proper food. But he was starting to worry that it was something infinitely more sinister. The hot sweats, aching joints and constant shivering felt horribly familiar.

He feared he was experiencing the onset of something terrible, for which he could only really blame himself.

The training camp for 2 SAS, at Philippeville, Algeria, had lain close to a stagnant swamp. The SAS commanders had soon realised the dangers it posed. Not only could the trainees be hit by bouts of malaria – a potential killer – while stationed there, but if not treated properly the disease could strike again at any point in the future, including on operations. In an effort to minimise the risk, they'd put each man on a course of anti-malarial tablets. However, twenty-something Harold 'Tanky' Challenor, being fit and strong-minded, felt he'd had no need. He had been determined to rebuff the 'attentions of the mossies' by sheer willpower alone.

But one day, while playing cards, he was seized by a fit of 'uncontrollable shivering'. At first, he didn't understand what it was. But on seeing him in such a state, his comrades recognised the symptoms. Challenor had been struck with malaria, and it was entirely his own fault for not having taken the medication. It took ten days for him to fight it off and return to his duties.

Now, as Challenor trudged along, with Wedderburn hobbling beside him, he realised that the dreaded malaria had returned. With all his joints aching, his teeth rattling 'like castanets' and his whole body shivering uncontrollably, Challenor faced no option. He would have to fall upon the charity of any villagers they might run into. If not, he was as good as dead. Wedderburn was in little better shape, being all-but crippled.

Finally, they neared a village nestled in a fold in the mountains. Seeing the two fugitives' desperate plight, the locals took pity upon them. But along with the sympathy, which abounded, there was bad news. The village was seething with enemy troops. On learning this, Challenor figured the game was up. He turned to Wedderburn and urged him to push on alone, for there was little point in their both being captured. The SAS lieutenant refused even to countenance what Challenor was suggesting. 'We were in it together,' Challenor would later remark. 'The SAS knew no other code.'

They were spirited away to a large townhouse, and the doctor was summoned. After giving Challenor several injections, and doing his best to treat Wedderburn's feet, he left them in the care of the householders, who told them they could stay as long as they needed. But they felt far from safe; the enemy were all around. Even as Challenor was lying in bed racked by fever, he could hear enemy troops conversing in German on the streets below the window. His nerves were utterly frayed.

For days they rested, using the time to husband their strength and hone their Italian. By using the phrasebook he carried, and conversing regularly with their hosts, Challenor was able to gain a better grasp of the language. As both men suspected, being able to speak Italian might prove crucial for whatever lay ahead. To be able to converse freely with the locals, and to potentially pass themselves off as Italians, might well prove a lifesaver if they came across German patrols.

But as both also appreciated, they could hardly remain in that village – their sanctuary – for ever. The risk to the locals was just too great. Most knew exactly who they were and where they were billeted, yet apparently not a soul ever thought to betray them, even less to ask for any form of payment. Late one night they gathered their things, bade farewell to their hosts, and once again headed off on their epic trek to find the Allied frontline.

Pressing on, the weather took a turn for the worse. As they trudged south, fierce gusts of wind and snow began to blast into their faces. Shortly, Wedderburn's feet had ballooned in size again, and were so swollen as to resemble a 'couple of pumpkins'. Worse still, Challenor's malaria had returned with a vengeance. If they didn't find somewhere to shelter, they were either going to die of hypothermia, or they would have to give themselves up to the enemy. To do the latter would open them up to Hitler's Commando Order, which would very likely mean one outcome: torture and execution. Throwing themselves on the mercy of the Germans was not an option.

After covering some 400 kilometres on foot across such inhospitable terrain, it was the cruellest of outcomes: either die of hypothermia, or at the hands of a murderous enemy. And so it was almost as if by a miracle that they stumbled upon the village of Coppito, which lay some ninety kilometres north-east of Rome. Here they were told of someone who had never refused to help any Allied soldier in need of sustenance or shelter. And in the autumn and winter of 1943, there had been many such troops in desperate need.

On 8 September 1943 – the day after the Speedwell raiders had parachuted into Italy – the Commander-in-Chief of Allied forces, General Eisenhower, had announced on UN radio that 'The Italian Government has surrendered its armed forces unconditionally.' Upon hearing this, any number of Italian soldiers had simply abandoned their posts to return home. The gates of POW camps had been thrown open, and many of those incarcerated had made good their escape. Anticipating this turn of events, the Germans had moved swiftly to take control of the camps. But they were not to have it all their own way. There were many Italians, particularly those who lived in the mountains, who felt a burning contempt for Mussolini's Fascists and their Nazi allies. Likewise, many were driven by a sense of common humanity, as Challenor saw it, believing that any stranger in need of shelter or sustenance should be helped.

One such family had extended whatever assistance they could to any Allied soldier who presented themselves. They were the Eliseios, who lived on a small farm near Coppito village.

The matriarch, Mama Domenica Eliseio was around fifty years old. Challenor would describe her as 'small, plump and swathed from toe to toe in heavy black', with 'dark brown, birdlike eyes' that were full of motherly care. She and her family had planned to emigrate to Australia before the war, her husband having gone ahead to find work. But due to the outbreak of hostilities, the family had been unable to join him. That had left Domenica and her two children, twenty-one-year-old son Mimino and twenty-year-old daughter Anita, to run the farm in his stead.

It was a Sunday afternoon sometime in early November – the ailing fugitives had lost track of time – when the two benighted SAS men stumbled into Mama Eliseio's yard. Gathered at a table, eating a meal alfresco, was the matriarch and her two children, Mimino and Anita. And sitting across from them, enjoying a veritable feast, were three British POWs. Challenor and Wedderburn's approach was eyed furtively, for they were dressed to all intents and purposes like German soldiers with German weapons slung over their backs.

Seeing the look of alarm on the faces of the escaped prisoners,

Wedderburn sought to calm their fears. 'Take it easy,' he muttered, exhaustedly. 'We're British Paras on our way to the lines, and we're just about all in.'

After shaking hands all around, the two men were offered some food. It was like manna from heaven. They ate ravenously, chatting to their countrymen between mouthfuls. This was the first time in an age that Challenor and Wedderburn were able to get news of what was happening with the wider war. Until then, they'd had no idea just how the Allied advance was progressing. The soldiers were able to fill them in. As far as they were concerned, it was not good news. Not good news at all.

Challenor and Wedderburn learned that the advance had stalled near the River Sangro, some 130 kilometres further south. A major battle was still raging there. The very thought of another massive trek across the mountains, with all the usual obstacles in their path – wild rivers, plunging valleys and rough, snowbound terrain – didn't fill them with any eagerness to continue. This was especially so, with Wedderburn's feet being so bad and Challenor sensing his malaria really starting to bite.

Their dire predicament must have been clear for all to see, for Mama Eliseio spoke up almost immediately, insisting the two fugitives should stop with them, to rest and to eat. Neither man was in any fit state to argue.

For the next few weeks Challenor and Wedderburn enjoyed the hospitality of Mama Eliseio and her family, as they slowly recovered their good health. They kept a low profile, sleeping in a small hut, and only going to the farmhouse for meals. Over time a deep friendship developed between the two British soldiers and the Eliseios. However, Challenor and Wedderburn were acutely conscious of the danger they were putting their hosts in, for the farm looked down over a village that was crawling with enemy troops. Discovery could happen at any time, which would doubtless mean a violent and horrific death for all.

To lessen the danger somewhat, Challenor and Wedderburn suggested that they swap their uniforms for some civilian clothes. Clearly, the chances of being found out to be British parachutists would be much reduced if they could make like locals. A tailor was summoned, and soon enough the two men were kitted out in smart new suits, paid for from their stores of lire. Now looking decidedly less conspicuous, and with Wedderburn's feet improving and Challenor's malaria abating, they were able to repay the kindness shown by the Eliseios by helping out on the farm. They busied themselves feeding and mucking out the livestock, and immersing themselves in the way of life of their hosts. Gradually, the reality of the war seemed to recede, until it felt remote indeed.

In this manner the weeks flew past. Challenor, being around the same age as Mimino and Anita, grew very fond of them. He flirted shamelessly with Anita, vowing that he would wear his new suit 'when I marry you'. Mimino, who had taken on the role of being head of the household in his father's absence, was 'a fine young man, strongly built and very good looking', Challenor observed.

In this way Christmas Eve 1943 came around. As was tradition in the local area, the villagers called on each other, quaffing wine and enjoying the festivities. A crowd moved from house to house, gathering more and more locals. Keen to have a good time, Challenor tagged along, and subsequently drank more alcohol than was perhaps advisable. Finally, the party of revellers ended up at the local church, where Midnight Mass was about to take place.

As he took his seat at one of the pews, Challenor instantly

sobered up. Seated across the aisle from him were a number of German soldiers. Realising that to leave suddenly would only draw attention to himself, he forced himself to remain until the end. Once outside, the enemy troops started a snowball fight. It was now that the effects of the alcohol really hit, as Challenor threw up violently in the snow.

As he staggered away from the vomit-stained whiteness, he turned to the Germans and yelled out: 'God didn't hear you, you bastards!'

Fortunately, either due to his slurred speech or the fact that the soldiers were busy with their antics, they seemed not to hear.

While the following day was Christmas 1943, it seemed to mark a turning point in their fortunes, all for the worse. There appeared to be a significant increase in enemy activity, as more and more escaped Allied POWs were hunted down. German troops poured into the area. For Wedderburn and Challenor, it was obvious that to stay would lead to their discovery. After a lengthy discussion thick with emotion, they decided that the time had come to go their separate ways, at least for the time being. They hoped that by splitting up, should one be discovered the other would still have a chance of getting away. Challenor went to hide in one of the many caves that peppered the mountain slopes above the farm, while Wedderburn took refuge with a woman named Philomena, who lived on the village fringes.

Their plan was to wait for the Germans to give up their manhunts, before reuniting and continuing on their way. At first Challenor feared he'd got the worst end of the stick, having to stay in a rat-infested cave in the bitter December cold. However, at three o'clock in the morning of 27 December he was woken by the sound of 'rapid firing' and the snarl of motor vehicles.

Shortly, Challenor was to learn what this signified. When Anita next came to the cave with his food, she gave him the dire news: Wedderburn had been captured by the enemy, and the lady who had been sheltering him had been taken outside and shot.

While he was deeply worried about the fate of his friend, Challenor knew there was little he could do to help. He feared that once the Germans discovered Wedderburn was SAS, they would assume he was not alone and increase the intensity of the hunt. Trying to muster his strength in that freezing cave, Challenor prepared to move. Finally, he decided he couldn't risk endangering the Eliseios any longer, lest they suffer the same fate as Wedderburn's erstwhile protector, Philomena.

On 20 January 1944, he made his move – setting out for the British lines, do or die. The frontline was, he knew, somewhere south of the city of Chieti, around a hundred kilometres away. Although his mind was made up, he knew it would be far from easy getting there. The malaria was threatening to make another appearance, and to make matters worse the weather was terrible. With only a thin suit to wear, he was bound to struggle, as he was already feeling groggy and shivering after weeks in that cave.

Typically, Mama Eliseio tried her best to dissuade him. 'Stay here,' she argued. 'We can hide you. The weather is bad and you are sick.'

But Challenor told her that his mind was made up. That being the case, Mama Eliseio got Anita to escort him as far as the Popoli road. Together, they would look like a courting couple, as opposed to one ailing Allied soldier on the run. From there Challenor could strike out alone. It was a tearful moment when Challenor left Anita standing at the roadside. They had grown very close in the months they had spent together.

Challenor would later remark about Mama Eliseio, in his auto-biography, *SAS and the Met*: 'Even now, forty-five years later, I feel a lump in my throat when I think of her.'

Challenor walked all day, until he was just a short distance from Popoli town. As he approached he heard the sound of aircraft engines rumbling in the sky, followed by the distinctive whistling as their bombs were released. Looking to the heavens he spied the distinctive roundels of RAF bombers, which were raining down their ordnance on the town. Bright flashes filled the horizon as the bombs exploded, ripping walls apart and throwing masonry and timbers in all directions. Entire buildings burst into flames, lighting up the sky with an orange glow, as palls of thick dark smoke rose high into the air.

Just ahead of him a car skidded to a halt. The occupants, a German and an Italian, jumped from the vehicle and immedi-ately took cover. Glancing at Challenor, the German called for him to join them. Caught in a growing fog of malarial fever, and taken by surprise, Challenor made the schoolboy error of crying out a reply in English. 'Don't worry,' he yelled, 'they're mine.' Just as on Christmas Eve, his words seemed to go unheeded by the German. However, they'd not escaped his Italian companion's attention.

When the bombing stopped the Italian approached and asked if Challenor was English. Too tired and cold to pretend otherwise, he confirmed that he was, at which point the man whispered: 'I'll see you here at midnight. Wait for me. I can help.'

Deciding to trust in his offer of assistance, Challenor waited until it grew dark. After standing around for hours, and fearing he was about to freeze to death, he decided he could tarry no longer, and he set off in search of shelter. Eventually, he found a derelict, boarded-up building near the railway line. After checking he could not be seen, he broke in and kindled a fire within the cold hearth. 'Shivering from the bitter cold' and 'shaking from malaria', he moved as close to the flames as possible to get warm, and shortly he'd fallen asleep.

Challenor awoke later to feel an intense pain in his back. It took him a second or so to realise that he was on fire, a burning ember having fallen onto his jacket. After managing to extinguish the flames, he checked on the damage. His back seemed fine, but there was now a large hole in the rear-side of his jacket. He searched around for more wood to burn, but could find none. Fearing he would perish of malaria or frostbite if he stayed where he was, he decided to press ahead. Daybreak could not be so far away, and the hope of reaching British lines at Chieti drove him on.

Cutting a vagabond figure, Challenor set forth. He kept telling himself that one last massive effort would bring him safely to Allied positions. As he neared what had to be the frontline, the roads became jammed with enemy transport. Throwing himself into the snow, or into ice-filled ditches, to avoid being seen, he made painfully slow progress. Exhausted, semi-delirious with malaria and freezing cold, he did not notice, until it was too late, that he had stumbled into yet another village. As he inched forward, his head bowed, he was stopped dead by someone shouting at him . . . in German.

Before he had a chance to react, a torch was shone into his face, causing him to blink and to raise his hands to shield his eyes. He still carried the pistol he had deployed with, stuffed in one pocket, but there was no time to pull it out, cock it and fire. He would have to bluff his way through this. Using the Italian he had learned over the past few months, Challenor explained to the German soldier, who was pointing a rifle at his chest, that he was a farmer who had lost some of his cows during the bombing. He was simply out and about searching for his missing livestock.

Either the soldier was unconvinced by Challenor's story or unable to understand his Italian. He motioned the lone fugitive to a nearby hut, where a group of German troops were warming themselves over a fire. A sergeant approached and when Challenor repeated his story, the man sent for an interpreter. It was then that Challenor knew the game was up. Speaking too quickly for him to understand, it soon became clear to the interpreter that Challenor was no native Italian.

Challenor response was to give a resigned shrug. 'Englander,' he muttered. 'Englander.' He was almost past caring.

Shortly, Challenor had been disarmed of his pistol, and his SAS-issue silk escape map had been confiscated. That done, he was allowed to stay in the hut overnight, the German sergeant giving him some hot soup and letting him thaw out at the fireside. The following morning, he was taken to a nearby headquarters building, where he was handed over to a high-ranking German officer.

'You are armed, equipped with a map, and dressed in civilian clothes,' the officer informed him. 'This is a serious matter. I am required to hand you over to other people.'

Challenor knew quite well what that euphemism signified. 'Other people' – the dreaded *Geheime Staatspolizei*, aka the Gestapo. His mind racing, he figured he had to think of some reason that would force them to treat him as a bona fide prisoner-of-war. If he could manage that, he might still come up with a way to escape. But nothing came into his head. Shortly, a dark car pulled up outside and two SS men strode purposefully into the room in which Challenor was being held.

One of the men wore the insignia of an officer. Without saying a word, the other strode up to Challenor and struck him with a 'pulverising backhander'. It sent him flying across the room. Another punch knocked him to the floor, whereupon the SS officer proceeded to kick him repeatedly in the stomach. Without further ado the two men hauled him outside and into their car. They drove him to SS headquarters in Popoli. Upon arrival Challenor was dragged into a courtyard at the rear of the building, where he was led to a wall riddled with bullet holes, and stained red with what he presumed to be splashes of blood.

They were trying to soften him up, Challenor figured, so further and worse interrogations were sure to follow. Once they'd finished delivering their chilling threat at that blood-stained wall, his captors led him back into the building. There he was paraded in front of another SS officer. Forced to strip naked, the SS men searched every part of Challenor's body. What exactly they were looking for, he had no idea.

Eventually, the new officer began to speak. 'You are not a soldier. You are a spy and will be shot if you do not help us.'

Challenor sensed that simply giving his name, rank and army number would not cut it with these types. Although he was still dazed from the beating he had taken, he figured he could get away with giving them information he reckoned they already knew, tinged with what he thought made a believable lie.

'I am in the Special Air Service Regiment,' he told them. 'I have been on an operation. I went down with malaria and an Italian stole my uniform.'

'Tell me more about the operation,' the officer demanded.

'It was a train-blowing job north of La Spezia,' Challenor replied, assuming this was something they would already know had happened.

The SS officer began to fire more questions at him; how many had been on the mission, what was their objective, and where had they come from?

'I have already given you more information than I am required to do as a prisoner-of-war,' Challenor replied, firmly.

'So far you have given me no details to prove you are a soldier and not a spy,' the Nazi officer countered. 'I say you are a spy. And you will be shot as one.'

With that Challenor was dragged away and thrown into a cell. The guards took it in turns to beat him, until all of his body seemed to ache like hell. His face was terribly bruised, his lips split, bloody and swollen. The fact that they took great pleasure in doing this did not go unremarked by Challenor. Over the next few days the beatings became routine – prior to each interrogation he would be given a sound kicking. He was to receive the worst of them all following another RAF bombing raid over Popoli, and partly he brought the savagery down on his own head.

Watching from his cell window as the RAF rained down carpets of bombs upon the town, Challenor noticed German soldiers scurrying in all directions in the yard below, desperate to find cover. Loving seeing them panicking like this, he began to shout abuse at his captors, laughing at them as they cowered from the bombardment. Upon seeing this barefaced show of defiance – this prisoner who took such open delight in their fear – one of them fired his pistol at Challenor's cell window, forcing him to dive for cover as well.

No sooner had the bombing stopped, than a group of German soldiers thundered into his cell, and proceeded to give him a particularly vicious beating, eventually leaving his battered body face-down on the mattress. Challenor vowed of this moment that if ever he were to make it back to Allied lines, and rejoined his unit, he would kill every German soldier he came across, no exception.

Not long after this, Challenor was hauled before the same SS officer as before, for more interrogation. When he refused to answer any further questions, the German declared. 'Very well . . . You will be taken to Aquila camp where the necessary documents will be prepared for your execution.'

The Aquila Prisoner-of-War camp – also known as Camp 102 – had been run by the Italians until the signing of the September Armistice. On that day, as Challenor well knew, the 'Italian Commandant had opened the gates and marched the POWs out into the hills, as . . . Germans were approaching,' Despite this brave act by the Camp Commandant, many of the escapees had been 'rounded up by German paratroops and taken back' to the camp. Aquila was now being administered by German soldiers, and it was there that the recaptured Allied soldiers were being housed.

Conditions in many Italian camps were horrific. Some POWs had starved to death, or, having lost all hope, had taken their own lives. But for Challenor, the move to Aquila represented a positive change in his fortunes. Condemned to death he might be, but at least he would get to spend his last days with fellow Allied troops. He also nurtured a spark of hope that he might escape, reminding himself repeatedly – 'while there was life, there was hope'. Given back his clothes, he was taken to Aquila camp, and marched into a large dormitory full of Allied POWs. These were regular soldiers, captured on the battlefields of Italy and North Africa. Unlike Challenor, they were in little danger of being put in front of a firing squad, for they did not fall under the ruling of Hitler's Commando Order. Challenor, therefore, had only one choice open to him, as he saw it. Escape or die.

Upon learning of his dire situation, the prisoners rallied round. Here was a young soldier who, like them, was guilty of doing nothing more than serving his country. If they could help in any way, then they would do so.

It had been drilled into Challenor during training that 'as a member of the SAS it was his duty, if captured, to escape.' No sooner had he arrived than he was looking for a way to break out. It did not take him long to find a possible weakness in the prison block's security.

The men of the SAS were selected not only for their physical attributes, but also for their ability to act on their own initiative and to think laterally. Tanky Challenor was no exception. After being at Aquila for just a few days, a plan of escape began to form in his head, one that was so totally outrageous and so completely off the wall, that if he pulled it off it would go down as one of the most ingenious and audacious breakouts of the entire war. It would take both courage and a massive quantity of brazenness to pull it off, attributes Challenor reckoned he could call on.

Nursing his battered and bruised form, Challenor gathered his fellow POWs and began to outline his plan. The dormitory in which they were incarcerated was on the first floor of a building situated close to the camp gates. At the rear was an exercise yard surrounded by double barbed-wire fences, with watchtowers either end. Challenor had noticed that the meagre rations dished out daily were delivered via a hatch leading into a ration store, which was connected in turn to an administration block. Each day a number of elderly Italian women would enter and leave the camp, seemingly without being challenged, to carry out cleaning and laundry duties. If Challenor could manage to squeeze through that hatch, there was just a chance that he might slip away disguised as an Italian cleaning lady.

Once he'd finished outlining his plan, at first Challenor was greeted with hoots of derisory laughter. But when it subsided and the prisoners realised he was serious, they set about helping him. As all appreciated, time was of the essence. The Gestapo could return at any moment. If Challenor was to survive, he had to get out of the camp quickly, otherwise a firing squad beckoned. A disguise was quickly fashioned. One prisoner gave Challenor a pair of knee-length black woollen stockings that he had picked up while on the run. Another donated a large piece of material he had been using to store his things, to use as a makeshift shawl. As many needles and thread as they could find were gathered, and a blanket that was crawling with lice was fashioned into a makeshift skirt. To complete his disguise, Challenor gave himself an ample bosom made up of balled-up wads of paper.

Snatching a few hours' sleep, Challenor began to have doubts that he could really pull this off, 'it seemed so hare-brained'. But the very next morning he seized the chance to put his madcap idea into action. Noting the hatch had been left open and unguarded, he donned his disguise. Not wanting to discard his long johns, due to the wintry weather, he rolled them up, pulling the black stockings on below them. Quickly placing a greatcoat around him, a group of prisoners walked Challenor out into the exercise yard. Shielding him from observation from the watchtowers, they ushered him towards the open hatch. For all intents and purposes, this was merely a group of prisoners getting some fresh air.

Upon checking the room beyond the hatch, and the corridor leading from there to the camp offices, it was confirmed that all was deserted. Waiting until they were sure the guards weren't looking, Challenor was lifted up to the hatch, and posted through it feet first. With the whispers of good luck ringing in his ears, he adopted a stooped position, like that of an old woman, and began to shuffle ahead. Passing only one other person, a German orderly who took no notice of him whatsoever, Challenor slowly made his way along the corridor, hardly daring to lift his head to see how close he was to the door leading to the front of the building.

After what seemed like an age, he was finally there. Turning the handle, he opened the door and stepped outside. Ahead of him, just thirty yards away, was the main gate; beyond that, freedom. With beads of sweat running down his forehead, and a sense that this just couldn't last, he tugged the shawl tighter around his shoulders and pressed on, trying his best to hobble like an elderly Italian peasant woman. Resisting the urge to quicken his pace, he inched past the two sentries manning the gate, who, like the orderly only seconds earlier, seemed to take no notice of him at all.

By now, his heart was thumping so hard he thought it would burst from his chest. The sound thudded in his ears like a machine gun. Deliberately keeping his eyes from glancing at the sentries' rifles, he focused his gaze on the handle of the gate, hardly daring to breathe. And then he was there. Placing his sweaty grip on the handle he turned it. Opening the gate, he stepped out of the camp and onto the road, expecting at any time to hear the order he feared most, as he was pulled to a halt.

No such cry came. But while he was outside of the camp gates, he was by no means home and dry. Passing a group of German soldiers waiting for their transport, it was now that the long johns he had pulled up to accommodate the black stockings began to fall down his legs. He was forced to cling desperately to their tops, to stop them tripping him up, as the soldiers watched on indifferently. Finally, Challenor allowed himself to breathe a sigh of relief. He turned a corner and figured he had done it. Somehow, his seemingly laughable plan had worked. When the Gestapo came to collect him for his execution he would be nowhere to be found.

He had dared . . . and he had won.

Alone in the Italian countryside, he could think only of heading to the one place he knew he would find sanctuary – the home of the Eliseios. A few hours later, after cadging a lift off a kindly old man with a donkey and cart, he knocked at that familiar door. At first Mimino did not recognise him, for he was still dressed as an old woman, but when Challenor revealed himself, he was dragged inside and 'deluged with affection'. After polishing off a hearty meal and accepting a change of clothes, he refused their appeals to stay: they had taken far too many risks already. Instead, he returned to his cave up the mountainside. Once there he collapsed on his familiar bed of straw. To Challenor, it felt like 'returning home after a long absence'.

It was now 2 February 1944. Challenor had been on the run for nearly five months, barring that brief spell in captivity.

His stay in that cave went on for longer than he had ever imagined possible. Once again, he fell into a malarial fever. Racked by terrible deliriums, he was only saved by Mama Eliseio and Anita's kind ministrations. From somewhere they had acquired some quinine – then the primary treatment for malaria. For weeks Challenor battled the illness, as they nursed him daily. Finally, on 1 April 1943, eight weeks after his daring escape from Aquila camp, Challenor came back to something like his normal senses. Feeling as if he had regained enough strength, he decided to resume his hike towards Allied lines.

A second tearful farewell followed with the Eliseios, before he set off once more. Challenor stuck to the mountains, heading over the Gran Sasso range, which climb to some 9,500 feet in height. While this was the most direct route towards the Allied frontline, the snow remained knee deep, and the going proved slow, exhausting and hazardous in the extreme. Below him, Challenor could see 'Germans digging in and setting up gun emplacements', so he knew he could not be far from the frontline.

Dogged by bouts of malarial delirium, after a while Challenor found he had gained a companion. As if from nowhere, he became aware of someone walking alongside him – a man, dressed like him in civilian clothes. The figure confided in Challenor that he too was an Englishman; another prisoner-of-war on the run. As Challenor was too sick to engage in deep conversation, they forged through snow and wind in a companionable silence. At any time that Challenor seemed to falter, this stranger spurred him on, offering words of encouragement: 'Keep going. Not long now. We'll rest soon.' Buoyed by those kind words, Challenor dug deep to find the reserves he needed to continue.

Finally, after what had been a gruelling ordeal in the snowy wastes, the two men wandered into a farm near to San Rocco, a small village only a few miles from the frontline. There they took shelter in a cowshed.

Despite being sandwiched between sleeping cattle, for the first time in an age Challenor managed to get a good night's rest, the warmth of the animals lulling him into a deep slumber. When he awoke the next morning the fever had all but subsided. Almost immediately he noticed that his mysterious travelling companion had gone, leaving him to ponder if he had actually existed at all. Had there really been a British POW walking alongside him, giving him the encouragement to finish his journey? Or had it all been a figment of his addled mind, brought on by his bouts of malaria? He would never be sure. Whether real or imaginary, the incident had given him a renewed vigour to make it to safety.

Challenor took stock of his situation. He was close enough to the front to hear the sound of Allied artillery as it pounded the German positions, only a few miles to the north-east. Below him snaked the wide, fast-flowing Pescara river, something he would have to find a way across, as the Allied positions lay on the far side. Looking for a good place to do this, he spied 'a low dam', which appeared to be watched over by a lone enemy sentry. With no other way of getting over the river, he made his way towards it.

Deciding to bluff his way across, Challenor approached the dam. Feigning a confidence he did not feel, he passed the German, nodding a greeting of '*Buon Giorno*'. The German sentry seemed completely uninterested, merely turning away, and allowing Challenor to make it safely to the far side. Moving off the main road he headed into the open countryside, pressing on towards British lines, the promise of success getting ever closer with each step. It was then that he ran into an Italian, who told him that he could help guide Challenor to the British lines. That man claimed to have smuggled other escaped POWs across. He didn't seem concerned when Challenor warned him he had no money left with which to pay.

The Italian led Challenor to a house where a group of South African airmen were also hiding out. Leaving the new arrival with them, he set off to see if he could find any more accurate information on the current Allied positions. Returning an hour later, the Italian looked badly shaken. He had just come across the bodies of two men. One was his good friend, who had also been acting as a guide, while the other was a POW. Both had been executed with a bullet to the head. Warning the five that he could no longer help, he quickly departed.

With their guide now gone, the South Africans decided to return to the hills and await the advance. Challenor, on the other hand, had had enough of the mountains. He vowed that he had not suffered all that he had, only to fall at the final hurdle. He was so close to the British lines that he could see the muzzle flashes, as their artillery pounded the German positions. He resolved that he would head on alone.

As he stole forward, he came across a sign in Italian, warning that any civilians found in the area would be shot. As he was no longer in uniform, he would need to take great care. Day was giving way to night, and he decided to press on through the darkness. He kept hearing the distinctive sound of voices speaking in German and the growl of vehicles. Each time he was forced to dive for cover and to hunker down in the shadows. Approaching the small village of Guardiagrele, he realized how close he was to the frontline. Guardiagrele had changed hands numerous times during recent heavy fighting. Again he heard German voices ringing through the darkness. He was about to make a dive for cover when, from out of the shadows, stepped two German soldiers, their weapons levelled at him.

Recalling the signs he had seen warning that Italians would be shot on sight, he did the only thing he could think of to prevent himself from being killed. Raising his hands in the air he called out, 'Englander!' – moments later assuring them that he was an escaped British POW. Challenor felt 'sick at heart at having to give myself up when the British lines were so close'. He had come so far, only to have been thwarted at the very last obstacle. It was utterly soul-destroying.

His captors led him before an officer, who was dug in with his unit on the slopes of a nearby hill. Again Challenor fell back on the story that he was an escaped POW and that an Italian villager had stolen his British uniform when he was stricken with malaria. That was why he was dressed in civilian attire. The officer seemed to accept this at face value. Challenor was held there for the remainder of the day, as they sheltered from a heavy artillery bombardment being laid down by British forces positioned not far away.

As evening drew in, the officer ordered Challenor to be moved further away from the bombardment. He was to be dealt with at a later time, when things had calmed down a little. The hut to which he was taken was occupied by three German troops, who had orders to keep a close eye on their lone prisoner. To Challenor, each appeared 'grey-faced and red-eyed', and to be suffering from the effects of being months under intense fire.

In one corner of the hut was a large barrel of wine. The long-suffering German troops weren't about to pass up such an opportunity. They proceeded to quaff copious quantities, waving Challenor over to join them. After all that he had endured, he figured a couple of mugs was the least he deserved. A few hours later, and 'quite drunk', Challenor passed out asleep on the floor.

He awoke to a bright early morning. The sun's rays cut through the dirty windows, throwing shafts of light onto the table behind. Seated there, and looking much the worse for wear, were his three guards. Although Challenor himself was feeling the effects of the alcohol, another 'crazy idea' came to him.

He had travelled hundreds of miles through one of the harshest winters in recent memory. More than once he had come close to death due to malaria and at the hands of the enemy. He had been captured; he had escaped, dressed as a washerwoman. He had made it all the way to the frontline. He could not let it end here. He owed it to himself, but equally to Lieutenant Wedderburn, and to all those who had helped him on his way. That included the men in Aquila POW camp who had helped fashion his disguise; the many, many Italian people who had aided him, each at great risk to their own personal safety. He owed it to the ghostly stranger who had spurred him on through the mountains, when he had been on the verge of giving up. And he owed it most of all to his 'second family': Mama Eliseio, Anita and Mimino, who had saved his life on more than one occasion.

Without them, he would be dead by now. His resolve stiffened by such thoughts, he vowed to make one final bid for freedom.

Noting the state of the three Germans, Challenor hatched his plan. Taking off his shoes he placed one in the middle of the hut, where all could see it. No man ever tried to escape wearing one shoe. He then wandered to the door, which had been left ajar. Making as though to clean the remaining shoe, he gripped it in his hand, even as he stole a glance at the hungover guards. They stared indifferently, clearly thinking he was going nowhere with nothing on his feet. A moment later he had placed the second shoe on the floor, and was 'off like a hare', leaving the three enemy soldiers sitting at the table.

169

Challenor didn't bother to look back, to see if they were giving chase.

Instead, he ran as fast as his legs and stockinged feet would carry him.

On he ran, heading towards the south, away from the sun, on a bearing he reckoned would lead him towards British lines. As he dashed ahead, falling occasionally due to his own pounding hangover, his feet were cut to bits on the sharp rocks. But he blanked the pain from his mind. He simply kept on running, and turning away whenever he heard German voices. Through bushes he thundered; in and out of gullies and over rocks and boulders. He paused only to take shelter whenever he heard movement or the sound of German soldiers that he simply couldn't dash past.

Eventually, he sensed that he was on his own. Finding a gully in which to shelter, he paused to take stock of his situation. His feet were a mess – bloody, shredded and agonising. Peeling off his long johns, he tore them into pieces and proceeded to wrap the rags around his feet like bandages. Thus crudely dressed, he hobbled onwards, making for where the British lines had to be. He figured he had to be in no-man's-land, that area sandwiched between the German and the British frontlines.

He was so close now.

And then, once again, he heard what he most dreaded: German voices.

An enemy reconnaissance patrol was heading back towards their own lines. As yet, they were unaware of his presence. Quickly he dived for cover. As soon as they had passed him by, Challenor was back on his feet and he plodded on. A few minutes later, he heard another voice ringing out. But this was no

German, nor even an Italian. The one word was barked out in English, but not in an accent he knew or recognised.

'Halt!'

'Take it easy, chum,' Challenor yelled back. 'I'm English.'

It was then that a huge-seeming Indian trooper emerged from the cover of a wall. Grabbing hold of Challenor, the soldier proceeded to search him thoroughly. All the while, Challenor was trying to explain just who he was – an SAS saboteur returning from an operation deep behind enemy lines. Finally seeming convinced by his story, the Indian soldier took Challenor to a forward command post, where he was questioned by an officer. There it was confirmed that Challenor was indeed who he claimed to be.

For the first time in seven months, he could relax.

As if in a dream, he was offered a seat on an ammo box with his back against a tree, while a cigarette was thrust into one hand, a mug of steaming tea into the other. As he sat there, over and over Challenor repeated the words like a mantra – 'I've done it, you bastards. I've done it, you bastards. I've done it, you bastards.'

He had escaped against all the odds. He'd defied death countless times, and he had made it home.

But sadly, many others who had taken part in Operation Speedwell were not to be so lucky. After two failed escape attempts, Challenor's Speedwell partner and friend, Lieutenant Thomas Wedderburn, was to spend the rest of the war in a POW camp in Germany. He would at least survive the war. Once the Allies had uncovered the fate of Captain Patrick Dudgeon and Gunner Bernard Brunt, their bodies were disinterred and reburied in the Military Cemetery in Florence, in adjoining graves. The bodies of Sergeant William Foster and Corporal James Shortall were also disinterred and reburied at the Staglieno Military Cemetery in Genoa, likewise side by side.

The larger Speedwell stick, led by Captain Philip Pinckney, experienced mixed fortunes. Pinckney himself went missing following the drop, never to be seen again. Lieutenant Anthony Greville-Bell reported that although Pinckney's voice 'was heard on the ground', they were unable to locate him. After waiting for hours, they moved out. Greville-Bell assumed command, splitting the men into two groups of three. They went on successfully to derail four trains, before making their escape south, Greville-Bell's party reaching safety on 16 November 1943. Greville-Bell was awarded the Distinguished Service Order (DSO) for his actions during Operation Speedwell.

The Eliseio family emigrated to Australia, in time Mimino becoming a thriving farmer.

As for Tanky Challenor, for his part in Operation Speedwell and his subsequent escape, he was awarded the Military Medal (MM). The final part of his citation reads – 'Throughout the seven months spent behind enemy lines this NCO displayed the highest courage and determination.' Following his epic escape Challenor rejoined the SAS and got more of the action that he craved, serving with distinction following the invasion of France until the end of hostilities.

After the war he joined the Metropolitan Police where he rose to the rank of Detective Sergeant. He became the scourge of the underworld, being a constant pain in the sides of many a gangland boss. However, his wartime exploits were to cast a long shadow. On the verge of a nervous breakdown in 1963, he was deemed unfit for service and was discharged from the police.

*

During the course of their operations deep behind enemy lines, the men of Operation Speedwell had proved themselves to be the very best the British Army had to offer. They had succeeded in all of the mission objectives, destroying multiple trains and damaging several rail lines, not to mention tunnels. However, they were badly let down. The plans were hurried, and they dropped into theatre with no means of communication; the only information they could get on the ground came from friendly locals and any POWs they encountered. More to the point, they were sent in with no proper plan of extraction, simply being told to 'do their stuff' and then make their own way back to British lines. There was no chance of them heading for the coast to be picked up by boat or submarine, despite their area of operations being just thirty miles from the Mediterranean Sea.

The fact that *any* of the thirteen made it back at all was testament to the men themselves and their steely fortitude, especially bearing in mind the brutal predations of Hitler's Commando Order. All thirteen displayed the vital attributes required of SAS soldiers: courage, tenacity, flexibility, resilience, intelligence and toughness. These qualities would prove crucial for the fight that was to come. For another, far larger operation was in the offing, for which the services of the SAS would be called upon as never before.

As Operation Overlord – the D-Day landings – got under way, so the missions of the SAS would spawn yet another of the war's greatest tales of escape.

Chapter Four

RETURN OF THE LOST

Duault, Brittany, France, 17 June 1944

The man at the wheel of the black Citroën Traction Avant saloon car had no idea where they were heading. Riding in the vehicle with him were three more German military policemen, while a few yards ahead, in a second such car, there was a similar party. But even the driver of the lead Citroën appeared uncertain of their whereabouts. By now, it had become apparent that they had taken a wrong turning, a narrow country lane stretching a long way behind them, and seemingly leading absolutely nowhere.

The lead car nosed ahead uncertainly, its driver trying to work out where they might be, and what on earth they should do. All anyone seemed to know was that they were somewhere between Bohal and Saint-Marcel, deep in the countryside of Brittany, on France's far north-western region.

Suddenly, from out of nowhere there came a tremendous, ear-splitting howl. It rose to a crescendo, filling their ears like some kind of hellish banshee. A fraction of a second later the car in front exploded, as whatever shell or missile had been fired tore into it. The heatwave from the explosion rolled over the second vehicle, forcing the occupants to duck down instinctively. They could only imagine those up front had been killed instantly, for the vehicle had been torn apart and blasted into chunks of twisted, smoking wreckage.

Unbeknown to them, they had quite by chance stumbled upon the largest Maquis hideout in the whole of Brittany, the Maquis being the French resistance groups that had been armed and trained by the Allies. Raising his head, the driver of the second vehicle glanced in his rear-view mirror, checking whether there was any chance of reversing out of danger, before whoever had shot at them reloaded their weapon and fired again. Probably not, he told himself. They were sitting ducks.

Only one option remained. The four Germans flung open the Citroën's doors and piled out onto the roadway, scrambling away as fast as they possibly could. They were convinced that to stay inside would bring a horrible, fiery end, just as had been suffered by their comrades. By now, their corpses were being consumed by the furious conflagration, as flames raged through the mangled wreckage of the vehicle. A pall of thick black smoke rose high into the early evening sky, marking the position of the attack for all to see.

As the four men ran for it, bullets began to snap past their heads and to rip up the ground all around them, as a large body of French resistance fighters gave chase. Sensing there was no chance of getting away, three of the fleeing figures stopped, raising their hands above their heads in surrender. A few moments later they were surrounded by rough looking partisans, young Frenchmen dressed in all manner of clothing. Among them were a few wearing what looked to be British Army uniforms, and each held British-made weapons with which they menaced their German captives.

But one of the Germans appeared to have got away. No matter how far the Maquisards searched, there was no sign of the missing man anywhere. Reluctantly, they gave up trying to find him and headed back to their positions, one prisoner short. This was bad news. Bad news indeed. For that German soldier now knew exactly where the Maquis base was situated. If he made it to the nearby town of Malestroit, just over three kilometres to the north-east of there, they were in little doubt that he would raise the alarm. The enemy would then surely return, and this time it wouldn't be just eight men in two black sedans.

The German military had formidable resources in Brittany – almost forty thousand men at arms, including elements of the 5th Parachute Division, plus 'hardened White Russians from a Waffen-SS division, artillery units, coastal defence infantry and a Luftwaffe infantry division specially trained to hunt down parachutists, complete with dogs. For the Maquis of Saint-Marcel, which included in their number a contingent of Special Air Service parachutists, this was not good news.

Those SAS hailed from 4 (French) SAS Regiment, and they had played an extraordinary role in Operation Overlord, the June 1944 Allied invasion of Normandy. They had been the first Allied soldiers to land on French soil, serving as the spearhead of Overlord. Indeed, rather than the vanguard being formed by the pathfinders of the British 6th Airborne Division, or the forward elements of the US 101st or 88th Airborne Divisions, it had consisted of a few dozen SAS troops.

Though intimately connected to Overlord, their mission hadn't taken them into Normandy. Instead, at around 2340 hours on the night of 5 June 1944 – so in advance of the main Allied invasion force – thirty-six soldiers of 4 SAS had parachuted into Brittany. These men were all French. They had fled their homeland to join the *Forces Françaises Libres* – Free French Forces – under the command of General Charles de Gaulle and the Allies. Each had volunteered for 'Special Service' and had been put through the same rigorous selection process as their British and Commonwealth comrades. Now, after the long years of Nazi occupation, they were back on French soil, determined to kick the reviled enemy out of their homeland.

Formally, their mission was to 'sever, as far as possible, all communications between Brittany and the remainder of France' with 'complete liberty to undertake the tasks ... in whatever manner' those on the ground considered best. By cutting off Brittany from neighbouring Normandy, their aim was to prevent enemy reinforcements from being rushed to the landing beaches and driving the Allies back into the sea. To say their mission was of vital importance was the understatement of the century. They could not afford to fail.

Initially, they had been split into four patrols of nine men. Two were to set up a drop zone in the north of Brittany, code-named 'Samwest', and two were to do similar in the south, that DZ being codenamed 'Dingson'. They were then split again into groups of three, with orders to execute widespread sabotage of the railway lines that ran through the region. Those actions were crucial to preventing German military units from heading to the Normandy beaches, once the invasion force had got ashore.

Those vital sabotage tasks completed, the SAS were then to

establish two key bases of operations – one at the forest of Duault in the north, close to the Samwest DZ, and one at Saint-Marcel in the south, adjacent to the Dingson DZ. These areas had been selected by British high command due to the scarcity of German units they harboured. From those remote bases, it was hoped the SAS would be able to move with relative freedom. SAS Lieutenant Pierre Marienne was charged to take command of the camp at Saint-Marcel, while Lieutenants André Botella and Charles Deschamps were to run Duault.

Once those bases and DZs were established, the SAS were charged to carry out further actions, 'attacking railways, cutting telecoms, [striking] opportunity targets e.g. attacks on soft vehicles, sentries etc.' With large numbers of Maquis existing in the area, they were to link up with their forces, to help harass and tie down German troops, and until they could link up with Allied forces, once they had broken out of the Normandy beachheads.

Immediately after the D-Day landings had taken place, the news spread across France like wildfire. The SAS and local Maquis commanders found themselves inundated with volunteers hungry to fight. Patriotic young men and women, sensing the end of the era of Nazi occupation, were eager to play a part. Shortly, the numbers in the Brittany camps had swelled to some six thousand fighters. As the size of the volunteer force kept growing, air drops were called in to deliver supplies, as Allied aircraft began parachuting in arms and ammunition to thousands of mostly untrained partisans.

More SAS began dropping in, including 4 SAS's commander, the one-armed Colonel Pierre-Louis Bourgoin, who joined the Dingson group at Saint-Marcel. A large, good-natured man with pale blue eyes and thick, curly, fair hair, he'd lost his right arm

SAS founder, David Stirling (above left) and Blair 'Paddy' Mayne, the man who took over command when Stirling was captured in February 1943. At the very outset they stressed that theirs was an egalitarian unit, requiring freethinking self-starters – men who, if captured behind enemy lines, would never cease striving to escape and to re-join the SAS.

December 1940, senior military figures inspect the men of No. 11 Special Air Service Brigade (11 SAS) at their training ground, RAF Ringway, near Manchester. Two months later, thirty-six of these fledgling airborne troopers would parachute into Italy on the daring Operation Colossus, the first ever such mission by British forces anywhere in the world.

The Colossus raider's target was the Tragino Aqueduct (above left, shown in a painting of the mission). But one 'stick' – six men, led by Captain Gerrard Daly and with Sapper Alfred Parker in their number – were dropped in the wrong valley. The Colossus raiders' daring achievements would hit the press, garnering headlines in both the British and American newspapers, but also winning grudging praise in Nazi Germany itself.

A group of the Operation Colossus raiders – also known as 'X Troop' – held in a prisoner-of-war camp in Italy. It was from such incarceration that Sapper Alfred Parker would break out with his close friend, Lance Corporal George Dent, making a desperate bid to reach Allied lines.

In February 1940, Lieutenant Anthony Hough volunteered for winter warfare training, joining the likes of David Stirling, in Chamonix, in the French Alps. But it was to be in North Africa that Hough would first see action. By the summer of 1942 he had joined the ranks of the SAS, waging war across the desert wastes.

Hough (above left) took two of his stalwarts from his previous unit into the SAS: Alfred Handscombe and Mick Levy. They'd forged an unbreakable bond while soldiering across the barren desert, plus larking about in their downtime (as shown above and below). Deployed on SAS Operation Palmyra, a mission to harass German General Rommel's supply lines, Hough's jeep-born patrol hit the enemy hard, but it would end in a last-ditch stand and then capture. So began Hough's herculean and death-defying escape.

Twenty-one-year-old Harold 'Tanky' Challenor (above left) nursed an 'intense hatred' of the Nazis, even before parachuting into Italy, as part of SAS Operation Speedwell. This was a daring mission to sabotage German rail links, which were hurrying reinforcements to the front lines. Hunted by an enemy hell-bent on entrapping the SAS saboteurs, brave Italian families like the Eliseios (above, right) sheltered Challenor and his comrades.

Deployed on Operation Speedwell in September 1943, Challenor would spend seven months behind enemy lines, facing capture, torture and execution by the SS and Gestapo, before escaping and making it back to friendly lines. He went on to rejoin the SAS, serving with distinction after the D-Day landings – pictured (above) in a jeep nicknamed 'Little Tanky' at the village of L'Isle-sur-Seriene, in north-central France.

Summer 1944, British and US forces dropped weapons, explosives and supplies to the French Resistance in preparation for the D-Day landings. But even before Allied forces had hit the Normandy beaches, SAS units had parachuted in to link up with the Resistance. Once such unit, of the 4 (French) SAS Regiment, fought a massive battle with the enemy before all contact with them was lost.

With scores of SAS unaccounted for, SAS high command dispatched Major Oswald Cary-Elwes (above left), a high-spirited devil-may-care officer, to parachute into Brittany to find the missing men. Cary-Elwes was fortunate to have his steadfast batman, Corporal Eric Mills (above right), at his side. Cary-Elwes had cut his eyeteeth at war in some of the wildest parts of West Africa (below). His and Mills' exploits across Brittany would prove fraught and testing, as they battled the Gestapo, the SS, French collaborators, and German patrols, to track down their missing SAS brethren, and then to execute the daring escape that followed.

In December 1944 SAS commander Major Roy Farran (above left, front row, with sub-machine gun) sent Captain Bob Walker-Brown and a squadron of SAS, to drop behind the lines in Italy. Their mission was to spread havoc to the rear of the enemy's Gothic Line, ensuring that the SAS would become the hunted, so drawing thousands of enemy troops away from the front. Laden with weaponry, including mortars and Vickers machine guns (above right), Walker-Brown made his mission a die-hard reality; elite German Alpine troops were dispatched to hunt the SAS force. Their subsequent escape over snowbound Italian mountains became the stuff of SAS legend.

in Tunisia in February 1943, while serving with the euphemistically named Inter-Service Liaison Department (ISLD), a cover name for the British Secret Intelligence Service (SIS). The vehicle he'd been riding in had been attacked by a German warplane, causing him multiple injuries. Regardless of that, he'd gone on to volunteer for the SAS, being appointed 4 SAS's commander despite being missing the one arm.

To say Bourgoin was an iconic figure was an understatement. For the French SAS, he was a brilliant leader and an inspiration. Bourgoin landed in Brittany on 10 June 1944, the British having provided him with a special parachute, decorated in the colours of the tricolour – the French national flag – under which to jump. At the same time as Bourgoin had dropped in, so too had the British SAS liaison officer, Squadron Leader Pat Smith.

But forty-eight hours after Bourgoin and Smith's arrival, the Duault/Samwest base had been set upon by a large body of German troops. Running battles had ensued, resulting in the SAS and maquisards scattering, forming smaller bands. Many had headed south to join their comrades at the Saint-Marcel/Dingson base, in the hope that that would evade discovery. By the evening of 17 June, there were some 200 SAS troops and close to 3,000 maquisards occupying the base, which was spread across a large farm called Le Bois-Joly, plus the châteaux of Sainte-Geneviève and La Nouette. The logistics of running such a group were challenging, and Bourgoin, plus his deputy, Lieutenant Marienne, were worried that the base was bound to come to the notice of the enemy.

But it had been quite by chance that they had been discovered by that patrol of German military policemen, riding in their two Citroën saloons.

*

As Bourgoin and Marienne fully appreciated, now that the Germans knew where they were, they had to move quickly. Separating into smaller groups made perfect sense, but it was not going to be easy. Their camp had amassed a huge stockpile of weaponry and ammunition, including scores of Bren light machine guns and bazookas. Even as the SAS commanders set about distributing the weaponry and supplies, and getting their men on the move, the enemy struck. The convoy of Citroëns had blundered into their base on the evening of 17 June. At dawn the next day the trap was sprung.

At Le Bois-Joly farm, lying towards the southern border of the SAS–Maquis base, a large body of German soldiers stealthily approached through the fields. Once they were around a hundred metres from the nearest watch post, which was manned by five maquisards, they opened fire. Those young men stood no chance, as their bodies were riddled with machine-gun fire, all five being killed instantly. Sadly, a stray round ricocheted away and struck a young girl who was watching over some cows in a neighbouring field, and she too was killed.

With that explosion of gunfire, the camp was roused and the SAS and Maquis went into action. Though they were massively outnumbered, the route leading into Le Bois-Joly farm ran uphill, across wide fields golden with wheat. The terrain provided little cover, and the lie of the land gave the defenders the advantage. As they crawled through those crops in their grey-green uniforms, creating furrows through the tall wheat, the German troops were horribly exposed. Letting rip with a murderous barrage of rifle and machine-gun fire, the Maquis and SAS delivered a fearsome onslaught. Very quickly many of the Germans lay in bloody heaps among the crops, either dead or severely wounded.

Still they came on relentlessly, seemingly determined to annihilate all within that camp. Lobbing smoke grenades to hide their progress, and supported by machine-gun fire, the first of the German troops managed to rush the farm. Beyond Le Bois-Joly, their chief aim was to take the nearby Château of Sainte-Geneviève, assuming that to be the SAS–Maquis command post. Due to the sheer weight of numbers, the defenders were forced to retreat. Abandoning the farm, they pulled back to a line of trees a short distance away, but not before leaving a large number of German dead in their wake. The battle had been fierce and bloody, for the Maquis and SAS knew they were fighting for their very survival.

With Le Bois-Joly farm now in their possession, the Germans brought forward mortar teams and began to pound the trees up ahead. Bombs rained down all around the defenders, blasting hot shrapnel in all directions. By way of response, well directed and concerted blasts of Bren gunfire ripped through the enemy ranks, as the SAS and maquisards blasted away at the advancing Germans, knocking many to the ground. With outstanding skill and incredible bravery, they actually managed to push the Germans back, and after a fierce firefight they retook Le Bois-Joly.

But by that stage they'd suffered many wounded. A handful of Willys jeeps had been parachuted in, intended for executing hit and run operations against the enemy. Now, those vehicles were loaded with the casualties, and tasked to ferry them to the nearby Château of Sainte-Geneviève, to receive first aid. From there the most desperate cases were rushed to the Château of La Nouette, a kilometre-and-a-half to the west, using the sunken lanes that were so typical of this region. Bourgoin was using La Nouette as his command post, and from there the hope was to spirit the most critically injured to safety.

Despite the needs of the wounded, four of the jeeps were to be used for a very different purpose. Bourgoin's deputy, Lieutenant Marienne, took that phalanx of vehicles and went on the offensive, raking the German positions with deadly accurate bursts from their Vickers K rapid-firing machine guns. The highly trained Marienne used those vehicles in classic SAS fashion, opening up with a devastating barrage, but pulling away again just as quickly, before zipping along to the next target. These were tactics that the SAS had perfected during their earliest days of operations – to hit hard, unleashing extreme violence, then speeding away before the enemy had the chance to respond.

Leading from the front, Lieutenant Marienne had himself suffered a wound to the head, but he remained undaunted. Witnessing his jeep 'coming out of the road to the [château's] abbey and into the full sunlight of the courtyard', a maquisard called Drennec spied Marienne 'standing up in it . . . a bloodstained strip of white parachute silk tied round his head. Everyone called him "The Lion".' Yet despite such courageous resistance, the enemy kept bringing up more reinforcements.

Bourgoin radioed London for orders. He demanded to know how long Allied high command needed him to hold out. Reports were that the Allies were to land a second invasion force into Brittany, even as the fighting in Normandy raged. The enemy resistance had proved fearsome, and if this second invasion force was only a short time away from landing in Brittany, then Bourgoin might be able to hold his area, which constituted an ideal landing zone for Allied troops. If not, then he'd need to disperse his forces, for that was the only way to safeguard their survival.

With fighting raging around the borders of their camp,

Bourgoin gave the first evacuation order – that all female maquis were to disperse. There had been many such young women in the camp, acting as *agents de liaison*. They'd formed an essential part of the French resistance, relaying messages from place to place while riding their bicycles, and often passing through German checkpoints with those precious rolls of paper hidden in their clothing, their hats, or even in the bicycle frames. Those caught faced being handed over to the Gestapo, where bestial torture and interrogation would follow. Any who survived were destined for the concentration camps. Here at Saint-Marcel, as the battle raged all around, they had been caring for the wounded, as well as acting as runners between the different command posts. But with so many enemy forces attacking, and the camp being at risk of becoming surrounded, it was time for them, at least, to pull out.

As the day wore on and Bourgoin awaited his orders, the enemy began pulling in heavy reinforcements from their nearest bases – armoured car and artillery convoys, boasting the kind of weaponry that could inflict serious damage on the defenders. The German commanders were clearly going all out to smash the Saint-Marcel Maquis, plus their SAS brethren. Forces mustered, at 'two o'clock they attacked hard along a two-and-a-half-kilometre front'. The enemy units consisted of a mixed bag of Germans and 'White Russians' – soldiers hailing from Russia who had volunteered for the SS and were battle-hardened fighters. The attackers boasted far superior firepower, and faced what was largely an untrained band of volunteers. While resistance proved fierce, the enemy eventually 'broke through as far as the Château of Sainte-Geneviève'.

The defenders refused to give up the château. One of them, SAS

Sergeant Gaston Navailles, though wounded twice already in the fighting, climbed onto the building's roof, dragging with him his Bren gun and a heavy load of magazines. Firing well-aimed bursts from that vantage point, the enemy began to drop, as his bullets tore into them, leaving the courtyard below strewn with bloody corpses. But Navailles was struggling to hold on; there were simply too many attackers. A small number of enemy troops managed to break into the château and make their way to the 'big bedroom' below Navailles' position. They immediately began to fire up into the ceiling, hoping to hit him through the roof.

Realising his position was growing desperate, and with no way of taking out those below with his Bren gun, Navailles pulled a grenade from his pocket, ripped out the pin and dropped it down the chimney into the hearth of the bedroom underneath. A moment later, there was the crump of an explosion. The firing stopped. With the threat from those within the château neutralised, Navaille and a few others managed to hold on to the building.

But as Bourgoin fully appreciated, things were getting increasingly desperate for his beleaguered force. He radioed for air support. At around four o'clock a flight of Allied fighter-bombers roared overhead and let rip with their rockets, causing an untold number of casualties among the enemy, blasting armoured cars and artillery pieces to smithereens. Thick clouds of smoke from the resulting fires drifted across the battlefield, which echoed to the cries of the wounded.

Still the enemy pressed home their attack, and 'by the end of the afternoon, the Germans were in the thickets and coverts of Sainte-Geneviève'. With the château surrounded, the woods were now ablaze, black smoke rising high into the air. With the defenders fighting furiously at close quarters, hurling grenades and using small arms fire to try to beat back the enemy, the heavens opened. A torrent began to fall across the area, curtains of rain blanking all from view. Under the cover of that downpour, those forces defending the farm at Le Bois-Joly had to withdraw for a second time, lest they get overrun.

It was an hour after that first air-strike that a message came back from London, ordering Bourgoin to abandon his camp. The planned landings in Brittany had been cancelled, at least for the time being, and he and his men were to do whatever it took to save themselves. They were to disperse, regroup into smaller units and carry out guerrilla fighting and sabotage wherever possible. As they pulled out, they were to destroy any arms and ammunition they could not carry on their persons. This included a significant ammunition dump which they had built up from the repeated air drops.

Bourgoin knew any withdrawal would be far from easy. He needed a ruse – some cover under which to begin pulling out. There were wounded to evacuate, and that made the process all the more challenging. The most seriously wounded were to be taken to a 'clinic run by Augustinian nuns in Malestroit', the nearest town. But some of the injured were so badly hurt that moving them would undoubtedly result in their deaths. There was nothing to do but leave them to the mercy of the Germans. To gain as much time as possible for the evacuation, Bourgoin ordered his men to launch a counter-attack.

Lieutenant Marienne, who'd been in fierce combat all that day, was still roaming the area with his jeeps, blasting any targets that came into range. His part in the counter-attack was to redouble his efforts. Others were to push hard and take as much ground as possible, to buy enough time for the evacuation to be executed. The counter-attack proved spirited but bitterly fought, and it wasn't long before the Maquis and SAS were surrounded on three sides. There was only one way out – to the west, in the direction of the town of Sérent, although that route would likely be closed to them shortly.

It wasn't until eleven o'clock that night, with his men fighting a fierce rearguard action in the pouring rain and the darkness, and hounded by 'crack SS troops', that Bourgoin abandoned the base at Saint-Marcel. Before doing so, he sent a final message to Britain stating that they were surrounded and were pulling out. As a last act of brilliant defiance, the arms cache containing the excess weaponry was blown sky high in an almighty, thundering explosion. As the weapons dump burned fiercely, and further explosions lit up the immediate vicinity, a convoy of trucks, cars and jeeps containing the last of the Maquis and their SAS comrades slipped into the shadows of that rain-soaked night.

Incredibly, the SAS and Maquis had left over four hundred enemy corpses in their wake. But they'd lost thirty of their own men killed in action, as well as very many wounded. With those they were forced to leave behind, the SS typically gave no quarter, murdering many of them as they lay defenceless on their stretchers. Sadly, SAS Sergeant Gaston Navailles, who had defended the Château of Sainte-Geneviève so valiantly, would not escape their predations. Badly wounded, he'd made it to the shelter of an abandoned house in the village of Callac, where he was treated by a local woman doctor.

But Waffen-SS soldiers would discover him there, and they shot him where he lay.

*

As a blanket of rain and a burning darkness enveloped the scene in Brittany, so Brigadier Roderick McLeod, commander of the SAS back in Britain, was growing worried. Knowing of the fierce fighting that had erupted around Saint-Marcel, after Bourgoin's last broadcast, late on 18 June 1944, all had fallen silent. All he could presume was that he had several hundred SAS on the run in Brittany, with absolutely no idea exactly where they were, let alone what their fate might be.

Had all his men been captured or killed in the fierce fighting around Saint-Marcel? Were they still in active combat, but with no means of requesting any support? Was this chiefly a communications issue – had they lost all their radios, so couldn't get in touch? Whatever the cause for the sudden silence, McLeod needed to know what lay behind it. He reasoned the only thing he could do now was to send someone into the area to find out exactly what had happened. There was no other option.

McLeod figured he had just the right man for a mission such as this – the wonderfully named Major Oswald Aloysius Joseph Cary-Elwes.

'Born on 14th November 1913, Oswald Cary-Elwes was the youngest of eight children,' runs an entry in the *Old Amplefordian News*, the newsletter of Ampleforth College, the boarding school where Cary-Elwes had been educated. His father, Charles, was a champagne merchant and, like him, Oswald had become a fluent French speaker and wine connoisseur. At Ampleforth, he'd excelled in sports, particularly boxing and rugby. Crucially, two of his schoolboy contemporaries had been the Stirling brothers, David and Bill. While David had founded the SAS in North Africa, Bill had gone on to raise 2 SAS, the second SAS regiment. 'An adventurous and popular figure,' Cary-Elwes had opted for a military career largely in memory of his elder brother, Wilfred, who had been killed on the Western Front in 1917, aged just eighteen, while serving with the Irish Guards.

Cary-Elwes had been 'commissioned into the 2nd Battalion, the Lincolnshire Regiment in 1933'. After postings to Malta and Palestine, he'd found himself at Western Command HQ in Chester, when war broke out. From there he'd been posted to the Nigerian Brigade, based at Lagos, Nigeria, West Africa, as the Brigade Major, before joining the 1st Army in North Africa. A veteran of Operation Torch, the November 1942 Morocco and Algeria landings, shortly thereafter he'd been asked by Bill Stirling, David Stirling's brother, to join the newly formed 2nd SAS Regiment.

Once he'd completed the vigorous training regime, he'd taken part in 'SAS raids into Sicily and was in operations in Italy, including the landing at Taranto'. Throughout those missions, Cary-Elwes had shown the kind of attributes required to command an SAS unit, leading from the front with a calmness and a steely determination, and by example. He 'walked with long relaxed strides, his rifle balanced on his shoulder', one of those who served with him would observe, and was 'bright-eyed and fresh complexioned, with a dazzling smile, a handlebar moustache, and an evident joy in being alive'.

Indeed, nothing much had seemed to faze Cary-Elwes. In September 1943 he'd led a group of SAS soldiers in a daring mission deep behind enemy lines, to rescue prisoners held in a concentration camp at Pisticci, in southern Italy. They were about to be transported north, no doubt to the death camps in Poland and Germany. Using the SAS's trademark Willys jeeps, Cary-Elwes had taken and held a key railway junction, enabling a train, which had been hijacked by the SAS, to speed through, steaming towards Pisticci camp. Once there, the SAS had rescued 180 inmates, taken the camp commandant prisoner, before steaming the train back down the same tracks, returning to Allied lines.

Sometime before that epic rescue mission, Cary-Elwes had recruited one of his stalwarts to the ranks of the SAS in fabulous style. A tank commander in North Africa, Charles 'Charlie' Hackney had twice had his Crusader tank blown up beneath him, he alone being 'lucky enough to escape.' Arriving back at his lines after the second horrific incident, 'dirty, exhausted from lack of sleep and with his clothes in tatters,' Hackney was ordered back out again, commanding another Crusader and crew. He 'refused point blank' to go. Facing a court martial, he was placed under close arrest, soldiers with fixed bayonets standing guard.

Then a stranger materialised before him. Tall, ramrod straight and with a magnificent moustache, the officer struck Hackney as having a distinctly 'aristocratic air'. It was, of course, Cary-Elwes. Cary-Elwes asked the condemned man to explain exactly why he was under arrest. After hearing Hackney out, Cary-Elwes told him that if he could be outside, kit packed and 'ready to move off in the officer's jeep', he'd spirit him away to join the SAS. A thousand-mile journey across the desert had followed, at the end of which lay the SAS base. There Hackney began his training. When his parent regiment, the 4th Hussars, discovered what had happened, they ordered the fugitive to be returned, to face 'court martial'. But SAS founder David Stirling reckoned that Hackney was worth 'more alive than dead, so . . . the order was ignored'.

In January 1944 Cary-Elwes was back in Britain, in Ayrshire, Scotland, serving in a unit which formed the link between the 'French and British SAS troops', including 4 (French) SAS.

His fluency in the French language, his natural good humour, plus his charm and tact, made him a popular figure with the men, many of whom he'd got to know well while soldiering in North Africa and Italy. As far as Brigadier Roderick McLeod was concerned, all of that made Cary-Elwes the natural choice to be dispatched to Brittany, to find out what on earth had happened to the missing men.

Time being of the essence, McLeod drew up some hastily drafted orders for what was to be known, fittingly, as 'Operation Lost':

> You will take a small reconnaissance party . . . and will drop on a DZ to be selected by you to the west of the Dingson area . . . Your task is: a) To discover what has happened in the Dingson area and to report the situation to me as soon as possible. Your report will include an appreciation as to the number of SAS troops and Maquis who can be reconstituted in the Dingson area, together with an estimate as to their organisation and value; b) To contact Cmdt Bourgoin or the senior surviving French officer in the area as soon as possible . . .; c) In the event of being unable to contact any of the more senior officers . . . you will take charge of the situation yourself and will organise the forces available . . .; d) To organise the reception of arms and equipment for the Maquis.

Those Top Secret orders also contained instructions for Cary-Elwes to 'influence . . . Bourgoin that the SAS troops and the Maquis may . . . give the greatest . . . assistance to the operation for the capture of St. Malo'. Saint-Malo was the Brittany port-fortress which the Allied commanders very much coveted. An airborne operation to seize it was being mooted, planned 'for the next moon period' – the time when there would be enough ambient light to mount such an assault. But Cary-Elwes was under strict instructions not to reveal this to anyone, bar Bourgoin.

He was also to brief French commanders on the ground that the Allies were 'interested in the preservation of facilities in all ports in Brittany and every effort should be made to get in touch with personnel working in the docks and request them to prevent destruction to dock facilities'. From Cary-Elwes' orders it was clear that Allied commanders were seriously considering landing a second invasion force, this time in Brittany, in an effort to take the key ports and to outflank the Germans.

With his orders committed to memory and burned, as instructed, Cary-Elwes gathered together his small team. First and foremost there was his ever-faithful batman, Corporal Eric Mills – a batman being a soldier assigned to an officer as his personal assistant. Cary-Elwes and Mills had been together since the North African campaign, Mills taking care of the major's admin, as well as fighting alongside him in combat. Mills was blessed with a great 'sense of humour and a loud laugh which kept the spirits of many around him up' whenever the bullets started to fly. After the war, he was to describe how, when caught up in a tight spot, 'It wasn't the bullets that went whistling by that worried me, but the ones that went thud.'

Mill's ability to 'laugh in the face of danger' and his undying good humour had endeared him to Cary-Elwes, and he was never far from his commander's side. Each morning, 'I called him with a cup of tea,' Mills recalled, 'which he never drank but he demanded to know if he had got it.' As far as Mills saw it, his role with the SAS major was 'just to look after him, guard him'. As Mills fully appreciated, Cary-Elwes cut a spirited, devil-may-care figure, even when on ops behind the lines. 'He took some bloody guarding and all,' was how he described his role.

Cary-Elwes and Mills would be joined by a contingent of six French SAS, including Lieutenant Fleuriot, plus Sergeant Mati and a team of three signallers. Corporal Mills was the only man in the party who 'could hardly speak a word of French, let alone hold a conversation' in that language, as he readily confessed. Their drop was to take place in an area close to where the Saint-Marcel base had been located, it being the last known position of the missing Colonel Bourgoin and his men.

The evening of the drop – 22/23 June – was 'a typical summers night, warm with no wind', noted Mills, in his diary. Normally, those would be ideal conditions for a parachute jump, but for the one problem: it was a moonless night and they would be leaping into pitch darkness, onto ground with no reception committee. Wherever exactly they chose to put down, it was likely to be swarming with enemy troops on the lookout for fugitive SAS and Maquis. But there was nothing they could do about that right now.

With their equipment stowed on the aircraft, the eight SAS men climbed aboard. As the plane rumbled down the runway and lifted into the night sky, they settled into what would be a two-and-a-half-hour flight. 'Everybody's nerves were on edge,' Mills would reflect later. 'We were to jump behind the enemy's lines into we knew not what, but all were full of hope, and we put our faith in the pilot not to drop us on an enemy camp.'

As they neared the DZ each of the men got to their feet to

check their straps and that their kit bags were firmly lashed to their right legs. They shuffled towards the exit, with Cary-Elwes in the lead, Mills at number two, and with Sergeant Mati and the signallers behind. Lieutenant Fleuriot and one other man brought up the rear. A few moments later the jump light turned from red to green. With barely a moment's hesitation Cary-Elwes stepped into the void, immediately followed by Corporal Mills.

While the SAS major may have been first through the door, he actually loathed parachuting. Being first out was a way to hide his fear from the others, men he now had to lead into the unknown. As Mills hit the blast of the slipstream, he was horrified to see his kitbag torn away, even as the silk canopy of his 'chute snapped open above him. Relieved as he was that his parachute had worked, the loss of the kitbag was not good news.

Once on the ground the men gathered. Cary-Elwes quickly assessed the situation. It had been a decent landing considering the circumstances: just 'two of the party were slightly injured', with 'one Frenchman with a sprained ankle'. The main problem was that three of their kitbags had disappeared. Among other things, they contained the Eureka transmitter – a device used to guide in aircraft to drop zones – all of Cary-Elwes' kit, which included one of their radios, plus all of Lieutenant Fleuriot's kit. Fortunately, they still had one radio remaining, so contact with McLeod in Britain would still be possible.

As Cary-Elwes studied their maps, he worked out that they had landed adjacent to the road running between the towns of Ploërmel and Sérent. Of course, unbeknown to Cary-Elwes, it was in the Sérent direction that Bourgoin had led his men, following their breakout from the battle of Saint-Marcel. Not wanting to remain near the roadway, Cary-Elwes led the group on a seven-kilometre hike, moving in the direction of Sérent. Finally, they came across a field ringed with high hedges, which was a decent enough place to lie up. There they settled down to wait for whatever the morning, and daylight, might bring.

With dawn, Cary-Elwes resorted to the only thing he could imagine doing, in an effort to locate the missing force of SAS. He wandered into the nearest hamlet, and in his excellent French he began asking questions. With such a large camp of Maquis and SAS having until very recently been located near by, surely someone had to know what had happened to them all. Frustratingly, he found that few of the locals were prepared to talk. They seemed highly suspicious of this tall SAS officer, in his neat uniform, who kept asking questions about the whereabouts of Colonel Bourgoin and his fighters.

Eventually, Cary-Elwes figured out the source of the locals' reticence. They doubted if he and his men were who they claimed to be. It turned out that both German soldiers and the Milice Française – a French pro-Nazi militia that worked closely with the Germans – had managed to get their hands on some SAS uniforms, presumably from those of Colonel Bourgoin's men taken prisoner or killed. Thus attired, they were busy doing the exact same thing as Cary-Elwes, in their attempts to track down and capture the Maquis and SAS. The locals simply couldn't trust the SAS major's bona fides. If they got it wrong, they would put themselves in terrible danger, for the enemy were already carrying out horrific reprisals against anyone they suspected of harbouring either SAS or Maquis.

Gradually, Cary-Elwes persuaded some to divulge snippets of information. Bit by bit, he was able to piece together some of what had happened. As he would report later, it was clear that Colonel

Bourgoin's camp had 'entirely broken up after the battle . . . and that the Germans had remained in the area until Wednesday 21st June'. German troops were still regularly patrolling the area and carrying out search operations. Although this was worrying news, it meant that some at least of his comrades had escaped after the battle.

Cary-Elwes decided to split his small force in two, so they could cover more ground as they began their search. Cary-Elwes together with Mills and two of the French SAS would make up one party, with Lieutenant Fleuriot leading the remainder. Agreeing to rendezvous in a patch of nearby woodland later that night, they set out. It was to prove a highly unsuccessful day – both groups were continually met with the same reluctance to talk. On one occasion, Cary-Elwes and his men came across a farm. According to Mills, the farmer's wife 'looked just as if a bar of soap was unknown to her'. Regardless, they sought her counsel, revealing that they 'were English parachutists and friendly'. The reply they received was replete with suspicion: 'Maybe . . . but maybe Boche in British uniforms.' It was becoming irksome.

They returned to their rendezvous at the woods. Lieutenant Fleuriot reported that he too had suffered similar fortunes. However, he had scored one signal success – he'd managed to procure some bread, butter and Breton cider – a local drink similar to mead – which all tucked into, for they were famished.

Despite the obvious dangers – Cary-Elwes and his men risked capture, torture and worse, by continuing the search – they did not give in or relent. But it wasn't until 25 June, their third day on the ground there, that they detected the hint of a breakthrough. It was midday when Cary-Elwes approached a remote farmstead. The farmer demonstrated the same stubborn reluctance to talk, but Cary-Elwes could tell from the man's demeanour that he knew something. The farmer went as far as explaining that if he gave them any information, and they turned out to be Germans, 'his wife and five children would . . . be shot and his farm burnt'. He was keeping quiet out of fear of Cary-Elwes and his men not being who they claimed to be.

Cary-Elwes knew that somehow he had to allay the man's fears and prove that they truly were British and French forces of the SAS. That gave him an idea. Before deploying on the mission, a verification phrase had been given to the BBC that was specific to Operation Lost. They were to transmit it for several days at six o'clock p.m. precisely. If he were to return at that time with a radio set, and the farmer heard that coded message, would that prove their authenticity, he demanded. The farmer conceded that it might.

At the agreed time, Cary-Elwes was back with the radio set primed to go. And while they failed to get it turned to the right frequency in time to hear the broadcast, upon seeing the wireless kit and their know-how, the farmer seemed convinced. To allay his fears still further, Cary-Elwes handed the farmer his identification card, telling him to take it to his nearest Maquis or SAS contacts. If they could get it to Colonel Bourgoin, or any of the other surviving SAS commanders, they would be able to vouch for him. The farmer agreed to give it a try. After indicating the woodland in which they were hiding out, Cary Elwes departed.

At midday the following day, a Frenchman turned up at the camp. Having explained that he was a Maquis guide, he asked Cary-Elwes to accompany him. They made their way to a nearby farm where, waiting for him, was Colonel Bourgoin. Finally, after an epic and fraught search, Cary-Elwes had found his man. As

Bourgoin explained, his precautions had been entirely necessary. 'The whole area was full of Germans hunting for him and they had put a large price on his head,' Cary-Elwes confirmed. So keen were the enemy to find Bourgoin that they had arrested all one-armed men in the district. But the French colonel remained undaunted. He'd re-established his operations, dispatching bands of Maquis across the region, each with small groups of SAS embedded in their units, to arm and train them, and to lead them on sabotage missions.

Having finally linked up with Colonel Bourgoin and his group, Cary-Elwes and his men allowed themselves to relax just a little. Eric Mills was to write of this time: 'We were all very pleased with ourselves and celebrated with having a wash and shaving, the first since our arrival on French soil.' With the weather taking a turn for the worse, and the rain pouring down in sheets, Cary-Elwes and his crew were relieved to discover that the farmer who had let Bourgoin use his property as his headquarters remained more than eager to help. Accommodating the new arrivals was the least he could do.

After a hearty meal of 'soup, then omelette, roast veal, stew with potatoes', several of the new arrivals joined a group of Maquis, who 'retired to the wine cellar where barrel upon barrel of cider awaited our consumption'. After two hours of solid drinking, Corporal Mills declared himself in no fit state 'to combat anything at all, much less our enemy, the Boche'. Thankfully, there was to be no need for soldiering that evening, for in the pouring rain the enemy were likewise keeping a low profile.

As part of the 'Operation Instruction' from Brigadier McLeod, Colonel Bourgoin was to give Cary-Elwes 'the greatest possible assistance to the operation for the capture of St Malo', as well as information on other key ports, chiefly Vannes to the south and Morlaix to the north. Whatever information Bourgoin and his men could glean, this was to be passed to Cary-Elwes with all urgency, to deliver in turn to Allied high command. Ideally, this was to include plans of German port defences, enemy troop numbers and anything else that could assist with an Allied landing in Brittany.

That agreement struck, Cary-Elwes and Bourgoin decided to divide forces. It made little sense having two precious radios – the one that Bourgoin had salvaged from the recent battle, and now Cary-Elwes' set – at the same location. As Cary-Elwes would report it, 'to avoid swelling the numbers of his Headquarters . . . I should go with my party to join Lieutenant Marienne.' Incredibly, Lieutenant Marienne had survived his injuries and his daring jeep sorties during the fighting around Saint-Marcel, and was now commanding a second band of SAS and Maquis, based not far away.

As all had realised, following the battle of Saint-Marcel, they would need to disperse into smaller groups to avoid detection. There was no way they could allow such a large camp to form again. The Germans were on the hunt and boasted far superior numbers and firepower. In fact, it had only been due to the bravery of the fighters at Saint-Marcel, plus a huge dose of luck, that so many of them had managed to get away.

A system for arming and training the scattered groups of Maquis was now in place. Each had a small band of SAS attached to it, and their job was both to instruct the maquisards in weapons use and tactics and to request air drops. All requests for air missions were coordinated by Bourgoin from his new headquarters. He would radio Allied high command with his shopping list of weaponry and supplies, and with instructions as to where to make the drops. This gave the SAS colonel overall control of all that was going on, but still the challenges were legion.

As there were no radio links between Bourgoin's headquarters and any of the Maquis groups dotted about the area, *agents de liaison* bore the brunt of the message-carrying. These courageous women, some as young as sixteen, would cycle mile after mile, often in atrocious weather, relaying messages to the scattered groups, and often returning the same night, bearing replies. Mostly, they were ignored by enemy patrols, the German soldiers refusing to believe that these bright young women – many no more than girls, really – might be capable of espionage and sub-terfuge. But as time went on, this would change. As Cary-Elwes would become painfully aware, some of the couriers would get 'captured and tortured by the Germans for information, but none gave anything away'.

If Cary-Elwes and his men could link up with Lieutenant Marienne and bring their radio set into use there, that would prove invaluable, and for all the obvious reasons. Their plans with Bourgoin settled, they decided to divide forces. Too many in one place for too long was bound to draw the attention of the enemy. Instead, Cary-Elwes took his team into some nearby woodland in which to hide out, before they made their main move. Shortly, a guide arrived to take them to Lieutenant Marienne's base, which had just migrated to Guéhenno, a small village lying ten kilometres to the north of Bourgoin's headquarters. Shifting to Guéhenno reflected how Lieutenant Marienne and his men were constantly on the move, in an effort to fox the enemy.

Thankfully, the terrain in this part of southern Brittany allowed for a degree of free passage. Small fields with high hedges, linked together by winding lanes, enabled small groups to travel without being seen, unless the enemy were moving along the same route. Still, it was crucial to have a guide. With the area crawling with enemy troops, Cary-Elwes decided to travel at night to avoid detection. And so, in that fashion, the eight SAS and their guide slipped through darkened lanes, shielded by shadowed hedge-rows. They made it to Marienne's base just before dawn on 1 July 1944, so barely a week after they had parachuted into Brittany.

On 24 June Marienne had been promoted to the rank of cap-tain in the field. His new base of operations was headquartered in and around a remote farmstead. The camp was located 'around the edges of a field with men posted at each corner,' as Cary-Elwes noted. There were not so many fighters gathered – less than twenty – which made it discreet enough. And although it was pouring with rain when Cary-Elwes and his men pitched up, he noticed how the sentries remained steadfast at their posts. Captain Marienne clearly ran a tight ship and was rightly taking no chances.

In his diary, Eric Mills described their arrival: 'We were shown to a ladder and a loft and here we spent a couple of hours resting. At early dawn we moved out and were led to a nearby hide, a cornfield with a ditch and shrubs, so that one could hide both from the air and other prying eyes.'

Captain Marienne's appearance was striking – testimony to the ferocity of the battle of Saint-Marcel. The SAS captain had fought furiously, so much so that he had earned the nickname 'The Lion of Saint-Marcel'. And despite the wounds he'd suf-fered, he was now responsible for leading a band of SAS and maquisards. Tall, dark, lean, his hair flecked with a few white hairs at the temples, Marienne gave off the aura of being both battle-hardened and a born leader of men. Yet at the same time it was clear that the toll of operations, and the fatigue of combat, lay heavy upon him.

Cary-Elwes and his men got busy right away, bolstering the French captain's set-up. They'd brought with them their precious radio set, and could now establish a second communications hub, calling in supplies of weaponry and rations direct from Britain. This would prove invaluable, and for the week that followed it became their chief task to organise supply drops for the groups in their area, while liaising with Colonel Bourgoin. Almost nightly, the rumble of engines could be heard high in the dark skies, as a flight of Allied aircraft thundered in to drop supplies to pre-arranged DZs. But Cary-Elwes was under no illusions: if they could hear the planes, then so too could the enemy. To him it seemed virtually a miracle that none of the drops had yet been compromised.

On the night of 8 July, Cary-Elwes received new orders from headquarters. He was tasked to move forty kilometres north, to link up with Lieutenant Henri Deplante, another of Bourgoin's deputies. Deplante's SAS and Maquis group were waging guerrilla warfare around the town of Guern, an area of key strategic importance to the Allies. Guern lay inland of the major German naval base at Lorient, a site from where U-boat wolf packs harassed Allied shipping. The KIII U-boat pens at Lorient were massive reinforced concrete structures, cathedral-like in scope and size. Despite innumerable sorties, they had been immune to Allied air-attacks. Cary-Elwes felt certain that the move north to Guern had to concern that Lorient base.

The hunt for the Guern Maquis and SAS had proved intense. Not only were German agents and Milice dressing as British parachutists, in an effort to track down their adversaries, they had resorted to other, more crafty ploys to locate their whereabouts. On one occasion, a wicker basket had been discovered in a field not far from the SAS–Maquis bases, with a parachute attached to it. Inside the basket was a pigeon. Strapped to the bird's leg was a tube containing a questionnaire, at the top of which were stamped the words 'On His Majesty's Service'. To all intents and purposes, the document looked genuine. The questionnaire asked for details of German positions around the SAS–Maquis base. Lieutenant Deplante had managed to get a radio message sent to London, asking whether the questionnaire was genuine. The pithy response was: 'Pigeon likely dropped by enemy . . . suggest make a pigeon pie!'

Before setting out, Cary-Elwes determined that his signals team, plus their all-important radio set, were best employed remaining with Captain Marienne. Their work was too vital to disrupt. So it was that on the night of 22 June, Cary-Elwes set out, taking with him his trusty deputy, Corporal Mills, plus two of their French SAS comrades, and the local guide.

Mills, for one, was relieved to get moving. He'd grown increasingly anxious about the time they had spent in the one location, with a body of fighters that kept growing. 'I was getting rather nervous again as to safety here, as there were by this time some twenty French parachutists besides partisans all gathered in one place, and our whereabouts was certain to be heard of by the Boche.' Mills's misgivings were to prove somewhat prescient.

While the distance to Deplante's Guern base was only forty kilometres as the crow flies, the group would need to cover a lot more ground to avoid enemy garrisons and patrols. Often they had to double back on themselves, or take wide diversions around key positions. The way ahead also required a constant change of guides, for as Cary-Elwes would report, 'these guides have intimate knowledge of all the lanes within five kilometres of their homes and complete ignorance of what lies beyond.' Frequent stops were made at farms along the way, for refreshment and to gather intelligence. Invariably, 'refreshment' took the form of the local cider that seemed to be the staple drink of the Bretons. After a while Mills could stomach the vinegary brew no more. It 'gave me the runs,' he recalled, 'so I was sticking to milk as far as possible!' Shortly, he'd earned the nickname, *Le petit caporal qui ne boit que du lait* – the little corporal who only drinks milk.

The weather of that late spring worsened dramatically. During their second night on the road the 'rain began to pour down', as Mills noted, morosely. This made the heavy packs they carried all the more burdensome, as they became sodden wet. The small group reached a village. As it was dark and all seemed quiet, they decided to press on through it. On high alert in case enemy soldiers were stationed there, they proceeded along the main thoroughfare with great care. They made it through safely but had actually been incredibly lucky. As Eric Mills would later note: 'There were, we were later informed, enemy in the village but whether they had a sentry on or not, I do not know.'

But even as those four SAS were pressing through the rain-lashed darkness, so disaster was to strike at Captain Marienne's base, the location they had only recently vacated. Marienne's band of mixed SAS and maquisards had carried out a number of daring sabotage operations, further stirring up the fury of the enemy. In light of this, a Milice collaborator named François Munoz had managed to infiltrate a small Maquis band, which acted as a satellite to Captain Marienne's group. Dressed in a

British parachutist's uniform, Munoz convinced them that he was an Allied soldier looking for Captain Marienne. The Maquis gave him the name of a man who could help, a wheelwright in a nearby town. Subsequently, this man was also fooled by Munoz and he pointed out a farm where he thought Captain Marienne had established his base of operations.

Munoz reported his findings, and was joined by a large force of mixed Milice and German troops. Maurice Zeller, the head of the Milice in the area, also joined the party. They managed to slip into the farmyard undetected, finding eight maquisards sheltering in a barn. After tying them up and beating them with rifle butts, they discovered that Captain Marienne and a number of SAS were hiding out in the nearby woods. Soon enough, they had surrounded the tents in which the SAS contingent were resting. It included Lieutenant Fleuriot and Sergeant Mati, two of those who had parachuted in with Cary-Elwes at the outset of Operation Lost. They were dragged out, lined up against a nearby wall, and tortured in an effort to make them talk.

Ignoring the protestations of Captain Marienne, who pointed out that they were bona fide Allied combatants serving in uniform and should be treated as prisoners-of-war, the nightmare continued. Finally, the SAS were marched to a nearby farm, where they were reunited with the maquisards. Marienne, incensed at their treatment, stepped forward, barking out: 'Remember, we are soldiers!' But his demands that they be treated in line with the Geneva Convention fell on deaf ears. Forcing him at gunpoint to lie face-down in the farmyard, the German troops grabbed a number of the maquisards, plus SAS Sergeant Gabriel Jadet. Jadet was dressed only in his underpants, having been dragged from his tent earlier.

All were forced against a wall. The first burst of machine-gun fire knocked many to the ground. Sergeant Jadet, who'd been standing next to a young maquisard who had dropped dead, knew that this was it. If he didn't act in the next few seconds, then he too would be left in a bloody heap on the cobblestones. Somehow, mustering a superhuman strength, he broke free and made a run for it. Leaping 'like a young deer over a hedge that he would never normally have been able to clear', he ran as fast as his legs would carry him, as machine-gun bullets blasted past his head and tore up the ground all around him. Eventually he slipped away into the darkness.

But with Sergeant Jadet having broken free and fled, the Milice and the German troops turned their ire back on their captives. Captain Marienne was to get the worst of it. Over the next few hours they beat and tortured him so badly that he was to perish in that dark farmyard, due to the terrible injuries they inflicted upon him. But he had remained resolute and unwavering to the last, like the 'Lion' of his nom de guerre: he died without giving anything away about any other Maquis groups. And of course, Captain Marienne had known so much and could have betrayed so many.

Unable to extract any more information from the others, the Milice commander, Zeller, gave the order. Even as the SAS soldiers and maquisards lay helpless on the ground, they were to be shot. Alongside them, the farmer on whose land they had been sheltering was also to be murdered, along with two of his farm workers, a father and son. Once the butchery was over, all of which was carried out in front of a group of women cowering in one corner of the farmyard – the dead men's sisters, daughters and wives – the killers took out a camera and snapped a number of photographs of their murderous handiwork. Some of them were smiling and laughing. After setting fire to the farmhouse, they left the bodies of the dead where they lay.

Of course, Cary-Elwes and his men knew nothing of these terrible events, busy as they were with their trek north towards Guern. When they learned of the fate of Captain Marienne and his men, they were horrified. The loss of the French SAS captain and his band of fighters was a huge blow. Both Eric Mills and Cary-Elwes had grown worried about the risks, even as they'd spent time in captain Marienne's camp. In a detailed report, Cary-Elwes would conclude: 'In my opinion Marienne stayed too long in the same place and his presence there was much too widely known in the area.' If they hadn't moved on when they had, they'd very likely have shared the same horrific fate.

Pressing on towards Guern, Cary-Elwes and his party hit a natural obstacle, the River Blavet, a sizeable watercourse that empties into the Atlantic near Lorient. Finding a rowing boat, complete with a set of oars, they decided to use it to make the crossing. But once they'd pushed off, one of the oars snapped in two, the wood being rotten. With only one oar remaining, the boat began to spin in circles, as Cary-Elwes and Mills tried frantically to wrestle back control of the vessel. Comic though it would surely look to any bystander, they were being swept downstream at some pace. Using their hands as makeshift paddles, somehow they managed to make it to the far bank, and scrambled ashore. But where they had landed was anyone's guess.

By a stroke of good fortune, the guide who was with them managed to locate another trusted local guide, who knew the way ahead. As the rain continued to beat down, the four SAS pressed onwards, and finally they made it to Lieutenant Deplante's camp.

Right away Cary Elwes was impressed by Deplante's set-up, which he found to be run with real efficiency and security. 'It consisted only of himself, his wireless team of three, one parachutist and his "agent de liaison" [twenty-one-year-old Marie Krebs, code-named Marie-Claire]. He only stayed in one place for forty-eight hours and only a few people . . . knew his exact location . . . He successfully arranged almost nightly parachuting of arms and equipment to all the various Maquis in the sector over which he had an extraordinary measure of control.'

Lieutenant Deplante was a broad, well-built man with a restless energy and sparking eyes. But despite his rigorous security measures, the risks were legion now for any such bands of fighters in Brittany. In addition to Captain Marienne and his men's horrific demise, numerous other groups had been rounded up by the enemy. The longer they had to wait to be liberated, either by a second Allied landing in Brittany, or by a breakout by Allied forces from the Normandy beachheads, the more the SAS and Maquis risked suffering a similar fate. As Cary-Elwes was to reflect later, 'Every day more and more of the Maquis leaders and SAS were being rounded up, and this fact, not unnaturally, was beginning to affect the morale of those who were left.'

In addition to these losses, the dreaded enemy reprisals were cutting deep. As Cary-Elwes would report, those who were found to be sheltering SAS and Maquis would receive no mercy. 'Normal penalty for a farmer caught harbouring patriots or parachutists, is for both him and his family to be shot,' Cary-Elwes noted, grimly, 'or burnt with their farms. Where the resistance group can be traced to a village, or where the shooting of German soldiers can be attributed to men from that village, hostages of men, women and children are taken; they are tortured by having their nails drawn or eyes gouged out, shot, or hung on telegraph poles . . .' While such unspeakable brutality fuelled the locals' hatred of the Nazi occupiers, it also left a legacy of terror and fear in its wake.

Upon reaching Deplante's base, Cary-Elwes received a new set of orders. With Lieutenant Deplante's help, Cary-Elwes had managed to get his hands on detailed maps, delineating the key naval bases along the Atlantic coast, including Morlaix in the north and Vannes to the south, and with the U-boat base of Lorient lying between them. They included 'details of the defence plans of the ports', as Cary-Elwes noted, which would be crucial to any potential Allied landings. With those enemy documents in his possession, he was ordered to make his way back to Britain post-haste. With a 'second D-Day' in the planning, involving landings on the Brittany coastline, those captured papers were precious indeed.

While it was time for him to pull out – Operation Lost having been accomplished – the question remained as to how exactly he was to do so. As time was of the essence – those plans were needed back in Britain pronto – he'd need to settle upon some speedy means of escape. His orders from Brigadier McLeod had given him the one lead to help with their getaway. He had been passed the coordinates of a location where he would find a contact known simply as 'Robert'. Somehow, the mysterious Robert was to mastermind their flight back to Britain.

Upon checking his map, Cary-Elwes realised that the rendezvous, which was set near the town of Guingamp, lay some seventy kilometres due north of their present location. If they attempted that journey on foot, it could take a week or more to accomplish. In fact, moving only at night and in the pouring rain, which showed no sign of letting up, plus always being reliant upon guides, it could take for ever. There was only one option: to hit the road using a local vehicle. Cary-Elwes decided to do just that, taking only Corporal Mills, plus two maquisards who promised to rustle up a suitable vehicle.

It turned out to be a battered old van. Bizarrely, someone had rigged up the brake pedal to the vehicle's horn. So every time it slowed, the hooter rang out. No matter. Beggars could not be choosers. At midnight on 16 July 1944 they set forth, their Maquis driver sticking to the back roads all the way. Though their weapons were primed for trouble, and their eyes peeled, the journey proved remarkably trouble-free. It was to be their drop-off and the subsequent pick-up that was somewhat less straightforward. Having reached their destination – the coordinates on the map – the Maquis drivers left the two SAS men at the side of the road and drove away. At daybreak there was not a soul in sight, certainly no one here primed to link up with them.

With no other option, Cary-Elwes and Mills approached the nearest farm. Unfortunately, as Cary-Elwes noted, 'the farmer denied all knowledge of anyone of the name of Robert.' Eventually, Cary-Elwes was forced to conclude that they had been dropped at the wrong location, most likely due to 'a corrupted map reference from Brigade Headquarters'. Transcribing a six-figure grid reference delivered over the airwaves was famously prone to errors. Cary-Elwes and Mills were now in a similar situation to the one they had faced at the start of their mission, when searching for Bourgoin and the missing SAS. But of course, now they had no radio – no way of communicating with anyone, either in Brittany or in Britain.

Acutely aware of the time-sensitive nature of the intelligence he was carrying, Cary-Elwes was driven to desperate measures.

There was nothing he could do other than approach more of the locals, to see if anyone knew of, or could put him in touch with, the elusive 'Robert'. Time and again his efforts were rebuffed. No one knew of any 'Robert' or could offer any further assistance. Finally, Cary-Elwes and Mills ran into a young Frenchman who appeared to be somewhat more engaged. Once they had managed to convince him of their credentials, he seemed willing to help. He suggested they rendezvous in an isolated patch of woodland in a few hours' time. He promised to bring them some food, plus crucially, a representative of the local Maquis.

Though Cary-Elwes and Mills knew they were taking an enormous risk, they agreed to his suggestion. They had no other option, although it was obvious that as a means to set a trap for them, the woodland rendezvous was perfect. Enemy troops were on the hunt throughout Brittany, and both men were acutely aware of what the consequences would be if they were caught. A quick death would be the best they could hope for.

It was midday by the time the young villager returned. He'd brought with him another man, likewise dressed as a local. Both appeared to be unarmed, and there wasn't the slightest sign of any enemy troops as far as Cary-Elwes and Mills could determine. Thus reassured, they emerged from hiding. As promised, the villager had brought them food. More importantly, the man who'd accompanied him claimed to be a local maquisard. He introduced himself as 'Tristan', and let them know that he did in fact know of a man by the name of 'Robert' in the vicinity.

Tristan offered to approach Robert on their behalf. If Cary-Elwes' story checked out, then he would send guides to collect them. He also told the two SAS men that there was an RAF pilot by the name of Philip Fargher who'd been shot down recently, and was also hiding out in the area. Tristan asked that the British airman should join them on their escape back to Britain, if such a thing were possible. That agreed, they were taken to spend the night at a local farmstead, where the farmer, 'reassured that we were British, was only too pleased to have us', as Cary-Elwes would later report. There, Fargher joined them. Shortly, a guide arrived, with orders to take the trio to Robert's camp, not so far away, at Étang-Neuf, a small hamlet lying on the Trieux river.

The base was located adjacent to the village, 'in a large wood near a big lake', as Cary-Elwes described it. The lake measured maybe half a kilometre from end to end and was surrounded by dense forest. 'We entered . . . over a small bridge past sentries in all kinds of clothing, armed to the teeth with British weapons,' noted Mills. 'They were all young boys between eighteen and twenty years of age and very eager. I, a British Tommy, was looked upon as a kind of god among them and they plied me with questions . . . This, I think, was the best camp I had so far been into. It was like a film set.'

Likewise, Cary-Elwes was impressed by what he saw. 'Robert' turned out to be one Sergeant Jean Robert, a Frenchman serving with 4 SAS. He ran a first-class camp, crammed with over two hundred maquisards, each of whom looked to him as their natural leader. They were well-disciplined and comported themselves like well-trained fighters. 'Guards were mounted properly, organised parades held, and the Tricolour was hoisted with due ceremony at dawn and similarly lowered at dusk,' Cary-Elwes observed. While sentries were posted on all approaches to the woodland, Robert had also placed mines along the routes the enemy might use to attack, should they discover the location of the base.

The arrival at the Étang-Neuf base was also something of

a reunion. Cary-Elwes' former comrade, Squadron Leader Pat Smith, SAS liaison officer to the French, was also at the camp. Ever since parachuting into Brittany on 9 June, three days after the D-Day landings, Smith had been extremely busy. Constantly on the move to avoid capture, he'd spent his time organising supply drops for the Maquis. Despite his precautions, he'd come close to being caught on any number of occasions, for enemy patrols had been constantly on the hunt.

One of the Maquis groups he had assisted had recently been wiped out, almost to the last man. Forced into the attic of a farmstead, German troops had thrown in a number of grenades, setting fire to the house. All of those trapped inside had been killed. In his report on operations in Brittany, Smith was to stress the perils of such actions: 'Farms, attics, etc. in this area are very dangerous as there is never more than one exit.'

Smith declared that he too would join Cary-Elwes and his party on their journey back to Britain. A fifth member of the escape party was also presented, a Major William (Bill) Jones of the United States Army Air Force (USAAF). As with Fargher, Jones had been shot down some weeks back while flying sorties over France, and had evaded capture ever since. As Robert explained, the five of them were to form an urgent escape party, and would utilise a well-established ratline – escape route – back to Britain. To those in the know it was called the 'Shelburn Line' (sometimes also spelled Shelburne).

The Shelburn Line traced its roots back to the actions of two Canadians, Raymond Labrosse and Lucien Dumais. On 19 November 1943 they had landed at a clandestine airfield in France, with instructions from MI9 – the British Secret Service's escape and evasion specialists – to set up an escape line for downed Allied pilots, enabling them to reach Britain via Brittany. First, Dumais and Labrosse established a string of Paris safe-houses, at which Allied pilots could be furnished with civilian clothing and forged identification papers.

From there they would be dispersed by rail to Guingamp, a town in northern Brittany lying a few kilometres short of the coast. From Guingamp they would move north by truck, or sometimes on foot, to a further series of safe-houses, before reaching a last hideout just short of the secluded Plage Bonaparte (Bonaparte Beach) on the north Brittany coast. From there the evaders were to be picked up by one of the Royal Navy's fast Motor Torpedo Boats, this part of the process becoming known as 'Operation Bonaparte'.

As Robert revealed at his Étang-Neuf camp, it was via this route that Cary-Elwes and the rest were supposed to escape from France. For two days the men waited, during which time they exchanged their SAS uniforms for civilian clothes. Cary-Elwes got an ill-fitting travelling salesman's suit, but he would just have to play the part as best he could. Mills's predicament was far worse. Due to his lack of French, he would have to pretend to be mentally unstable and to gabble incomprehensible nonsense if ever they were challenged.

That decided, their photographs were taken, so false papers could be drawn up. For some reason Pat Smith was warned he would have to wait a little longer for his papers, and so would have to follow on later. They were also told to abandon all their weapons, for from now on they would be posing as French civilians. This didn't sit right with Cary-Elwes and Mills, who decided to hang onto their pistols, with Mills also pocketing a number of hand grenades.

During the night of 19 July – so some forty-eight hours after arriving at the Étang-Neuf base – the entire camp was suddenly put on full alert. 'Germans were reported coming our way in considerable numbers,' as Pat Smith was to report. 'I asked if they knew our location and was told they did.' Reportedly, a map had been captured by the Germans that displayed the locations of several of the Maquis hideouts. Corporal Mills, for one, was not to be fazed by any of this. He awoke to see 'young men, all excited . . . pointing Sten and Bren guns, rifles and revolvers in all directions and handling hand grenades like marbles. So I turned over and went to sleep . . . thinking it would be far safer for me to be in bed than walking around.' For whatever reason the enemy troops didn't materialise, the alert was cancelled, and Mills was able to sleep on through.

The following morning the four men prepared to set out, utilising a most novel form of carriage. Dressed like locals, they clambered aboard a horse-drawn cart, driven by one of the maquisards. 'The horse was a mangy old nag,' recalled Eric Mills, 'and the cart was what I should call a manure wagon.' He'd worked with horses all his life, being a ploughman before the war, so he would know. Still, maybe the parlous nature of their conveyance provided good cover. With Cary-Elwes seated beside the driver, Mills and the American pilot behind them, and the RAF pilot Fargher in the rear, the group set off on the thirty-kilometre journey to a safe-house at Plouha, a village lying just a few hundred yards from the Brittany coastline.

Progress proved painfully slow, for the driver was unable to coax much by way of speed out of the old nag. As they crawled through a string of small villages, there was no sign of the enemy anywhere. Sporting their civilian garb, and with their false papers, a buoyant Cary-Elwes had a spontaneous, if somewhat foolhardy, idea. 'Feeling somewhat overconfident of our disguise, I suggested to our driver that we should stop off at a bistro and have a drink. To this he agreed with alacrity and we went into a small cafe.'

Mills wasn't overly surprised at the spur-of-the-moment decision. Several times he'd caught the SAS major strolling down a Breton lane while whistling 'Oh My Darling Clementine', as if he didn't have a care in the world. 'I said, "Shurrup! You'll have all the Germans in the district at me!"' Mills recalled, of one such incident. 'It was like a bloody band walking down the street.' Mills had learned to act like Cary-Elwes' shadow. Everywhere the SAS major went, he went, on the lookout for trouble. Still, as they strolled into that village café, Mills would never forget what ensued.

'We all entered and took our places at a long table. The guide ordered our drink which came in a glass not much larger than a thimble. We were trying our hardest to be French and then took a sip of the liquid . . .' What these fugitives disguised as Frenchmen had failed to realise was that they'd been served local Calvados – a very powerful apple brandy. It was 'much stronger than whiskey . . . and seems to knock your head off your shoulders', Mills would reflect. Right then it caused a cacophony of coughing and spluttering, which meant the drinkers were soon attracting the attentions of the locals. 'As soon as my companions had recovered sufficiently, we left in haste!' Cary Elwes would recall.

The incident in the bistro proved that they could not afford to drop their vigilance. Remaining alert and watchful, and trying to keep in character – a shabby salesman, his mentally unstable friend, plus some locals moving from farm to farm – they managed to make it to the Plouha safe-house, yet another remote farmstead. On arrival, 'the farmer informed us that the officer in charge of the arrangements . . . would arrive shortly,' Eric Mills reported. A little later, he was there. Their MI9 contact turned out to be none other than the Canadian, Raymond Labrosse, one of the founders of the Shelburn Line.

As Labrosse warned Cary-Elwes, he was under orders to get the SAS major 'home as soon as possible, but so far he had not been able to make the final arrangements for a boat'. However much Allied Command were keen to get their hands on the plans and maps Cary-Elwes carried, without a boat they were going nowhere. For now, at least, the four men would have to lie low and wait. The following evening, a familiar face arrived at their hideout. It was Squadron Leader Pat Smith, who'd been spirited north from Étang-Neuf by truck. Dressed as a local Breton, he too carried all the paperwork to 'prove' he was a Frenchman. But regardless of their disguises and their false identities, no boat meant no onwards journey to Britain. They were so near and yet so far.

Two days and two nights passed, and still there was no further news. Then Labrosse was back at the farmhouse. With a certain air of mystery, he asked Cary-Elwes to accompany him to a nearby property that he was using as his own hideout. Once there, they made their way to the loft, where Labrosse had his wireless set up. Cary-Elwes was introduced to Labrosse's radio operator, a man whose job was one of the most dangerous of anyone operating clandestinely behind enemy lines. The Germans had perfected mobile wireless-hunting units, and the life expectancy of one of these operators was not high.

Cary-Elwes would later describe that radio operator as 'one of the toughest men I have ever seen'.

Cary-Elwes was briefed on progress of sorts. Labrosse and his radio man had managed to organise a boat to collect the five escapees. But before the pick-up could go ahead, they would first have to move to a final staging area – the last stop on the Shelburn escape line. After confirming the arrangements, Cary-Elwes returned to his fellow escapees, to ready them for the move. At nightfall, the five men climbed aboard yet another pony and trap and were taken to a dense patch of woods. From there they could distinctly hear waves crashing against rocks, the smell of the sea sharp in their nostrils.

For an hour they waited among those darkened trees, until finally a pair of figures appeared. They turned out to be MI9 operative Lucien Dumais – the co-founder of the Shelburn Line, along with Labrosse – plus a French resistance member, François Le Cornac. After brief handshakes, the seven men set off on foot heading towards the water. Or, as it transpired, to the fringes of Bonaparte Beach, for close to the shore lay the Maison d'Alphonse, truly the last stop on the Shelburn Line.

The house lay in a remote, secluded spot, enveloped by steep cliffs, and screened from prying eyes. A path led from there to the beach, and it was largely shielded from view by steep ridges rising on either side. The Maison d'Alphonse was owned by Jean Gicquel, a young farmer who lived there with his wife, Marie, and their six-week-old baby. Throughout the past year, the Gicquels had helped scores of Allied escapees get out of France. During all those operations, Bonaparte Beach had proved to be the perfect place for the Motor Torpedo Boats (MTBs) of the Royal Navy's 15th Flotilla to get close enough to shore and execute their daring pick-ups.

By the time the group arrived, it was close to midnight. The Maison d'Alphonse lay in total darkness. There had been no time to warn the Gicquels that a party of escapers would be arriving, and consequently the family had retired to bed. After banging on the door, a light came on and the young farmer opened up. He was asked by Dumais to feed and shelter the group for twenty-four hours, for they were to be picked up by MTB the following night. While Gicquel agreed to do so, he was shocked at the number of evaders there were, for he was used to housing only one or two at a time. Once the handover was completed, Dumais and Le Cornac departed.

The five escapers settled around a table, chatting and drinking cider by the light of an oil lantern. An attic lay up a flight of steps. That was where they were to sleep. After a while spent carousing, Marie Gicquel, who was seated nearby nursing the baby, warned the men to hush. She'd thought she'd caught the noise of someone moving outside. All fell quiet. Mills bent down so he could listen to any sounds coming under the door. 'I heard footsteps,' he noted. He signalled a warning, and in response Jean Gicquel made his move. Maybe it was Dumais and Le Cornac returning? Had they forgotten something?

Pulling the bolts back he flung open the door. But instead of seeing those two familiar faces, before him stood soldiers in German uniform. Instantly, Gicquel slammed the door shut again, and locked it, while at the same time ushering the five escapees up the ladder leading into the attic. As they hurried up those steps, the deafening sound of gunfire rang out, tearing apart the quiet of the night. Bullet holes had been blasted through the door.

'Pat Smith had the presence of mind to dash out the lights and the farmer just had time to push us up the stairs,' remembered Cary-Elwes. The yells from the enemy soldiers revealed them to be White Russians, which meant they would be serving with the Waffen-SS. They also sounded seriously drunk. As the fugitives scurried up the ladder, violent banging erupted from behind, followed by more shots.

On reaching the attic, they realised there was no way out, other than the means by which they had entered. Things were looking dire. They were dressed in civilian clothing, some were carrying weapons, and Cary-Elwes had in his possession the plans for the defences of the key German naval bases along the Brittany coast. If they were caught, it would be hard to argue why they should not be treated as spies. Their fates would be sealed. It would be torture first, with execution to follow.

Downstairs, Jean Gicquel had no option but to unfasten the door. With a wife and young baby to protect, he could not have the enemy troops setting fire to the house. Before he had a chance to remonstrate, the door was flung wide and the soldiers forced their way in. Pushing him to one side, they saw the ladder leading to the attic. Raising a sub-machine gun to his shoulder, one of them unleashed a long eruption of fire directly into the ceiling. 'Shots were now coming up through the floor and . . . crashing into the roof,' Mills recalled. 'Someone shouted up the stairs and fired a burst of machine gun up. I was ready with a hand grenade.'

Mills had pulled a grenade from his pocket and was primed to let it fly. But Cary-Elwes stayed his hand. As he rightly surmised, 'If we tried to blast our way out by throwing a couple of grenades down the stairs we would have blown the farmer and his wife to bits as well as the patrol.' As Pat Smith recalled, 'The Russians fired two bursts . . . into the attic but did not hit anybody. They finally told us to come down but we did not reply.' There was no way that any of them were prepared to do as the Waffen-SS troops demanded, no matter how many times they shouted for the 'terrorists' to show themselves. To do so would amount to a death sentence.

But what were they to do instead? With two pistols and a couple of grenades to hand, they were hopelessly outgunned. Cornered like rats with little possibility of escape, the Russians were bound to call in reinforcements. Or if not, they'd simply set fire to the place with them inside, just like they'd done with countless other groups of Maquis and SAS that they had trapped.

As a last-ditch effort, the five men managed to squeeze behind a wall that partitioned the attic. 'The only hope seemed to be to stay where we were . . . and if they came up after us, to lob the grenades into the other half and hope that the thin wall between would protect us,' Cary-Elwes noted of the moment. In truth, that was the only way they might kill the enemy, while at the same time trying to safeguard the Gicquels and their young child. Even so, things looked dire. 'We were all afraid, there is no doubt about that whatsoever,' Mills recalled. 'We were trapped.'

Incredibly, it was now that the enemy's thoughts turned to alcohol. As Cary-Elwes was to write later, 'Our visions of what might be going on downstairs were appalling, but we made no move and the demands for us to go down ceased. Instead, thick voices demanded "cognac", and, to our relief, we heard the farmer answer that he had some.' Shortly after demanding drink, things went deathly quiet. Apart from the sobbing of Marie Gicquel and the cries of the baby, the five hideaways could hear nothing more.

Straining their ears, the fugitives tried to make out what was going on. 'We kept very quiet in our upstairs prison and could hear moans coming upstairs,' Mills recalled. Having downed the cognac and seeing that not a soul had emerged from the loft, the enemy soldiers, 'not daring to go up . . . withdrew to the court-yard'. They took with them the Gicquels, Jean Gicquel having a bayonet menacing his back for good measure.

The moans that Mills had detected turned out to be coming from the most unlikely of sources. Some of the wild shots unleashed by the inebriated Russians had been loosed off into the shadows. Imagining there to be 'terrorists' everywhere, they had opened fire on an approaching figure. This turned out to be their own patrol commander, a German soldier, and he had been hit in the groin. Their injured comrade was in need of serious medical attention, for blood from his wounds was pouring onto the cobblestones.

Marie Gicquel was forced to administer first aid. Though she did her best to stem the flow of blood, it was clear that the injured man needed to be rushed to a hospital. But how to get him there? Jean Gicquel told the Russians that his neighbour owned a pony and trap. They ordered him to go and fetch it. From their position in the attic, the fugitives could overhear much of what was happening. 'Suddenly a horse and cart was heard drawing near and at last it stopped,' Mills noted. 'We felt sure that this was bringing reinforcements, but after a lot of shouting and moaning, the cart started to go away.'

Fearing for their patrol commander's life, the Russians headed off with his bloodied form laid out on the back of the cart. Jean Gicquel reckoned the Russians would blame their commander's wound on the 'terrorists'. They would be back, which meant that the escapees had to leave immediately. Once the cart was out of sight, he hurried back inside the house. 'We heard running feet in the parlour and on the set of stairs and the farmer was with us,' recalled Cary-Elwes. With the enemy gone, this was 'the one chance for us to get the hell out of it,' he warned. 'He did not have to tell us twice.'

Grabbing their few possessions, the five fugitives dashed outside, with Jean Gicquel leading the way. They now faced the worst of all conundrums. They desperately needed to hide, but they could not afford to stray too far. The Royal Navy MTB was due to collect them the following evening and, if the pick-up was still to go ahead, they had to somehow remain close at hand.

For Jean Gicquel and his family, this was the end of the line. They'd managed to assist well over a hundred Allied escapees, but all that was now over. The Germans would be here soon, seeking to hunt him down and kill him. It wouldn't just be the young French farmer they would exterminate; it would be his wife and baby too. As Gicquel explained, he needed to get his young family to a safe place, before he could do anything to assist Cary-Elwes and party. He pointed to some fields in the distance, and all agreed to hide out there until something more permanent could be arranged.

With that, the five fugitives hurried into the darkness.

Making their way to the nearby field of wheat, the only patch of cover the escapees could find was a ditch. Hiding out there, within sight of Jean Gicquel's farmstead, felt little short of suicidal. If the enemy mounted anything like a half-decent search they were bound to be discovered. But what else were they to do? For the remainder of the night they crouched in that ditch, cold, wet and miserable. But at least they were alive and not yet in captivity. They could actually see the distant glint of starlight on sea, knowing that over the horizon lay England and safety. They were so close.

Dawn. As the early July sun cast its rays over the cornfield, they were disturbed by the sound of people approaching. Fearing the worst, yet ever hopeful, Cary-Elwes peered over the top of the ditch. Above the corn, just visible in the half-light, he spied three men approaching. With enormous relief he recognised Labrosse and Dumais, the two Canadians who ran the Shelburne Line, plus Jean Gicquel. They'd come as soon as they could, and were there to escort the fugitives to a place of greater safety. There was good news: Gicquel had managed to spirit his wife and baby to a safe-house. Each of the five fugitives was given a Colt automatic pistol and a few grenades, in case they ran into those who were hunting them and needed to fight it out.

For the next couple of hours they walked, driven on by adrenalin. 'We travelled fast,' Mills recalled, 'moving in circles, each circle cutting the next so that dogs which may be put on us could not follow our tracks. Although for almost two nights we had had no sleep, we were now quite wide awake and really on the alert.' Coming so close to being captured had given the men a renewed determination to finish the job. But so too were the enemy determined to do likewise.

A force was even then bearing down on the Maison d'Alphonse. Having got their commander to hospital, the Waffen-SS troops had 'informed the Gestapo of the incident'. Gathering a large number of troops, including 'White Russians and Germans . . . Military Police and Gestapo', they launched a massive search for the Gicquels and for whoever they had been hiding in their attic. Stopping everyone they came across, 'they drew a blank to all their questions – no one was saying anything.'

The enemy descended upon the Maison d'Alphonse in force. Repeated challenges revealed that the occupants either had no intention of coming out, or they simply weren't there any more. The German officer lost his patience and ordered his troops to force a way inside. Finding it deserted, they looted anything of value. Enraged that the Gicquels seemed to have got away, the officer ordered the farmstead burnt to the ground. A short while later the Gicquels' home – the building that had served for so long as the last staging post in the Shelburn Line – was in flames. As smoke billowed into the air, it served as a warning that this was the price for harbouring enemies of the Reich.

But it was to be the Gicquels – and the French Resistance – who were to have the last laugh. As the flames licked around an outhouse, a huge explosion erupted, spraying shattered bricks and timber in all directions. Debris tore into the enemy troops, as a massive pall of smoke fisted high into the sky. By setting alight the farmstead, the German troops had inadvertently detonated a large cache of weapons and ammunition that the Resistance had been hiding at the farm.

'The column of smoke rose a hundred yards in the air, visible for many miles,' the air thick with burning. Cary-Elwes and his fellow escapees could guess what was happening. Their former refuge was aflame and the hunt was on. Jumpy enemy troops began opening fire at the slightest perceived provocation. Their nerves were on edge, due to the repeated attacks by SAS and maquisards across the length and breadth of Brittany. Every patch of woodland seemed to harbour an armed band. 'Russian soldiers . . . started firing for no apparent reason . . . Germans were shooting at anyone who didn't stop at their controls . . . and many people were forced to take refuge . . .'

As Eric Mills reflected later, 'We could hear the church bells in the distance,' as they peeled out the call to the locals. Many took sanctuary within their walls. The fugitives could also see trucks buzzing back and forth along the roads. They'd been taken to a well concealed hideout – a 'place with lots of gorse bushes', as Mills noted in his diary. 'It was an area that had run wild and although it gave us no cover from the air, it was just the thing for ground cover.' This was the last resort for the five escapees. Keeping utterly silent, they would have to remain here undetected, until nightfall.

With Jean Gicquel being known to the enemy, a decision was made that he too would have to be spirited to safety across the English Channel. It was simply too dangerous for him to remain in Brittany. Though there seemed to be enemy patrols on all sides, the escape was declared on for that night. Allied high command 'regarded the return of Lost mission personnel as imperative', especially since Cary-Elwes was carrying documents that were vital to the Allied war effort. Despite the risks, all measures had to be made to spirit the fugitives home. Plans were put in train to escort the escapees to Bonaparte Beach under a heavy Maquis guard, around twenty-five strong.

As the evening shadows lengthened, their escorts began to materialise. Armed to the teeth with Bren and Sten guns, the Maquis cut a piratical crew. As the sun dipped below the horizon they set off, with a pair of scouts leading the way. Moving through the darkness, the column of men were taking every care not to make any sound that might give them away. Should the enemy spot them and a firefight ensue, the MTB would be forced to abandon the pick-up. Silence and stealth were critical now.

As they approached the path leading to the beach, they were

warned to tread with the greatest care. In particular, they were to avoid stepping on any of the handkerchiefs that were laid out before them, each of which glowed a faint white in the moonlight. A seemingly bizarre instruction, it had a life-or-death reason behind it. Earlier, and with painstaking care, a young French girl, Marie-Thérèse Le Calvez, had used a knitting needle to seek out the mines that had been planted on the path. Gently probing the earth, she'd placed handkerchiefs upon any that she'd found, marking each one. Due to this incredible act of bravery, the fugitives were able to slip through that minefield unscathed.

A coil of barbed wire marked the end of that field of death. Once they'd clambered over it, they were free to make their way down to the beach. Some of the escorts remained on the cliffs above, their Bren guns guarding the approaches. Cary-Elwes and his five escapees – with Jean Gicquel now included in the party – stepped onto the Plage Bonaparte at just short of midnight. 'It was very dark, no smoking or talking, only very low whispering,' Mills recalled. 'Our guards had taken up their positions and the minutes ticked slowly by.'

By now, the weather had improved, early summer in Brittany ushering in a balmy, windless night. The sea was calm, waves lapping gently against the sandy beach. Cary-Elwes and the others settled down to wait. This was it. After the long weeks of operating behind enemy lines, they were so close to escaping the dragnet set by the enemy. As the minutes seemed to drag painfully slowly, the time for the pick-up approached: 0100 hours on 24 July 1944. Bang on cue, one of the Maquis leaders took out a torch and began signalling out to sea. This was the moment of truth, of course. Was the MTB really out there, cloaked in the darkness?

After a short while the sound of oars could be heard splashing against the water. And then out of the dark sea emerged three small rowing boats, each holding a number of heavily armed sailors. They leapt out into the shallows and hauled the boats ashore. Cary Elwes was amazed to spot a familiar face among them. Major John Verney, another veteran of the SAS, had accompanied the Royal Navy on the trip. Verney, already the recipient of a Military Cross, had himself escaped from enemy captivity, in 1943. He'd been determined to ride on the rescue vessel, for Operation Lost had been a triumph and he wanted to be there to help bring the men home.

The boats were crammed with stores for the Maquis. These were quickly unloaded, the arms and ammo being spirited into the darkness. That done, the escapees boarded the craft and the sailors pushed off, taking them swiftly out to sea. A few minutes later, once everyone was safely aboard the waiting MTB – number 502 – the skipper gave the order to proceed with all speed for Dartmouth. This was a route the boat had plied many times before, when picking up airmen and escaped POWs who'd run the Shelburn Line. But due to the attack on the Maison d'Alphonse the previous night, this would be the last. The Shelburn Line was now defunct, its cover well and truly blown.

As Cary-Elwes, Jones, Fargher, Smith and Jean Gicquel settled down for the journey, Mills was finally overcome with fatigue. After enjoying a bowl of hot soup and smoking a cigarette, he decided to get his head down for the remainder of the four-hour trip. 'I lay down on a bench and went to sleep, and when I woke I was covered with a sailor's coat and another under my head,' he would recall.

As the MTB zipped across the calm surface of the English

Channel, carrying some very brave men within its hull, Cary-Elwes reflected upon all that had transpired in Brittany. With Operation Lost, he was satisfied he'd achieved the mission objectives. He'd established contact with the lost legions of 4 SAS, and arranged countless air drops to deliver arms and supplies. And then he'd gone one step further. Through his French resistance contacts, he'd obtained those plans of the defences of Brittany's naval ports, still firmly secreted about his person. Those he would now be able to deliver to Allied high command.

But all of this had come at a cost.

Half of the men who had flown in with Cary-Elwes had been brutally murdered by the enemy, something that was hard to stomach right now. But that only gave him a greater determination to do his bit in ridding the world of the evil that was Nazism. Now, sitting on the deck of that speeding MTB, he felt a sense of achievement. To his side, sticking to him like glue, as always – albeit comatose to the world – was his trusted batman and friend, Corporal Eric Mills.

Upon arriving safely back in England on the morning of 24 July 1944, Cary-Elwes was rushed to SAS Brigade Headquarters. There he was finally able to deliver his precious papers. With that done he decided he deserved a little downtime, a champagne-fuelled celebration. 'I went in a party to the Dorchester [a top London hotel],' he wrote, 'and I don't think Bollinger '28 has ever tasted so good.'

Allied plans to launch a second series of landings, in Brittany, never came to pass. With their forces breaking out from the Normandy beachheads, on 1 August 1944 US forces pushed south and west, taking Brittany and many of its chief ports. By

September 1944 the region had been largely liberated. The ports of Saint-Nazaire and Lorient were surrounded and put under siege, enemy forces finally surrendering the following May.

As well as delivering those papers, Cary-Elwes provided a detailed report to Brigadier McLeod as to the state of affairs in Brittany at that time. This included information on the political situation and morale of the Maquis; an assessment of the enemy's strengths; the best type of equipment to be sent in to assist the Maquis and, importantly, an assessment of their fighting value – all of which had been requested by McLeod. Although he had reservations about some aspects of their martial capabilities, Cary-Elwes described the Maquis thus: 'All Resistance troops are suitable for guerrilla tip and run operations, small raids on W/T [wireless telegraphy, or radio] stations, isolated posts and all forms of sabotage.'

Two weeks after returning to Britain, Cary-Elwes found himself parachuting back into Brittany, once again with his batman Eric Mills at his side. They were in time to greet the US Armoured forces as they advanced to seize the territory. There he once again linked up with Colonel Bourgoin, when the task of dealing with the last German strongholds in Brittany was given to the newly formed French Forces of the Interior (FFI). For the remainder of the war he fought with distinction with the French SAS, soldiering throughout northern France and Belgium, and was awarded the Croix de Guerre and Légion d'Honneur by the French. He was also Mentioned in Despatches.

Post-war, Cary-Elwes remained in the army, serving until his retirement in 1968. After a period serving with the British Military Mission in Paris, he saw action in Palestine, in 1948, with his parent unit, the 2nd Battalion, Royal Lincolnshire

Regiment. He went on to perform various roles, including a spell as assistant military attaché in Cairo, and serving as a liaison officer and instructor at the French School of Infantry in Saint-Maixent-l'École. He would also see service with SHAPE (Supreme Headquarters Allied Powers Europe), and as 'head of the British Military Mission to the Commander-in-Chief of the French Army in Germany'. His final posting was to the Ministry of Defence where he was involved in the standardisation of equipment for NATO forces.

Cary-Elwes' wartime exploits in France would be recognised further when, in 1984, on the fortieth anniversary of D-Day and the French SAS's landings in Brittany, he joined his comrades at the Arc de Triomphe in Paris, and was awarded the Médaille de la Ville de Paris by Jacques Chirac, then President of France. This was in recognition of 'his great services to France'. He died on 2 January 1994 at the age of eighty.

Corporal Eric Mills, Cary-Elwes' devoted batman, settled in Barnack, near Peterborough, after the war and became a 'handy-man'. In total, he had parachuted behind enemy lines five times on operations with the SAS. For his service in France he was awarded the Croix de Guerre and, twenty-five years after the liberation of France, he returned and met again many of the people he had served with during that time.

Colonel Pierre-Louis Bourgoin, the one-armed commander of 4 (French) SAS, had become the most wanted man in Brittany during his time operating there. In September 1944 he commanded forces that attacked a large column of German troops, taking three thousand prisoners, and seizing huge amounts of equipment in the process. On Armistice Day, 11 November 1944, Bourgoin led the parade down the Champs Élysées in

Paris, after first accepting the Légion d'Honneur, on behalf of the 2nd Parachute Fighter Regiment, formerly the 4th SAS, from Charles de Gaulle. After the war, Bourgoin moved into politics and worked tirelessly for the rights of veterans and war victims. He died in Paris on 11 May 1970. He was buried in Plumelec, Brittany, not far from where his SAS deputy, Captain Marienne, and his group, were murdered on 12 July 1944.

For the orchestrator of that massacre, Maurice Zeller, justice was to come swiftly. On 4 May 1945 he was arrested while trying to escape into Switzerland. He was tried, found guilty and executed by firing squad on 17 July 1946 near Rennes. Justice had been served.

Jean Gicquel, whose farmhouse, the Maison d'Alphonse, had been used as the final staging post of the Shelburn Line, returned to Brittany in December 1944 to be reunited with his young family. Although he and his wife, Marie, struggled to make up for 'the loss of home and possessions they suffered in helping the Allied cause, they were ... highly regarded', Gicquel being elected to the office of Deputy Mayor of the local town. He died in 1977.

The daring operations carried out by the SAS and Maquis in Brittany from June to August 1944 prevented thousands of German troops from moving north, to threaten the D-Day invasion forces. Their work was an invaluable contribution to the overall success of Operation Overlord, fully endorsing the *raison d'être* of their deployment to Brittany.

As the SAS had fought bravely in France throughout the latter half of 1944, so another vital mission was about to take place, hundreds of miles away in northern Italy. There, the men of

2 SAS were about to parachute into a veritable hornet's nest, seeking to create as much mayhem, fear and confusion among enemy forces as possible.

This would lead to one of the most daring feats of escape and evasion of the entire war, in a mission commanded by one of the SAS's most daredevil officers.

Chapter Five

GHOSTS OF THE MOUNTAINS

Rossano Valley, Italy, December 1944

Major Gordon Lett, of the Special Operations Executive (SOE), glanced towards the grey winter skies. The drone of aircraft engines could be heard echoing over the white-topped peaks lying to the south-east. A fleet of warplanes was inbound, and Lett had with him a small group of Italian partisans who had laid out the distinctive markers on the snowy hillside.

Earlier that day a lone Douglas C-47 Dakota twin-engine transport aircraft had passed over this area – the Rossano Valley – dropping canisters of supplies. They'd thumped into the snowy wastes of what was a strikingly desolate scene, especially since the burned-out remains of Chiesa village lay near by, testament to the savagery of the enemy actions in recent days. Riding in those inbound aircraft should be thirty-four parachutists, as Lett understood it. Thirty-three would be battle-hardened soldiers of 3 Squadron, 2 SAS, while the other was a fellow officer with SOE.

Aboard those distant warplanes, the atmosphere was tense

and silent. The roar of the Dakota's Pratt & Whitney Twin Wasp radial engines drowned out any chance of conversation, not that these men were feeling decidedly chatty. All knew exactly what they were dropping into here. Some grabbed the chance to smoke, while others closed their eyes in an attempt to sleep, for who knew when they'd next get a proper chance to rest. From the briefings they had been given back in Brindisi, the city lying on Italy's southern Adriatic coast, each knew they were in for a hell of a time of it once they got boots on the ground.

In the lead aircraft rode the mission commander, Captain Robert 'Bob' Walker-Brown, a veteran of both the North African desert campaign, and recent SAS missions behind enemy lines in France. The ground they were passing over was in parts familiar to him, for he'd spent time in an Italian POW camp the previous year. Alongside him was the SOE officer, Lieutenant Christopher 'Chris' Leng, who, along with two others, would be dropped first, to ensure that the drop zone (DZ) was safe. As they'd not heard from Major Lett for a number of days, Walker-Brown had to be certain that they weren't about to drop into a trap. In effect, Leng and his fellows were to act as the guinea pigs.

The lead aircraft began to judder violently as it ran into turbulence, not uncommon when flying over this mountain-girdled valley. Fighting the controls, the pilot was able to wrestle the Dakota back onto course. He circled the Rossano Valley, scanning the terrain below for something that would indicate the location of the DZ. And then he saw it. A group of figures, dark against the snow, with distinctive marker-flags laid out on the ground. The pilot flicked the switch to turn on the jump-light adjacent to the exit door, the signal for the parachutists to make ready. Spying that red light blinking on, Leng clambered to his feet, clipped his static line to the hawser running along the aircraft's ceiling, as he waited for green-for-go.

One of the air crew hauled open the Dakota's side door, ready to hurl out a row of heavy supply canisters, which were lined up on the aircraft's floor. The sudden blast of ice-cold air barrelled into the fuselage, the noise increasing tenfold. To Leng's rear, Walker-Brown and the rest of his stick were on their feet too, each buddy-checking the man in front's straps and buckles. They needed to be ready to go, as soon as Leng gave the signal that all was well in the valley below.

Several thousand feet below, Major Lett waited anxiously. He saw the lead Dakota circle the valley, as if the pilot was nervous to commit to the drop. Those six transport planes were packed full of vital assets – both men-at-arms, to help him wage war here, and also supplies. After a few moments, the lead plane broke away from the formation and swooped towards the DZ, its side-door yawning open and revealing a row of metal containers waiting to be shoved out. With the partisans waving and shouting excitedly, all of a sudden the air above was filled with parachutes as the canisters were released.

And then Lett spied what he most wanted to see – among those drop-containers were three human figures. They drifted to earth beneath their 'chutes, each seeming to make a fine-enough landing in the thick snow, which offered a cushioned, if chilly, landing. One of the figures appeared very pleased with himself, seeming to hop about in joy, while another took up a defensive posture, just as they had been shown to do, in training. It was the third of the three who, after gathering up his silk 'chute, approached the partisans.

That was how the newly-arrived Leng, and the veteran SOE

operator, Gordon Lett, met. As they shook hands, the former laughingly compared their rendezvous with that of Stanley and Livingstone. Of course, Leng's actions had been courageous in the extreme, for no one had known if the DZ lay in friendly hands. Greetings done, Leng fired a single green flare from his Very pistol, the signal to those orbiting in the aircraft above that all was good, and that they should deploy.

Five days earlier, Major Lett had received a radio message that the SAS were headed for the Rossano Valley, to join him and help wage war here. He'd asked for a postponement until 27 December 1944, so he could secure the DZ and make ready for their arrival. But after losing all communications – the Rossano Valley was notorious for having bad radio reception – he wasn't certain if the SAS were coming or not. It was only upon receiving the earlier supply drop, and now with Lieutenant Leng standing before him, that he knew that the mission – codenamed Operation Galia – was definitely on. It was Lett's job to facilitate the SAS's endeavours on the ground, and no one could be better qualified to do so.

Incredibly, the courageous and spirited Major Gordon Lett had been in the Rossano Valley for over a year, aiding the Italian resistance – the partisans – to wage a secret war deep behind enemy lines. He knew the topography like a native, as he did the capabilities of the local fighters. How Lett had come to be in this extraordinary position was an epic tale in itself. After escaping from an Italian POW camp following the Armistice, in September 1943, he'd wandered into the Rossano Valley by chance. It was to be a serendipitous turn of events. Quickly, he'd abandoned all thoughts of making his way to Allied Lines.

Instead, he'd opted to stay right where he was, and to use his skills and training to aid the fledgling Italian Resistance.

Having made contact with Allied high command, Lett had been 'recruited in the field' by SOE, as he'd pulled together a network of partisan groups, which became known as 'The International Battalion'. They consisted of a mix of local villagers, former Italian soldiers and Poles – the latter, like Lett, fellow escaped POWs. SOE had codenamed Lett's mission Operation Blundell Violet. He'd teamed up with a Colonel Vulgo Fontana, an ex-Italian army officer who was the partisan leader overseeing operations in the region of La Spezia, the northern port city. Between them, they'd pulled together the semblance of an effective fighting force. However, it had not always been the easiest of operations. Some of the so-called partisans had proved less keen than others. Some seemed more interested in what they could gain for themselves, rather than protecting the local civilians or engaging with the enemy.

The arrival of the SAS was designed to put real steel into the partisans' backbones. Being the expert on the ground, Lett would be able to provide the British raiders with guides, extra trusted men and local knowledge. Crucially, he would also be able to supply the all-important mules, with which to transport weapons and ammunition to those areas where he wanted the SAS to hit the enemy hard. But first, he and Lieutenant Leng had to get the SAS parachutists safely down on the ground.

Having spied the green flare arcing into the sky, the orbiting aircraft homed in on the valley. Once again, the air was peppered with parachutes, but this time they seemed to fill the entire expanse of sky. Over two hundred supply canisters, each suspended beneath its own silk 'chute, plus thirty-one human forms, began to float towards the drop zone.

Lett had chosen this area as the DZ – codenamed DZ 'Huntsville' – for it lay in the heart of the Rossano Valley, which was partisan central, as far as he was concerned. This was their redoubt, and it was relatively easy to guarantee safety here. Surrounded on all sides by high mountains, and with the passes covered in thick snow and ice, the terrain alone made it extremely hard for enemy troops to penetrate here. But secure though it might be, Lett was no parachutist and the area he had selected wasn't exactly ideal.

DZ Huntsville lay on 'the steep side of a terraced vineyard', making it difficult for those coming down to judge their angle and best approach. As a result, a number of the SAS suffered injuries on hitting the slippery, ice-bound and snow-coated slopes. A few had drifted dangerously close to a gorge that lay in the bottom of the valley, which would have been fatal had any gone over. Walker-Brown himself had suffered a rough landing. Upon hitting the ground, he'd slid away, falling a further ten feet into a gully. He would later report that DZ Huntsville was 'unsuitable for dropping personnel'. But overall they had been incredibly lucky. All thirty-four paratroopers had made it down intact, despite a few cuts, bumps and minor injuries.

Bob Walker-Brown and Gordon Lett were no strangers to each other. They had first met while they'd been held captive in Campo 21, at Chieti, in 1943. From their shared experiences there, each held the other in high regard. With the light starting to dim as the cold winter's day faded, Walker-Brown gathered together the thirty-two men under his command, so they could be addressed by Lett. What the SOE man had to say didn't give them the greatest sense of comfort or ease.

The area in which the Operation Galia force was slated to

operate was fraught with danger. While the closest enemy were a four-hour march away, some of the partisan groups they would come across were distinctly unreliable, and especially the communist Red Brigades. Lett could guide them as to who was and who was not to be trusted, but caution was the rule of thumb. Due to the fierce winter conditions, their mission was likely to prove arduous going, and they faced an enemy who had already responded with real ferocity and savagery to any partisan-led operations.

The men of the SAS would have expected no less. This was what their briefings back at Brindisi had intimated. Equally, this was the type of thing they lived for. Each was a volunteer, and due to the SAS's intensive training and selection process they were the elite of the elite. No matter what the conditions, no matter the privations, each was determined to give a good account of himself, and to take the fight to the enemy no holds barred.

Even so, Operation Galia was to prove decidedly different from other such SAS missions. The terrain alone dictated it. With no suitable road networks, the use of the SAS's ubiquitous Willys jeeps, which had proved so effective in the deserts of North Africa and across the French countryside, was a non-starter here. Operating in the depths of Italy's Apennine mountains, the only means to travel was by foot or mule train. Indeed, Lett's mules would have to carry the SAS's heaviest firepower – their 3-inch mortars, plus Bren light machine guns – to the target areas. And that meant any chance of making a quick getaway would depend upon just how fast they could make the mules move.

Once Lett's briefing was done – it was best to know the worst – he and Walker-Brown got the troops billeted across the small villages and hamlets that lay scattered around the valley. A quick meal and early to bed was the order of the day – for the next morning they were expected to get busy.

Shortly after dawn on 28 December 1944, Walker-Brown gathered his men. The squadron had been split into six sticks – a stick being an SAS patrol of five or six men. Walker-Brown would command HQ Troop, which would have a link via radio to 2 SAS's Major Roy Farran, back at Special Forces Headquarters (SFHQ), in Bari, which lay some 850 kilometres to the south. Heading up No. 1 stick would be Sergeant Wright, with Lieutenant James Riccomini leading the men of No. 2 stick. Riccomini had been the one who had appeared so pleased with himself, after landing successfully the previous day – hopping about for joy in the snow. That was largely because it had been his first ever parachute jump into combat. Nos. 3 and 4 sticks were to be led by Sergeant Rookes and Lieutenant Gibbon, with Lieutenant Shaughnessy heading up No. 5 stick.

The previous evening Walker-Brown had chatted to Lett about possible points of attack. Keen to get the mission under way, he issued his orders. Typifying the way in which the SAS tended to operate, he'd decided to give his men free rein to select their own targets, at least within the areas he was assigning to each stick. In essence, in each of those regions they were to choose their own best means to create chaos and mayhem. 'Each troop to make its way down into the valley to attack transport,' Walker-Brown declared, 'to attack any small enemy posts, to use explosives at opportune places and above all to maintain constant activity.'

For now, Walker-Brown decided to split his forces. One half – three sticks – would fan out from the Rossano Valley, heading in all directions to seek out the enemy. With those sticks on the move, the remainder would stay where they were, gathering up supplies from the drop and hiding them for use at a later date. A second – reserve – radio had also been dropped, and this would need to be safely stowed away. With local guides and interpreters distributed across the three patrols setting out, 'Lieutenant Gibbon and his men moved to the area of the Pontremoli–Aulla road,' Walker-Brown reported, 'Lieutenant Shaughnessy and his stick to the area Aulla–Reggio [Emilia], and Sgt Rook's [sic] party to the Pontremoli–Cisa road.'

Communications were going to prove challenging, as Walker-Brown fully appreciated. Radio sets were too bulky for such small, fast-moving patrols. Each stick carried only a very rudimentary, lightweight radio receiver. Should Walker-Brown need to communicate an urgent order, the only means to do so was via a complicated and cumbersome relay system. He would first send a message to Farran, at SFHQ, who would then forward it to SAS headquarters in Britain. From there the message would be passed to the BBC, who were then to make a special, coded broadcast that it was hoped would be picked up in Italy by the patrol who needed to hear it.

This labyrinthine system of signalling was made all the more challenging in that Walker-Brown himself hadn't yet managed to establish communications with Farran, due to the ring of high peaks that surrounded the valley. As a fallback, he could attempt to rely on the local runners that Gordon Lett was able to furnish via his partisan network. Lett himself also had a radio, with a link to his SOE bosses in Florence. But he operated it from the village of Albareto, some considerable distance away in the lower-lying Gotra Valley, for the very reason that at least from there he was more or less guaranteed to be able to make contact.

With such limited communications capability, each SAS patrol

241

would be working pretty much in isolation. Their one rallying point – at which they were to muster for resupply, or if any stick fell into dire straits – was the Rossano Valley.

On 29 December, with all supplies found and safely cached, Walker-Brown led the remainder of his force out of the valley, heading south towards the village of Pieve. With him went Major Lett as his guide, and the SAS column was laden with a 3-inch mortar and dozens of high-explosive bombs. Beyond Pieve lay the Via Aurelia, the coastal road that linked the port cities of La Spezia and Genoa. Along the Via Aurelia, Walker-Brown planned to spread chaos and mayhem, hitting enemy transport columns. But the going proved tough, the mules slow and reluctant travelling companions. Laden down with such weighty ordnance, the pack animals stumbled over the ice-encrusted passes, the SAS troopers likewise struggling with the winter terrain. After resting overnight at Pieve, they moved on, heading towards the town of Serò, Walker-Brown's intended base of operations, which overlooked the Via Aurelia.

As the SAS column struggled onwards across the punishing terrain, so disaster was to strike back in the Rossano Valley. A further supply drop had been scheduled for that morning. Despite the best efforts of SOE agent Lieutenant Leng to have it postponed because of forecast bad weather, the drop took place regardless. Having released its load, one of the aircraft was attempting to leave the valley, but the pilot was clearly having trouble clearing the mountains. Hit by stormy conditions and heavy turbulence, he lost control of his aircraft, and the C-47 Dakota crashed into woods near a small farm on the north side of the valley. All seven crew were killed. This would have unforeseen and dire consequences in the days to come.

But Walker-Brown was oblivious to that air crash, and was busy preparing for action. He and his men were scheduled to attack that very night, 30 December. The route leading down to the Via Aurelia was steep, the path cutting through treacherous, snow-covered gullies. After steering the SAS troopers to their final destination, Major Lett left them in the hands of local guides, returning the way he had come. Walker-Brown selected a quiet stretch of road along which to set his ambush. Near by lay the town of Borghetto, where the German military – plus those Italian Fascists still loyal to the Nazi cause – had billeted one of their key garrisons.

As they made their final approach, Walker-Brown left the mules – relieved of their crushing loads – with the guides. They took to a narrow track that snaked down towards the highway, each of his men laden with weaponry and ammo. The night thickened, the darkness providing a cloak of cover. Along the fringes of the roadway lay a belt of trees – perfect cover from which to strike. In among those stout trunks Walker-Brown positioned his men, his Bren gunners flanking the mortar crew, whose weapon was zeroed in on the road.

As the tension mounted, there was the first stab of distant light that cut through the darkness. A vehicle appeared to be approaching. More lights joined that first flash of illumination, as a convoy of trucks grumbled around the distant bend. A military convoy was heading right into the heart of the SAS's ambush. As the vehicles drew within range, Walker-Brown gave the order to open up.

Immediately, the Bren guns spat fire, spraying bullets into the leading trucks, peppering the cabs and sides. As the windscreens disintegrated under the onslaught, so the crump of mortar fire joined the deafening cacophony, SAS troopers dropping their 10-pound shells into the firing tube. Lobbed up to target the road ahead, the rounds crashed down among the now stationary vehicles, spraying red-hot shrapnel in all directions. Further fire from the Brens raked the wider area, as enemy troops leapt from the trucks, desperate to find cover. One by one the stricken vehicles exploded, the burning carcasses lighting up the night sky, and throwing a pall of thick, black smoke high into the air.

Seeking to annihilate the entire convoy, Walker-Brown pressed home his attack. The screams of the injured carried clearly to the ambushers, as their tracer-fire flared across the roadway. So massive was the din created by the ambush that it must have carried to Borghetto. As the SAS raked the burning convoy with repeated bursts of fire, so the Germans brought up their own hardware: an armoured car, boasting a 20mm machine gun, raced into view. While the SAS's Brens didn't have the grunt to pierce its armoured sides, the effect of being pummelled by hundreds of light machine-gun rounds had to prove immensely intimidating. With tracer ricocheting off its thick armour, the German gunners fired in wild abandon into the trees on all sides, being unable to pin down their hidden attackers.

Finally, Walker-Brown gave the order to pull out. This was now the 'scoot' phase of a textbook 'shoot and scoot' SAS attack. Or at least it should have been – but without their trusty jeeps to execute a rapid getaway, things were to prove more than a little fraught. Unable to speed off into the welcoming night, the raiders faced a 450-metre uphill slog back to the mules, lugging with them the heavy mortar, their Bren guns and any remaining ammo. With Operation Galia having been mounted with such urgency, they'd not had time to source any white winter uniforms, and so they stood out against the snow. 'Scrambling up an absolutely snow-white background was rather bad for the adrenalin,' as Walker-Brown would later reflect.

Walker-Brown and his fifteen men were buoyed up by the success of their attack, and the adrenalin rush that had come with it. They tore up that steep hillside, weaving their way through the trees, as behind them a long line of enemy trucks were burning fiercely. Walker-Brown had little sense of the exact number of enemy casualties, though he would later report: 'Three enemy were killed instantly and one died later in Borghetto hospital. The number of wounded is unknown.' Having suffered no casualties of their own, the SAS commander led his men to the nearest village where they could lie low. They arrived as dawn was breaking on 31 December 1944.

Of course, there was a much deeper strategic purpose to Operation Galia than simply randomly shooting up Nazi troops and supply columns. During the summer of 1944, German forces had been engaged in a fierce fighting withdrawal, as the Allied armies advanced up the spine of Italy. In an attempt to hold back the British and American forces and prepare for a counter-attack, Field Marshal Albert Kesselring, the German commander-in-chief in Italy and a Hitler favourite, had established a last bastion of defence. The Gothic Line was a string of massive fortifications that stretched for over three hundred kilometres, running along the heights of the northern part of the Apennine mountains.

By the autumn of 1944, the Allied advance had stalled on the Gothic Line, just as Kesselring had intended. Worse still, that December the Germans had launched a sustained counter-attack, driven on by Hitler's urgings that Italy should not fall. The enemy onslaught had fallen chiefly on the US Army's African-American 92nd Infantry Division, famously known as the 'Buffalo Soldiers'. It had come hot on the heels of the German military's attempts to capture Castelnuovo di Garfagnana, a key transit point lying in the depths of the Apennines, situated to the east of La Spezia. As Kesselring's focus had turned upon the Buffalo Soldiers, Allied commanders feared it presaged a much stronger German attack to come.

Operation Galia was designed to be a crucial element of the Allied riposte. By dropping a force of SAS raiders to the enemy's rear, the aim was to convince German commanders that a potent force of Allied paratroopers straddled their vital supply lines. By hitting roads leading through the area, the SAS saboteurs could tie up troops destined for any counter-attack. If the enemy could be convinced that such a potent force was operating in their area, they'd be forced to commit masses of troops to dealing with the threat. That in turn would give the Allies time to mobilise rein-forcements, bringing in further troops to bolster the line. But all of that would take time, a commodity the Allies were very much short of. By hitting the enemy where they least expected it, the SAS were to buy them that time.

On 4 December, Supreme Headquarters Allied Expeditionary Force (SHAEF) had offered up one squadron of SAS to carry out this vital mission, to be aided by local partisans on the ground. Colonel Brian Franks, by then the commander of 2 SAS – the sister regiment to the original 1 SAS – allocated command of Galia to Bob Walker-Brown, giving him a free hand to select his targets at will. His was to 'operate with partisans . . . and harass the enemy lines of communication . . . with the objective of (a) Influencing the enemy to hold troops in the area, and result in reinforcements not being sent to the main battle area ... (b) Delaying any enemy withdrawals along the routes Spezia–Parma and Reggio-Emilia [sic].' By carrying out repeated daring attacks, it was hoped the enemy would conclude there were hundreds of Allied paratroopers on the ground, and so divert significant forces away from the front.

With his first strike of the night of 30 of December, Walker-Brown was starting to make of his orders a reality on the ground. Despite the elation resulting from that initial attack, the aftermath was not to be entirely positive. It was now that Walker-Brown would learn of the aircraft crash of the previous day, in which the C-47 had ploughed into the hills above the Rossano Valley, with all aboard killed. As a result of the losses, the United States Army Air Force (USAAF) were refusing to drop any more supplies to the Huntsville DZ, which was deemed too risky. This knee-jerk reaction represented a serious problem for the SAS on the ground.

But it was to be a second piece of bad news that discomfited Walker-Brown the most. Word had reached Major Lett that Lieutenant Shaughnessy, plus the men of 5 Stick, had been captured on their way to Vecchieto, from where they had planned to attack the Aulla–Reggio Emilia road during the same night as when Walker-Brown's force had struck. After marching for hours in the searing cold, Lieutenant Shaughnessy's stick had taken shelter from bad weather in what was nothing more than a cowshed, near the small village of Montebello di Mezzo.

Early the following morning they were rudely awoken. Yells in Italian were quickly followed by a grenade, which exploded at the doorway to their hut. Outside was gathered a large number of the Brigata Nera – the Black Shirts Action Squads, Italian Fascist paramilitaries who served alongside the forces of Nazi Germany. It turned out that Lieutenant Shaughnessy and his men had been given up by a local spy, their tracks in the snow being followed to the shed in which they'd taken shelter.

As Shaughnessy led his men outside with their hands in the air, the leader of the Fascists noticed that their Italian guide, Chella Leonardo, was wearing a distinctive badge that marked him out as a partisan. The seven captives were marched into the centre of the nearby village, whereupon the local population were ordered out of their homes. With the main square crowded with locals, the Brigata Nera got to work.

Forming two lines, they forced Shaughnessy and his men to run the gauntlet, each being assaulted with sticks and rifle butts as they passed. But the Fascist thugs saved the worst for Chella Leonardo, the guide. As he entered the line he was seized by two of the Brigata Nera, who unleashed a savage assault using sticks and clubs. After beating Leonardo to a pulp, they tore off his uniform, and the leader of the Brigata Nera approached. Grabbing the battered partisan by the hair, he put his pistol to the young man's head and pulled the trigger. Another shot was fired into his body, after which the Brigata Nera strung his corpse from a nearby lamppost, to serve as a warning to the locals of the kind of treatment in store for anyone caught assisting the SAS.

With that, Lieutenant Shaughnessy and the rest of his men were taken away in a truck to an unknown fate. Upon hearing this news Walker-Brown was incensed. Immediately, he set to work organising a revenge attack on the Germans. He vowed to give them a New Year's present they would remember for the rest of their lives – at least, those who survived. He planned to attack the main German garrison in Borghetto. As well as seeking vengeance for the beating of his men and the murder of their guide, Walker-Brown set out three key objectives for the coming mission: 'To make the presence of the SAS known to the enemy in the quickest possible time; to create uneasiness among the garrison troops on the Genoa–Spezia road and to stop enemy movement' on the same highway.

The majority of the Italians in the area were very supportive of the partisans and the British. But they were paying a heavy price for their allegiances, suffering terrible reprisals at the hands of the German occupiers and Italian Fascists. Many were living in constant fear. They had recently suffered a *rastrellamento* – a sweeping-up operation against partisans – carried out by the Brigata Nera, working in conjunction with German troops. During this round-up the Nazis and Fascists had resorted to extreme violence and brutality against any suspected partisans. But they had also taken savage reprisals against the civilian population, burning down houses and killing anyone they suspected of harbouring their enemies.

This was designed to instil fear in the locals, and it had very possibly led to Lieutenant Shaughnessy and his patrol being betrayed. Although such *rastrellamenti* were vicious and cruel in the extreme, in truth it was just such a type of reaction that the SAS were looking to provoke. If they could goad the enemy into concentrating all their forces on seeking them out, then those same troops couldn't be sent to the frontline. It was a huge gamble, for in achieving it they were making themselves the focus of the hunt, but it was exactly what they were here for.

On the night of 31 December, Walker-Brown and the men of HQ Troop, plus the two other sticks, set out along the frozen tracks and snow-covered hills, moving back towards Borghetto.

The plan was to attack the town at dawn with a force of some sixteen SAS, supported by fourteen partisans.

Via Lett's local intelligence network, Walker-Brown knew exactly which buildings should form the focus of his assault. Placing his mortar team a kilometre away, and situating the Bren guns on the high ground overlooking Borghetto, the SAS commander was ready for action long before sunrise. To cut off any enemy retreat, the partisans, led by the very capable Pippo Siboldi, took up a blocking position to the south of the town. Once Walker-Brown was happy that everyone was in position, he waited until there was sufficient light in which to see their targets. With the sun peeping over the mountain peaks to the east, he gave the order to commence the attack.

Instantly, the mortar team got to work, throwing bomb after bomb onto the enemy positions, blasting the target buildings into pieces. The ferocious bombardment was backed up with bursts from the Bren guns, aimed at any enemy soldiers or Bregata Nera who had the temerity to show themselves. In no time the SAS were having a field day, for the mortar team had got the range just right, scoring direct hit after direct hit. With the bombs raining down and the Brens blasting away, a German staff car was hit by a mortar as it tried to dash away. The bomb blew the vehicle to smithereens, transforming it into a mass of twisted, smoking metal.

The SAS pressed home their attack. There was movement to the east of the town, as a pair of trucks hove into view. Upon spying the devastation being wrought upon the buildings ahead of them, the drivers slammed on their brakes, bringing both vehicles to a halt. Spying this, Walker-Brown ordered his Bren gunners to dash closer to the roadway, and to turn their fire on those stationary vehicles. Swiftly his men raced ahead. Moments later, both vehicles were riddled with Bren fire, the bullets smashing into the cabs, shattering the windows and tearing into the engine blocks. Shortly, both were burning fiercely.

Back in the heart of Borghetto town the mortar bombs continued to rain down. Due to the sustained ferocity and accuracy of their attack, the enemy must have concluded they were facing a far superior force, for it wasn't long before German troops began to abandon their positions and flee south. Siboldi and his partisans did their best to stop them, but there were just too many. With the enemy in full flight, Walker-Brown gave the order to cease fire. It was time to pull out.

One thing was for sure now. After their attack on Borghetto, the enemy would know this wasn't simply a group of partisans on the rampage. This had to be a team of highly trained and well-equipped Allied troops, for their work with the mortars and the Brens was just too damn good. While Walker-Brown was unsure just how many enemy they had killed, writing later that 'the number of casualties is not known,' the psychological impact of the assault was clear. 'The entire enemy garrison withdrew from Borghetto and did not return for 24 hours,' he reported, meaning here at least the enemy were running scared.

Their job done, the men gathered their weapons and headed back into the hills, to begin the long and arduous trek back to the Rossano Valley. The following evening, 2 January 1945, they reached it. During that ferocious attack on Borghetto they had exhausted their supply of mortar bombs and used up their Bren ammunition – much of the entire lot that the C-47s had managed to parachute into the Rossano Valley. They sought a resupply from the stocks that lay hidden, but Walker-Brown knew that if they kept up such a relentless pace of operations, it was only a matter of time before they'd run out of ammo.

At Rossano, Walker-Brown also discovered that Lieutenant Gibbon and the men of No. 4 Stick were waiting for him. They'd failed to locate any targets on the Aulla–Pontremoli road, which just seemed deserted of enemy forces. They'd returned for fresh orders. Wasting no time, Walker-Brown ordered Gibbon to link up with Sergeant Rookes's No. 3 Stick, busy scoping out targets on the Pontremoli–Cisa road, to the north-east of Rossano. He was hopeful they would find richer pickings there.

With Lieutenant Gibbon and his men dispatched, Walker-Brown tried again to signal Major Farran, back at SFHQ in Bari. He was keen to deliver a report on actions to date, which would signify that Operation Galia was biting hard, just as Allied high command had intended. But again, any attempt to establish communications was thwarted by the girdle of high peaks on all sides. Ever since landing, a week earlier, Walker-Brown had still not managed to establish any contact. As far as SAS headquarters was concerned, the SAS commander and his entire squadron had disappeared into thin air. It was becoming a real issue.

But there were other, more pressing matters facing Walker-Brown, some of which proved enraging. While the SAS had been away, a group of unruly 'partisans' had visited the valley, preying on the local population and demanding money and food. Major Lett was extremely annoyed. He'd accompanied Walker-Brown on the Borghetto raid, and this was the last thing he had expected to discover upon his return. In his Operation Blundell Violet mission report, Lett outlined the extent of the problem, uncovering 'considerable confusion and a terrorised population owing to bad behaviour of partisans . . .' Lett's response was immediate and it pulled no punches. 'Gave orders . . . for expulsion of all patriots from area for military reasons and closed frontiers of Rossano Valley to all persons without special passes made out by Colonel [Fontana] at Command, or self.' This order would stay in force for as long as necessary, for guarding their redoubt in the Rossano Valley would be crucial to future operations.

As for Walker-Brown and his men, they had a very sombre task to carry out. The bodies of the seven US airmen who had died in the plane crash had been collected, and they were brought to Chiesa for burial. While the service was conducted by SOE Captain Chris Leng, the SAS gave the fallen airmen a formal guard, and they were buried with full military honours. That burial served to bring the events of the past few days into some kind of wider perspective. Despite two daring and successful attacks, not all was going in the SAS's favour. They had just buried seven US airmen, a full stick of six SAS had been cap-tured – fate unknown – a young Italian guide had been brutally murdered, and worst of all the Huntsville DZ was out of action.

Added to that the winter weather was starting to worsen.

Walker-Brown had much on his mind.

Back in SAS headquarters in Bari, so too did Major Roy Farran. Farran was already a legendary figure within the SAS. He'd won a Military Cross for actions in Crete, in 1941, was cap-tured, and earned a bar to that MC for his subsequent escape, earned a second bar for actions in Italy in late 1943, and finally a Distinguished Service Order (DSO), for his post-D-Day oper-ations in France. That last decoration had been awarded in the name of Major Patrick McGinty, the name Farran had adopted ever since escaping from German captivity, for by then the enemy knew his real name. In short, Farran – McGinty – was no fading violet, but even he was getting worried at the long silence emanating from Walker-Brown and his squadron.

At 1850 hours on 2 January 1945, he asked for a message to be sent to Walker-Brown by all possible means, with the caveat, 'Do not censor.' It read: 'Very worried about lack of news being sent us . . . If you are being hard pressed disperse as previously arranged. Remember that information is important, try to get though on air. The evening is the best time. Good luck and keep on moving.'

The following day, there was something of a breakthrough on the ground at the Rossano Valley. Due to a break in the weather, finally Walker-Brown was able to establish communications. During a short radio call, he was able to relay the good news about operations to date. His other key priority was to arrange for another supply drop, to replenish ammunition and food. But SFHQ repeated the previous warning, that any further air drops would need to take place outside the Rossano Valley. The Americans were steadfastly refusing to use DZ Huntsville, after the crash they'd suffered with the loss of all air crew on 30 December 1944.

Walker-Brown was not happy. The next-closest drop zone – codenamed DZ Halifax – was a five-hour march away, across heavy snow and ice. With the weather deteriorating, he just didn't believe it was a viable option. As he stressed to SFHQ, the reasons for maintaining Huntsville were compelling: '(a) easiest DZ for getting resupply to detached sticks as . . . approximately in the centre of the troop operations area, and (b) any enemy attacks . . . would have to come through under partisan observation of whose warning system we made use.' Farran and

Walker-Brown were of one mind, but their arguments to continue using the Huntsville DZ were rejected. The Americans refused point blank, and as they ran the fleet of C-47 cargo aircraft, the ultimate decision lay with them.

Though the American commander's obduracy angered him, Walker-Brown remained keen to go on the offensive. With that in mind, he ordered Lieutenant Riccomini and his stick to head to the Valeriano area, which lay a dozen kilometres north of the city of La Spezia. His mission was to carry out an assault on the bridge over the Magra river, which carried the main road running inland. It would be a daring attack, if Riccomini could pull it off, for the Magra river bridge lay just a few kilometres outside the city limits. As yet, Walker-Brown was still to hear if any of his other patrols had scored any successes. The pressing need to make the enemy think there was a much larger force operating in the area remained a priority. The attacks had to continue, until enemy commanders grew so enraged that they sent a large body of troops to seek and destroy the saboteurs.

After all, that was the entire purpose of Operation Galia.

With Lieutenant Riccomini's patrol dispatched, Walker-Brown remained in the snowbound Rossano Valley, repeating his requests for an urgent resupply drop. He asked for numerous items, including '50 light Arctic tents, 50 sleeping bags, 10 lightened Bren guns and 300 [mortar] bombs.' But all such requests went unheeded. Much that Farran was lobbying on Walker-Brown's behalf, the Americans remained immovable. And those much-needed Arctic tents and winter warfare clothing were proving highly elusive. Major Farran was trying to source that cold-weather kit from his base in Bari, in what everyone presumed was sun-kissed southern Italy.

On 6 January, Lieutenant Riccomini returned to the Rossano Valley, bringing uplifting news. It gave Walker-Brown a huge boost to his morale. Incredibly, forty-eight hours earlier Riccomini had managed to mine the bridge over the Magra. As he and his men had lain in wait, a German military truck had nosed onto the bridge. The mine had detonated, and during the explosion, and the follow-up Bren attack, Riccomini and his men had killed a dozen German troops and wounded a further eight. Not a single man of Riccomini's stick had suffered so much as a scratch. Striking with such daring and ferocity so close to a major port city like La Spezia, had to strike the fear of God into the enemy. It was just what Walker-Brown had hoped for.

Shortly, there was further good news. Walker-Brown's Nos. 3 and 4 sticks, led by Sergeant Rookes and Lieutenant Gibbon, had been busy on sabotage operations to the east of the Rossano Valley, north of La Spezia. While trying to blow a railway tunnel they were set upon by German forces, but in the resulting fire-fight all had withdrawn safely. On the road running west out of La Spezia, Sergeant Wright and his No. 1 stick had ambushed a German staff car, 'killing a high Fascist official and wounding three others'. This was music to Walker-Brown's ears. Striking so far and so wide – in all directions north, west and east of La Spezia – had to convince the enemy that a far larger force of Allied saboteurs was at work. It demonstrated how these unseen raiders could strike anywhere and at any time. And by killing that high Fascist official, it showed that no one, no matter their rank or status, was safe from such predations.

Walker-Brown was convinced that the plan for Operation Galia had to be working. Surely, German troops and Brigata Nera alike had to be on high alert now. At any time the SAS could spring from the shadows, hit them hard and with extreme violence, then melt back into the night. This was classic SAS hit-and-run tactics, albeit executed on foot and with mules, rather than utilising the speed and manoeuvrability of the Willys jeeps. The snowy hills and winter darkness were their cover, and with the expert guides furnished by Major Lett and his partisans, things were going well, despite the loss of Shaughnessy and his SAS patrol.

The one major downside remained resupply. The tussle with SFHQ – or rather, with the USAAF – continued. Walker-Brown was extremely reluctant to agree to switch the DZ to Halifax. It was simply too far away. With the weather turning from awful to horrendous, getting there, collecting up all the scattered containers, and hauling the kit back to the Rossano Valley would be exhausting in the extreme.

But by 9 January – some two weeks into their mission – Walker-Brown conceded defeat. Desperate for a resupply drop, a signal had been received that morning that simply stated: 'Sorry bad weather. Halifax (again soon) when possible.' Reluctantly, he ordered Riccomini and his stick to link up with Wright's patrol, and to head for the Halifax DZ at Pieve. That afternoon, Walker-Brown and his troop set out to follow, reaching Pieve well after dark and after the drop had taken place. At around 1530 hours a single Dakota had released a number of canisters, the load being scattered far and wide. Many of the containers had been looted by disaffected 'partisan' groups. The next twenty-four hours were spent recovering the stolen items, often at gunpoint.

Yet despite such trials and tribulations, Operation Galia was starting to bite hard. Reports began to filter in of the Germans moving troops into the area, to deal with the SAS threat. Sure enough, they were being pulled out of the Serchio Valley – the stretch of the Gothic Line at which they had been mustering, for Kesselring's much-vaunted counter-attack. This was music to Walker-Brown's ears. On hearing it, he decided to strike first and to strike hard. They would execute another assault on the Via Aurelia and the garrison at Borghetto, he decided. And they would do so that very night, moving the first groups out that evening.

With the January weather closing in, the going proved tough in the extreme. With snow and sleet blasting into their faces, keeping control of the heavily laden mules proved nigh-on impossible. Both men and animals found themselves slipping and sliding along ice-packed paths, only inches from plummeting into the chasms that yawned below. In places they had to battle their way through deep snowdrifts, which made for utterly exhausting going. Progressing at a snail's pace, this was exhausting work. All knew that at the end of their journey they would need to fight the battle of their lives, after which they would have to brave the same conditions as they made their getaway.

The boots the SAS wore proved unsuitable for such conditions, causing many to lose their footing. Lacking in winter camouflage, and with all the noise they were making, the element of surprise would be lost if they pressed on as they were. With several of his men in danger of succumbing to exhaustion and illness, Walker-Brown decided to rest up at the village of Serò, and launch the attack the following morning. As dawn broke on 11 January, the SAS and their guides, having rested frozen and aching limbs, set out for what was intended to be their most audacious attack yet. Leaving the job or mustering the main ambush party to Lieutenant Riccomini, who was proving himself to be a very able and courageous deputy, Walker-Brown took a single Bren and a number of men, and moved around to a position set some three hundred yards above the main German HQ building at Borghetto. Meanwhile, Riccomini, with five Bren gun teams, set up in a perfect position, commanding clear fields of fire along the road leading into the town.

From his vantage point, Walker-Brown could also see far along that road. To his surprise, he spotted two Brigata Nera Fascists sauntering along, and was very tempted to drop them with a burst from his Bren. However, he and his men held their fire, for there would be richer pickings soon enough. He didn't want the enemy to know they were there just yet. It was then that he heard the sound of motor vehicles approaching. As the noise grew louder, he spied a convoy of three vehicles, one of which looked like a captured British staff car towing a trailer. Tempted to open up on them, Walker-Brown again held his fire. The vehicles were headed towards where Riccomini had set up the main ambush party. As his deputy had more firepower at his command, Walker-Brown decided to leave them to him.

As the vehicles passed by, he was able to gaze down into them. The captured British staff car was carrying six German soldiers, one of whom was an officer. The following truck also pulled a trailer and was carrying a large number of German troops – no doubt, the escorts for the staff car. He counted twenty-seven in all. Disconcertingly, there were five women with the German troops. Though discomfiting, there was no way Walker-Brown could let the fact that there were female passengers dissuade him from proceeding with the attack. This was war. If those women got caught in the crossfire, sad as it was, there was nothing he could do about it.

As the convoy neared the town, all hell let loose.

With the vehicles coming within range, Riccomini gave the order to open up. In an instant the truck and staff car were riddled with fire from five Bren machine guns, each of which could unleash some 500 rounds per minute. Their combined firepower concentrated on that convoy proved utterly devastating. As the storm of bullets tore through the air, the vehicles burst into flames. The screams from the wounded added to the hellish noise, as those inside panicked and tried to clamber out, only to be cut down by the guns of the hidden raiders.

But not all had been killed. German soldiers bailed out and found positions from where to fight back, even as they were joined by others from the town's garrison. With bullets now coming back at them, as the Germans opened up, Riccomini made an extraordinary move. Calmly, he stepped out into the roadway, pointing out to his men exactly where they were to concentrate their fire. Ignoring the bullets as they flew past his head and ricocheted off the road all around him, he acted for all the world as if he were bulletproof. From that exposed position the young SAS lieutenant continued to direct the fire, forcing the Germans to fall back before their guns.

Taking his cue from Riccomini, Sergeant Wright likewise stepped into the road. Like Riccomini, he began directing the fire of his Bren gun team, and he too remained resolutely firm, even as the bullets flew close by. Eventually, after firing off thirty-two magazines from the Bren guns – a little short of 1,000 rounds – the order was given to pull back. As the two groups dashed into the cover of the trees, Walker-Brown glanced back at the scene of devastation. The vehicles were still burning furiously, having been hit with incendiary rounds, and many dead lay strewn across the roadway. In his report on the action, Walker-Brown would state that '26 were killed,' but the real figure, including wounded, was very likely far higher.

The SAS casualties were a solid zero.

As they made their way out of the ambush area, Walker-Brown was relieved to find that the enemy were not inclined to give chase. Or at least, not directly. Or immediately. But in truth, there was no way that the Germans, or their Brigata Nera cohorts, could let such an audacious second assault on Borghetto go unremarked or unpunished. Typically, though, their response was not to pursue and harry the British raiders. Instead, they chose to take out their frustrations and their anger on the local civilian population. Shortly, Walker-Brown learned that the Brigata Nera had begun to burn houses in and around Brugnato, a town situated along the route that the SAS had taken when preparing their attack.

Walker-Brown was a very particular kind of individual, blessed with a strong sense of right and wrong and a very distinctive mindset. In many ways he typified the one residing quality that was praised above all others in the SAS: the ability to think the unthinkable and then to put it into action. Enraged at the brutality of the Brigata Nera, and determined to put a stop to such actions, he ordered his men to make ready once more. They were heading back to Borghetto that very same day. And this time they would be taking the 3-inch mortar to give the enemy a right good taste of their own medicine.

Walker-Brown was just twenty-five years of age when he had been given command of Operation Galia. Born in Dallas, Morayshire, in north-east Scotland, his father was a doctor from Aberdeen and the son of a church minister. Being an only child, his mother had strongly objected to him being sent away to boarding school; he would remark later that she 'had very strange ideas about education'. At the age of eighteen he was sent to Sandhurst for officer training, securing a commission in the Highland Light Infantry shortly before the outbreak of the war. Self-effacing and humble to a fault, when he was asked, years later, why he had made the army his career, he would respond, 'Probably too stupid for anything else.'

In September 1939 he'd been in the regimental depot in Glasgow when he learned that Britain was at war, hearing the news with 'a mixture of foreboding and excitement'. Not long after hostilities had broken out, he was dispatched to Egypt as a platoon commander. Deploying from Cairo, his battalion 'moved up to the Western Desert', where he saw action against the Italians. From there he was sent to Somalia, taking part in fierce combat at the battle of Keren. 'It was very, very hard fighting in hot, steamy, humid conditions,' Walker-Brown would remark; 'we had to fight our way through thick, thick scrub under very heavy fire . . . we suffered some two hundred casualties.' He had shown an aptitude for acting decisively when under fire, an attribute that would serve him well in the years to come.

From Keren the battalion was sent to Cyprus to re-form and re-equip, after which Walker-Brown found himself once again waging war in the Western Desert, serving with the British Eighth Army. On 5 June 1942, while acting as the brigade navigator, he was in the lead vehicle as they advanced west. When the 22nd Armoured Brigade failed to show up to relieve them, Walker-Brown's battalion was set upon by the German 16th Panzer Grenadier Division. During intense fighting, he was 'wounded by shrapnel from a German air blast', receiving 'a nasty piece of shrapnel in my back'. As he lay among the dead and wounded, a German tank stopped just six feet away and began to fire round after round, resulting in him being 'completely deafened for about six months'.

With the battalion overrun, Walker-Brown was discovered by the Germans and taken prisoner. Laid out on the side of an enemy tank, he was taken from the battlefield, but it was during this time that he was wounded again, this time from British artillery. 'I had the unique distinction ... of being first of all wounded by the Germans and then shortly after by the British,' he would quip later.

Treated at a field dressing station, he was handed over to the Italians, taken to the port of Derla and shipped out to Naples. When his wound became infected – it was 'extremely septic and leaking pus all over the place' – he was sent for treatment at an Italian hospital. Eventually he was moved again, this time to a convent being used as a military medical station. Lodged in his back was the cause of all the infections: 'A piece of my cotton shorts ... a piece of my webbing equipment ... a brass buckle, followed by a very large chunk of shrapnel ... and literally hundreds and hundreds of maggots.' It was very likely those maggots that saved his life, preventing him from getting septicaemia.

His wounds cleaned, Walker-Brown made a relatively quick recovery. With no reason to keep him in hospital, he was transferred to a POW camp – the infamous PG21, Campo 21, at Chieti. And from there, once the Armistice had been declared, he had masterminded his first great escape of the war, making it safely back to Allied lines. After which he had volunteered for the SAS.

*

That was months ago, and Walker-Brown had other things to focus on in the early days of January 1945. Right now, he was busy preparing another daring attack, the second in two days, on the garrison town of Borghetto. Obviously, this was something the enemy would least be expecting. As well as wreaking revenge for the reprisals taken against the locals, Walker-Brown also harboured another, wider motive. 'By attacking Borghetto twice,' he would explain, '. . . the enemy would be forced to take action in order to prevent a third attack, either by reinforcing his garrison on the coast road or by attacking the SAS . . . with a large body of troops in order to clean up the area.' In other words, this was Operation Galia's mission statement writ large.

From their temporary base in the hills, Walker-Brown and his men set off down the now familiar track leading into Borghetto. Positioning himself at a vantage point, he had a commanding view of both the towns of Borghetto and neighbouring Brugnato, and the road bridge that ran between the two. Crucially, all of that terrain lay within easy range of their mortar. With everyone in position, Walker-Brown was poised to give the order to attack. But just as the mortar team took hold of their first bomb, the sound of an aircraft engine cut the air. Moments later a lone Republic P-47 Thunderbolt – a US fighter-bomber – came in low and fast. As the SAS men watched, the pilot released his bomb, pulling up sharply to bring the plane away from the target, Borghetto. But the expected explosion did not follow: the bomb must have been a dud.

In the vacuum left by that abortive attack, Walker-Brown gave the order to commence firing. As the first mortar exploded on the road below, he wondered if the enemy would somehow link the two – that USAAF warplane, and the explosions. Maybe they'd conclude that the SAS had the ability to call in airstrikes as and when they wished. That would be no bad thing, for it would serve to boost the sense that the British raiders were there in potent force.

In quick succession further bombs were dropped on the roadway. Almost immediately, the enemy began to appear. Panicking, they attempted to withdraw to the south, all the time being harried by mortar and Bren gunfire. As the Germans and their Brigata Nera allies drew back, they were chased by bursts from the SAS's carbines and Brens, many falling victim to the controlled and accurate shooting. Having made it across the main bridge, one platoon of German soldiers decided to put up a fight. Setting up two MG42s – the quick-firing machine gun nicknamed 'Hitler's buzzsaw' by the Allies – they began returning fire. But there was no accuracy to their shooting. Bullets slammed harmlessly into the trees or ricocheted off distant rocks, expending their force in the snow.

Quickly finding their range, the SAS mortar team dropped several bombs perilously close to the German gunners. Deciding that to stay where they were would mean certain death, the enemy abandoned their positions and fled into the hills. No sooner were they gone than the SAS came under fire from a 20mm cannon sited in the town's cemetery. As the bullets thundered all around, Walker-Brown had his mortar team turn their ire on that target. Soon enough, the well-drilled gunners were pounding that area, dropping a bomb right on top of the cannon. It blew apart the weapon, blasting those operating it into bloody shreds.

With the 20mm gun out of action, Walker-Brown got the mortar team to target the enemy positions in the town, blowing buildings to rubble and forcing those sheltering within to run, or to cower in fear for their lives. Although the enemy were returning sporadic bursts of fire, none of it was coming anywhere close. The SAS had the high ground and were firing from well concealed positions. The mortar team itself was hidden behind a ridge, while its fire was directed by Walker-Brown, who had eyes on the targets from the ridgetop above.

The effect of this attack proved devastating. The corpses of German soldiers littered the town, while others lay face-down in the river. As Walker-Brown noted, 'a number of the enemy were reported drowned in the river, presumably after having been wounded by mortar splinters, as the river is only two feet deep.' Aware of the successes they were having, the Bren gun teams began to move forward in a flanking manoeuvre, spraying deadly machine-gun fire into the streets of Borghetto. Magazine after magazine was expended, as they methodically worked their way through what had once been a German garrison town, these highly trained, war-bitten troops showing little fear as they purposefully and deliberately went about their task.

It wasn't long before several buildings had burst into flames, the smoke rising high into the afternoon sky. By now, the raiders had exhausted a vast amount of ammunition, and Walker-Brown began to consider withdrawing. They had caused untold damage to buildings and vehicles, and wrought heavy casualties upon the enemy. As he pondered his next move, a group of four Thunderbolts appeared in the sky. Seeing the action taking place beneath them, they swooped to attack. With engines roaring, two of the planes dive-bombed the town's bridge, while the others strafed the road, the bullets from their .50-calibre wing-mounted heavy machine guns ripping up the ground before them.

Once again, this led Walker-Brown to wonder if the enemy

would conclude that the SAS could call in air support whenever they felt like it. Of course, they didn't have that capability. They had no way of radioing in any kind of warplanes. Yet in truth, these air-attacks weren't entirely by coincidence. In his latest report to SFHQ, Walker-Brown had detailed targets for airstrikes, the garrison at Borghetto being chief among them. The American planes were acting upon that intelligence, and it was serendipitous that the SAS and the USAAF had struck at the same time.

Just as Walker-Brown was admiring the American pilots' handiwork, a powerful explosion burst upon the hillside not far from the SAS positions, throwing rocks, tree branches and chunks of ice in all directions. The SAS commander scanned the town, trying to spy out the source of the blast. It turned out that the Germans had 'brought up a 105mm field gun from La Spezia'. That weapon began to pound the slopes to all sides. But the German gunners seemed to have little idea where the British soldiers were located, their shells either falling short, or high and wide.

Walker-Brown decided it was time to withdraw. As the men gathered their kit and made their way up the hillside, they left behind them a scene of devastation. The target buildings had been reduced to heaps of burning rubble, and many German and Brigata Nera lay dead. In due course, intelligence received from Borghetto itself indicated that the attack had resulted in over fifty casualties for the enemy. As the icing on the cake, the SAS themselves had not suffered a single fatality.

With their ammunition all-but exhausted, Walker-Brown steered a route directly to Pieve, adjacent to the Halifax drop zone. By now, the weather was dreadful, and they had to fight their way through near-blizzard conditions. Worse still, Walker-Brown received warnings that his Nos. 3 and 4 sticks, under the command of Sergeant Rookes and Lieutenant Gibbon, were cut off. Drifts of thick snow, lying six-feet-deep in parts, had marooned those two parties on the far side of the Due Santi Pass, which lay some twelve kilometres to the north.

At the Halifax DZ there had been an air drop. A single aircraft had parachuted in a Vickers Mark I heavy machine gun, something that Walker-Brown had repeatedly requested. A .303-inch belt-fed weapon, it had an unrivalled reputation for copper-bottomed reliability and indestructibility, something that endeared the Vickers to every British soldier who ever got to use one. It packed a far heavier punch than the Bren, and while heavy, its worth in the kind of battles they were fighting would be immeasurable. Sadly, this one had not proved to be quite as indestructible as all had hoped. Upon release from the aircraft, the parachute had failed and the weapon had plummeted to earth, smashing itself to pieces on impact.

A courier had parachuted in along with the Vickers – a messenger sent by Major Charles MacIntosh, the head of SOE in Florence and Lett's key contact. He confirmed that the Huntsville DZ was a no-go as far as SOE headquarters and the Americans were concerned. It didn't particularly matter much just then. The weather had become so atrocious that no aircraft were about to brave those inclement skies. Finally, on 15 January the weather lifted briefly. A second resupply flight managed to sneak in. Two more Vickers machine guns were dropped, this time under fully functioning parachutes. But as further containers were shoved out of the aircraft and drifted to earth, the operation descended into something of a chaotic mess.

Learning of the drop and seeing the aircraft come in, partisans from various groups had gathered. They began grabbing canisters, and pilfering anything they could lay their hands on. As they attempted to drag kit away, Walker-Brown ordered one of his men to fire warning shot. That show of force had the effect he'd intended. The rogue partisans were forced to leave the immediate area, but they were far from happy. Taking up positions on the heights above, some of them began to take pot-shots at the SAS, their frustrations getting the better of them.

Incensed, Walker-Brown approached his radio operator, Ted Robinson, who at the time was carrying a Bren light machine gun. It was the perfect weapon to give those troublesome partisans a burst of fire, which was exactly what the SAS commander ordered. Robinson duly obliged, loosing off three magazines just above the heads of those who had been doing the shooting.

The Bren was one of the most accurate machine guns of the war. It had a maximum range of 1,850 yards, and was so deadly that some preferred it as a sniping weapon. Those searing bursts were enough to send the partisans on their way. Once the contents of the canisters had been gathered up, Walker-Brown urged his men to head back on the punishing trek to the Rossano Valley. That at least was a place where they could feel more comfortable and secure.

With his force now armed with those two Vickers machine guns, Walker-Brown was eager to get back into action. However, he knew that he had to be careful. Word had filtered in that the enemy were planning a major *rastrellamento*. Large numbers of German troops were being deployed to the area, to sort out the problem of the British paratroopers. On the one hand, the news was unwelcome, for it signified that they were about to become the hunted. On the other, it was a fantastic development, for it meant that Operation Galia had succeeded in its key objectives.

Typically, the news delighted Walker-Brown. Though he knew a major round-up was imminent, he radioed Major Farran at SFHQ, warning him that he intended to 'attack Pontremoli, which is very military'. If anything, that simple message was a studied exercise in understatement. Some two thousand German troops were now reported to be stationed at Pontremoli, a small city lying to the north of La Spezia, where they were readying themselves for the *rastrellamento*. To Walker-Brown's way of thinking, rather than waiting to become their prey, he would go hunting the hunters.

Together with Major Lett and Colonel Fontana, he drew up a plan for three coordinated attacks to take place. The first, led by Walker-Brown with his contingent of SAS, would be bolstered by a detachment of twenty reliable partisans. They would strike on the road leading into Pontremoli itself. At the same time a group of partisans, led by the very capable Dany Bucchioni, would head along the Magra river to the south of Pontremoli, hitting any targets they encountered. A third group of partisans would attack an enemy outpost near to Borgo Val di Taro, a town lying to the north of Pontremoli. In this way, the chaos and mayhem would be spread far and wide, but with Pontremoli lying at the epicentre of the action.

But while Walker-Brown was busy drawing up such an audacious plan of attack, his men were suffering. The cumulative toll of back-to-back missions, the punishing terrain, but most of all the bitter weather, meant they were dogged by fatigue, and some were falling ill. One, Corporal Johnson, had a wounded hand that was starting to turn septic. Others were falling sick to frost-bite and fever. But Walker-Brown remained undeterred.

It was 18 January when the SAS commander, together with those fit to fight, prepared to set off towards the village of Codolo, which lay not far from their target, Pontremoli. They left behind them a small group of SAS men who had been ruled unfit for duty. Before pulling out, a signal was received from Major Farran, congratulating all on their 'magnificent work' and urging them to 'keep moving'. Their exploits were being talked about and lauded in high places.

A forty-eight-hour march under punishing loads and in atrocious conditions lay ahead of the SAS raiders. By 19 January they were in position. They waited out the hours of daylight in hiding, before moving in under cover of darkness. It took hours of painstaking effort to inch their heavy pack animals down slopes slick with ice. The temperature plummeted as the icy chill of the night set in. The heavy Vickers machine guns made almost impossible loads, and at times it looked as if they simply could not manoeuvre them into position. But under Walker-Brown's firm tutelage they inched ever closer to the vantage point from which he intended to strike.

Eventually, they reached it. A snow-covered spur, it looked down over a wide expanse of the roadway, the sweeping bend below meaning that any convoys would have to slow to negotiate their way. As a bonus, the nearside of the highway was flanked by the Magra river, which offered little cover for any vehicles negotiating the route ahead, leading into Pontremoli itself. It was the perfect place for mounting the kind of ambush the SAS intended.

Walker-Brown placed the ever-reliable Lieutenant Riccomini in charge of the Vickers machine guns, their most potent firepower.

The SAS lieutenant had proved his mettle on more than one occasion during the past weeks, and Walker-Brown knew he was up to the task. After a short wait, the hidden raiders caught a distant sound that made their hearts leap – vehicles crawling along the icy road. In fact, the more Walker-Brown listened the more he figured they had traffic approaching from both directions. Moments later, his eyes confirmed what his ears had been relaying to him. 'We heard and then saw the head of a column coming towards us – armoured cars and two or three lorry-borne infantry [units]. At the same time from behind me . . . came a horse-drawn battery of German field artillery.'

It constituted a bonanza of enemy targets, especially as the two columns would converge at exactly the spot that the SAS's vantage point dominated. Shortly, Walker-Brown gave the order to open fire. Immediately the two Vickers opened up. The range was perfect, the skill of the gunners matchless. Streams of .303 bullets smashed into the leading truck, tearing apart the cab. Moments later it had careered off-route, ploughing into a large contingent of German troops who were marching along the roadway. With that first vehicle firmly out of action, the Vickers gunners swept their weapons from side to side, cutting down anyone caught in their fire.

The machine guns blasted away, pumping streams of blazing tracer across the river and lighting up its surface a fiery orange, as enemy soldiers scrambled for cover. Trying to escape from the carnage, some chose to throw themselves down the slope towards the freezing river, so desperate were they to find any route of escape, and no matter the risks involved. 'It was an absolute massacre,' Walker-Brown would reflect years later. 'There were horses and men throwing themselves down the steep slope into the river.'

As the Vickers continued their relentless work, chewing through their 250-round belts of ammo, it struck Walker-Brown that the enemy were gathered here in such numbers specifically to hunt down the British troops now attacking them. In the greatest of ironies, by shipping in hundreds of extra troops, the enemy had gifted the SAS more targets to take on, via their hit-and-run attacks. For long minutes the murderous fusillade continued, the gunners blasting through belt-load after belt-load of Vickers rounds. The concentrated fire ripped up the surface of the road, tearing into the scattered vehicles and bodies.

But just after midnight, something caught Walker-Brown's eye that sent a chill down his spine. Had it not been for their white-winter camouflage clothing not being quite as pristine as it might have been, he may never have seen them. Around a thousand yards away, and on the SAS's side of the river, a large column of German ski troops was heading in their direction. Sensing the danger – the hunt was on – he gave the order to cease fire. Collapsing the Vickers in double-quick time – the gun itself sat on a heavy and cumbersome tripod – Walker-Brown urged his men to get moving. That was easier said than done. The Vickers weighed some 50 pounds apiece, and each had to be lugged up the ice-bound slope that stretched high above.

But those guns had done such a magnificent job the SAS commander was loath to abandon them. Struggling, sliding, cursing and fighting for every yard of ground, the raiders began their perilous ascent, even as the German ski troops seemed to glide ever closer. As Walker-Brown and his men battled their way upslope, he spied a second group of fast-moving German troops advancing from the opposite direction – they risked being caught in a pincer-movement. There was worse news to come.

'A message came up from the back of the SAS column – "there are more Germans behind us",' Walker-Brown would note of the moment. They were in danger of getting surrounded, as they became hemmed in from three sides.

In a sense Walker-Brown had always known it was only a matter of time before the hunters became the hunted. Now that moment was upon them. Bizarrely, this was exactly what they had been sent in here to achieve – to make of themselves prey to a far larger enemy force. And in their twenty-five-year-old SAS captain, these men had the perfect officer to lead them out of the dire straits they now found themselves in. If anyone could get them out of this, surely he could. After all, Walker-Brown was no stranger to daring escapes, and there was no reason that this should unduly unsettle him.

In the late autumn of 1942, Walker-Brown had found himself languishing in Campo 21, at Chieti. He'd arrived wearing nothing but a pair of bloodied and ripped shorts and a blanket that he'd bastardised into a makeshift cloak. Even so, and typically, one of the first things on Walker-Brown's mind was whether there was any possibility of escape. But it was not until the following spring that he saw something that offered a possible route out. A concrete walkway surrounded the hut where he slept. On that path, covered in dirt, was a metal plate that resembled a manhole cover. Walker-Brown worked out that it could not be seen from any of the watchtowers or sentry boxes.

Seizing his chance, he levered open the metal cover. Below it lay a sump, some eighteen inches square and three feet deep. Although it was out in the open, and could be seen should any guard walk by, it lay close to one of the ablution blocks. If someone small enough could crawl into the sump and remove the bricks that formed the outer wall, then a tunnel might be dug from there. The spoil could be dumped between the double skins of the hut walls.

Excited at the prospect, Walker-Brown approached the Campo 21 escape committee with his idea. At the time, other tunnelling projects were under way, so this was a well-practised and accepted means to try to break out. Upon hearing Walker-Brown's proposal, the escape committee gave the go-ahead to start work on what was to become known as 'Tunnel 3'.

Walker-Brown sought out a suitable volunteer to start the excavations. It took the form of a diminutive officer of the Indian Army, who was somehow shanghaied into doing the job. Using a fire-poker to loosen the brickwork, he was able to break through the sump wall, and digging got under way. For the first forty feet or so the task proved relatively easy, for the concrete pavement above served as the tunnel roof. The soil and rocks from their excavations was dumped into empty Red Cross boxes, and then spirited across to the nearest hut, to be emptied between the walls.

But once the tunnel reached the end of the pathway, it had to be dropped down six feet or so, to ward against collapse. It proved tough going. Anyone with a phobia of confined spaces would never be able to brave it, for the tunnel itself was tiny. It was barely the width of a man's hips, with only enough room to worm one's way along. Had there been any kind of collapse, then the tunneller would have been buried alive. Eventually, the excavators hit a concrete sewer. It took a while to cut through, but while the smell was atrocious, it doubled as a useful staging post for any potential escapees. As an added bonus, there was now no need to pass the spoil back along the tunnel, for it could be dumped directly into the sewer system.

The rules of the camp made excavation work difficult. Spot roll-calls and surprise searches meant a quick exit was needed. Tunnelling parties tended to work at night, with makeshift dummies placed in their beds to fool any guard who might shine his torch along the rows of beds. The digging took months, but by the beginning of September 1943 they were almost there. Hitting the roots of a fig tree that they knew lay outside of the camp perimeter, they began to tunnel upwards. Finally, Walker-Brown and his team on Tunnel 3 were ready to go.

But it was then that everything changed. Having seen Sicily fall to the Allied landings, and British and American troops hit the Italian mainland, the Italians surrendered. Upon hearing the Stay Put Order issued by the camp's Senior British Officer, Walker-Brown had no intention of doing any such thing. He'd not spent the last six months excavating a tunnel, simply to hand himself over into German captivity.

A week after the Armistice was signed, German troops entered the camp in force. As they started to ship out the prisoners, those who had been digging tunnels now used them as places in which to hide. Walker-Brown and eight fellow escapees did exactly that in Tunnel 3. Due to the cramped confines, hiding there was far from easy. The air was thin and rank, and the heat oppressive – they could last only for so long.

After six hours or more their oxygen began running out. Concluding that the Germans must have left, they crawled back above ground. Sure enough, the camp was deserted. They wasted no time breaking out, Walker-Brown teaming up with two officers, Lieutenant Ken Bangham of the Royal Horse Artillery, and one other from the Durham Light Infantry. Moving only at night the three men managed to make swift progress south, exchanging their British uniforms for Italian farming clothing along the way.

Eventually, as they drew close to the city of Foggia, they could hear the sound of gunfire. Slipping forward to take a closer look, the three men were spotted by a group of heavily armed German soldiers. With weapons pointed at them, the section commander barked out a challenge.

'Englander?'

Unabashed, Walker-Brown replied, 'No, no, Italiano, Italiano.'

Moments later, each of them was handed an entrenching tool and told to start digging. As Walker-Brown was to reflect later, 'We presumed we were digging our own graves.' However, he was wrong. The German commander appeared to have swallowed Walker-Brown's story that he and his comrades were Italian villagers. Accordingly, the enemy troops were using the three men as labour, to dig slit trenches for them.

Shortly after putting their spades into the ground, they came under fierce mortar fire. They dived for cover, even as their German captors made a break for it, dashing out of view. Realising they were pretty much on the frontline, the three fugitives stayed where they were, hunkered down under the bombardment. Not long thereafter the area was 'overrun by a battalion of the Northamptonshire Regiment', as Walker-Brown would later describe it. Although the British troops were suspicious of the three men they'd captured, it was soon evident that they were who they claimed to be – three escaped officers from Chieti POW camp.

*

It was the winter of 1943 when Walker-Brown had been reunited with Allied forces. He returned to England and was posted to an infantry training centre in Aberdeen. After spending so much time in combat, followed by a very eventful period in captivity and executing a daring escape, this change in pace was not to his liking. In short, he was bored stiff.

His fortunes were to change one night, when he was enjoying a drink in a local pub. Noticing an officer who appeared to be armed to the teeth – 'covered in pistols, knives and God knows what' as Walker-Brown described him – he decided to investigate.

'What on earth are you?' he asked, intrigued.

'Oh, I'm in the SAS,' came back the reply.

'What's that?'

'The Special Air Service.'

The very look and poise of the man was enough for Walker-Brown. On the spot he decided that he wanted to be part of this unit, whatever the Special Air Service might prove to be. Persuading that soldier to give him his Commanding Officer's name and telephone number, he returned to his base and placed a phone call to Colonel Brian Franks, chief of the 2nd SAS Regiment. After explaining that he had spotted one of his officers in a pub and 'would very much like to join his regiment', Walker-Brown was invited for an interview.

Due to his extensive war service and the fact that he'd escaped from an Italian POW camp, the young officer impressed Franks right away. Walker-Brown was duly invited to join the SAS, bypassing the arduous selection process. He travelled south to join the unit, which was at the time busy making preparations for the Normandy D-Day landings, and the particular role the SAS was to play.

Parachuting into France with twenty men to support Major Roy Farran's SAS squadron, Walker-Brown was soon proving his worth. Linking up with the French resistance, he got busy on hit-and-run operations behind the lines in the Longes and Dijon areas, including attacks on German columns and radioing back targets for Allied air-strikes. In France, Walker-Brown proved himself an extremely capable special operations commander. Those attributes had made him the perfect candidate to lead the men of Operation Galia.

On Operation Galia, Walker-Brown's task had been deliberately to provoke the enemy, so as to become the hunted. In this, he and his men had proved themselves mightily successful. As a result of their January '45 assault on Pontremoli, they now had hundreds of German troops on their tail, hell-bent on avenging the deaths of those the SAS had left lying dead and wounded on that blood-soaked highway. The situation for this small band of SAS raiders was desperate. But if anyone could keep a cool head and lead his men out of there, Walker-Brown was that man.

As they struggled up that icy slope, the SAS commander was torn. Sticking to the well-worn track that stretched ahead was foolhardy, for it was the obvious route for the enemy to follow. Yet, for the moment at least, it was utterly necessary, because 'speed was absolutely vital'. But shortly, word came up from the back of the line that the enemy were hot on their heels. Above stretched the dark silhouette of a ridgeline. It lay about half a mile away. If they could just make that, they should be able to sneak over the top and slip from view.

It would be a hellish climb. They would be forced to leave the track and strike off across virgin territory. But if they kept to their present route they were finished, of that Walker-Brown felt certain. Beyond the ridge they could head for a friendly village, which lay about three kilometres away. With luck they could hide out there, slipping the trap the German troops had set for them. Yet not all could reach that ridgeline. Lieutenant Riccomini was dogged by an ankle injury. As Walker-Brown appreciated, one man couldn't be allowed to slow the entire column. Riccomini, accompanied by one SAS trooper and a partisan guide, would have to break off and try to follow the route of the Magra river, until they could reach the safety of the mountains beyond.

After bidding a quick farewell to those three, the main party pushed ahead. The climb to the ridge was murder, but somehow Walker-Brown and his party made it, and seemingly without being spotted. Eventually, sodden from thick coatings of snow and frozen to the bone, they entered the small village beyond. It was 0300 hours. On learning that the enemy were still close behind, Walker-Brown knew they couldn't stop for too long. Rallying his men, he got them ready to move. But a small number of the partisans that accompanied them refused to go on. Under the command of their leader, Nino Siligato, they argued that they would remain where they were, for they were in desperate need of food and of rest.

As Walker-Brown fully appreciated, this was tantamount to suicide. It would also very likely bring hellfire and damnation down on the villagers. Yet he had neither the wherewithal nor the time to persuade those partisans to do otherwise. He and his men set out. This time they made for an abandoned town, Noce, lying some ten kilometres to the west. There, they hoped to meet up with SAS Corporal Johnson, who had been tasked to move there with the SAS's radio and most of their mules. Three hours' desperate march later, Walker-Brown and his men reached Noce, only to discover that Johnson, his mules and the radio were nowhere to be seen.

Dawn was approaching. Back in the village that Walker-Brown and his men had vacated, sunrise was to be met by death and devastation. At 0715 hours, the enemy attacked in force. Having found shelter in some abandoned houses, Siligato and his partisans had kindled fires. They'd removed their boots in order to thaw out their feet after the freezing march. Even as they were warming themselves at the fireside, the enemy struck. Hearing the neighbouring house come under fire, Siligato dragged on his boots, grabbed his weapon and dashed outside. He was cut down in a hail of machine-gun fire, the bullets killing him instantly. A similar fate was to befall his comrades, all of whom were gunned down.

Hunkered down in the ruins of Noce, Walker-Brown received a runner from Lett, warning him that Johnson was not about to make it there any time soon. En route he'd stumbled across a German patrol. As he'd tried to steer a route around them, he'd come under intense fire. Most of the mule drivers had made a run for it and the majority of their stores were lost, including all of their radio equipment, their packs, food and sleeping bags.

Walker-Brown ordered his party to move out. Barely had they got under way, when the SAS commander spotted a large body of German soldiers 250 yards away, 'estimated at battalion strength . . . advancing in extended order', as he would later report. There was no way they could make a fight of it, and Walker-Brown made a snap decision to abandon the cumbersome Vickers machine guns, plus the mules that were carrying them. They needed to move silently and fast, if they were to stand any chance of slipping the trap. Disabling the weapons, they left them to the enemy, along with any other pieces of heavy kit. Speed and fleetness of foot was everything now.

Moving out, their weapons clutched in freezing hands, they were quickly spotted. The lack of winter clothing meant that they stood out starkly against the white of the snow. Moments later, mortar bombs began to drop around them, blasting snow, ice and rocks into the dawn skies. As fragments of razor-sharp shrapnel cut the air all around, Walker-Brown and his men somehow kept their cool. They paused to return fire, accurate blasts from their US-made M1 semi-automatic carbines cutting into the line of the advancing German troops.

Though heavily outnumbered, these dozen-odd SAS were conducting a well-drilled fighting retreat, as they sought to slow their pursuers down. Ahead of them lay a tree line leading up into the mountains. If they could only make it to that cover, there was a chance they could give the Germans the slip. Unleashing a few final blasts from their M1s, they began to run, Walker-Brown urging all to make a dash for that distant patch of trees. As they surged ahead, bullets tore past and slammed into the snowy ground, with mortar bombs exploding perilously close on all sides.

Miraculously, the lead figures made it into the trees. Pausing for an instant to catch his breath, Walker-Brown executed a hurried headcount. It was simply amazing: despite the onslaught, not a man in his party was missing or had been hit. Somehow they had braved that barrage of fire, emerging unscathed. But there was no time to tarry, or to marvel at their collective good fortune. Only one route offered any hope of safety. Up into the snowbound peaks, and over the Alta Via – the ancient, Roman-era trail that crossed the highest points.

Plagued by crushing exhaustion, it was only pure adrenalin that was keeping Walker-Brown and his men moving. It would have been so much easier to have rested up and warmed frozen limbs, back at that first village – but had they done so, they would all have been killed or captured. Only by fleeing into the most inhospitable terrain imaginable lay any possible hope of safety. But no one underestimated the difficulties that lay ahead. They had been on the move for hours now, for most of which they'd been hotly pursued by a far larger enemy force. They had been surrounded by German troops and twice escaped their clutches. As Walker-Brown fully appreciated, if they dropped their guard for only a few seconds it could spell disaster. They simply had to keep moving, and to stay one step ahead of the hunters.

They set off once more, keeping well away from any tracks or paths, and wading through virgin snowfields. At times the drifts lay waist-deep, but still they had to plunge onwards. It made the going nearly impossible, and proved utterly exhausting, especially for men such as these, who were already fatigued beyond what most could endure. They were hungry, soaking wet, shivering, and frozen to the core, yet still they pressed on. Every ten minutes or so Walker-Brown would change whoever was on point, rotating the most arduous task of breaking through the virgin snow. All the while he was acutely aware of how their dark uniforms would pick them out against the harsh whiteness.

On they went, climbing ever upwards. Eventually, they reached the high point, crossing over the Alta Via, after which they headed down towards the village of Groppo, which lay on the far side. But any hopes of rest or sanctuary were quickly dashed.

Upon reaching that village, they learned that it was sandwiched between two groups of advancing Germans. With no other option, they set forth again, finally reaching a further isolated village, Rio, at 1700 hours. Maybe there they could finally get some rest.

But it was not to be. Barely thirty minutes after settling down to thaw out frozen limbs, the high-pitched screech of an artillery round cut through the skies. Moments later, there was the boom of an explosion as the shell ploughed into a nearby building. No sooner had the sound faded away, than a second shot screamed into the village. The blast blew out windows and hurled masonry high into the air. Again, the SAS had been spotted, their uniforms being a dead giveaway. The enemy had brought up a 75mm field gun and were closing in once more.

Again, Walker-Brown had to get his men back onto their feet – for it was a question of run or die. With the light fading fast, their only hope lay in the coming blanket of darkness. Maybe, under night's cloak they could somehow escape. As the cold drew in, they managed to dash out of Rio village, heading north towards the flank of Monte Gottero, the peak of which rears to over 5,000 feet. This time it seemed as if they had slipped away without being spotted, the falling darkness being their salvation.

They settled in a thick grove of trees for what was to be a long night. After getting what rest they could at the foot of Monte Gottero, Walker-Brown and his team roused themselves the following morning. If they were to survive, then keeping moving was vital. The SAS commander knew that to choose the easy route now would only play into the hands of the enemy. He had no option but to push his men harder and further than ever he had before. The summit of Monte Gottero towered above them, the flanks glistening in their thick coat of snow and ice. Assuming the German commanders would never imagine that this desperate band of British paratroopers would make for those merciless heights, that was exactly what Walker-Brown intended now.

The thin line of figures trudged up the mountainside, their heads bowed and shivering uncontrollably, as gusts of icy wind drove snow and sleet into their faces. None so much as voiced a complaint. They knew instinctively that climbing the heights of Monte Gottero offered the only chance of safety. Practically crawling their way over the summit, they began to descend the far side, making for the village of Montegroppo where they hoped they might find some semblance of a safe haven.

Halfway down the mountainside, Walker-Brown spotted a group of men heading up towards them. He figured they had to be friendly, for none were dressed in winter camouflage kit, like their pursuers. As the two parties neared each other, he was more than a little surprised to see SAS Lieutenant Gibbon and Corporal Ford from No. 4 stick, along with a body of Italian partisans. The two parties rendezvoused. From Gibbon, Walker-Brown learned that they too were on the run. Their base had been overrun by a large force of German troops, and they'd only just managed to slip away.

In a sense, this simply confirmed what Walker-Brown already feared. The Germans were everywhere and had them pretty much surrounded. The only option was to push on to Montegroppo, for without rest and sustenance he and his men were going to perish, come what may. It was late in the evening of 21 January when they finally arrived. They found the village, which sat at the top of the Gotra Valley, to be full of partisans. There were around

285

twelve hundred in total, from various groups, all of whom were taking refuge from the *rastrellamento* that was in full force.

Feeling just a little more secure – the partisans were 'extremely well armed', as Walker-Brown described them – his men settled down to eat and to rest. But barely two hours had passed when a warning reached the village. A 400-strong force of German infantry was only an hour's march away. To Walker-Brown's surprise and disgust, on learning of the threat the partisans simply 'vanished into the mountains'. With no back-up with which to put up a fight, he was forced to move his men yet again. Seven kilometres further north lay the village of Boschetto. They would make for there.

Hours later they stumbled into that village, without having been cornered or trapped along the way. Thus far, they were remaining one step ahead of the enemy, but only just. At Boschetto Walker-Brown would learn more alarming news. German troops were no more than an hour behind them. They were warning any villagers that they came across that they were 'hunting British parachutists'. On the one hand that proved again that Operation Galia had achieved its objectives. But on the other, it did little to help the SAS's situation right then, with hundreds of enemy troops breathing down their necks. Gambling on the fact that the enemy would rest up during the hours of darkness, Walker-Brown ordered his men to bed down as best they could and to try to snatch some rest. They were dead on their feet, and without sleep they were done for.

At first light the following day, and in the knowledge that the enemy were moving in, he roused his men. Lieutenant Gibbon and Corporal Ford, along with their Italian fighters, decided to split from the main party. They would head back to the Belforte region, where they hoped to link up with the remainder of their stick. They knew that area well, and being such a small group they hoped to avoid enemy patrols. Bidding their farewells the groups split, Walker-Brown heading out of Boschetto, marching his men into the face of the rising sun.

Once again, they slipped out of an Italian village just as the net was about to close. Shortly, Boschetto was encircled by two thousand German troops. They stormed into the place with guns blazing. Walker-Brown, of course, knew little of this. For five hours he and his men trudged through hellish conditions. Eventually, they made it into the tiny hamlet of Buzzo. As Walker-Brown was painfully aware, by that stage his party had 'completed fifty-nine hours [of almost] continuous marching without rations or rest'. The men were exhausted beyond reckoning, himself included.

At Buzzo, he learned of a remote hut that lay high in the mountains beyond. It was a good hour's march away, but maybe if they could reach it, they could rest up properly there. Only with proper sleep and sustenance could they continue to evade the hordes of enemy troops now hunting them down; only by finding proper shelter and sanctuary would they be able to continue with their mission objectives. And so, once again, for what seemed like the thousandth time, the men grabbed their packs and their weapons and headed out, turning their faces to the mountain slope that reared high above them.

As they trudged up the steep hillside, in the valleys below buildings began to burn. The enemy were torching huts and houses, in an effort to flush out the elusive 'British parachutists'. Of course, Walker-Brown had no way of knowing the fate of the rest of his men. He had no way of telling how many might have been captured or killed. But of one thing he was certain. At that moment, hundreds of German troops who should have been massing on the Gothic Line were busy thereabouts, hunting for a few dozen SAS whose martial exploits had convinced the enemy that they were present in far greater numbers.

Finally, the ragged column of exhausted men reached that isolated hut. Entering it, they dropped their kit, and practically collapsed onto the floor, utterly spent. By now, they had been on the move for almost three days with barely a break. There was no doubt about it, without sleep they could go no further. For twelve hours solid they rested. For sure they had earned it, each and every one of them. They had frustrated and confounded the enemy at every turn. They had struck and struck again, before escaping from their clutches repeatedly. And one other thing was crystal clear to those men sheltering in that mountain hut: if they were this tired, then surely those pursuing them must also be feeling the strain.

All the following day, 23 January, Walker-Brown and his party remained in that hut, recharging their batteries. A group of trusted locals visited, providing them with food and intelligence. But shortly, the inevitable happened – German troops began to converge on the tiny settlement of Buzzo. Learning that the hunt was back on, Walker-Brown ordered his men to stand-to – to be ready to make an emergency getaway, or if trapped, to fight to the last round.

Hundreds of German troops streamed into Buzzo. Warned by locals that they were preparing to lay siege to their mountain hut, Walker-Brown ordered his men to move out. Knowing of a deserted village – Nola – that lay further back in the mountains, he figured they would head for that. Rested, fed and watered, the SAS felt thoroughly reinvigorated and they made short work of the journey, reaching those remote and ghostly ruins in two hours flat, despite the long climb across snow and ice that they'd just executed. When the enemy came to besiege the hut they had vacated, they would find it deserted. Their prey once again vanished.

And so the macabre dance continued.

By now, it was 25 January – almost a week into the *rastrellamento* – and as the evening shadows drew in, Walker-Brown decided it was time to execute a daring reconnaissance mission. Working on the assumption that the enemy had paid a visit to the hut and found it deserted, he presumed they had moved on from the Buzzo area. He needed to know for sure if the region was clear of the enemy, and if he could bring his men down from this eerie ghost-village. Accompanied by Lieutenant Leng – the SOE agent who had first parachuted into the Rossano Valley to check if the DZ was safe – and a partisan guide, he set off, the three figures edging into the gathering darkness.

Leng had only recently joined their party. As the *rastrellamento* had bitten hard, so he too had been forced to go on the run. By a roundabout route, he'd ended up bumping into Walker-Brown and his men. Moving with infinite caution, the three figures crept down the mountainside. After a while, they made it into a patch of woodland lying on the outskirts of Buzzo village. Ahead of them was a scattering of houses, their dark forms silhouetted against the white backdrop of the snow, and all washed in the silvery-blue light of the moon. There were lights showing in a few of the windows. The scene appeared utterly peaceful. Not a hint of German soldiers anywhere.

They stole forward, eager to find out if the enemy had indeed left. Suddenly, the stillness of the night was torn asunder by the deafening roar of gunfire. The attack took all three of them utterly by surprise. The blinding muzzle flashes revealed that they were being fired upon from a position just twenty yards away. In the blaze of light they spied the distinctive helmets of enemy troops. Bullets smashed into the ground all around and tore past their heads, as the characteristic bark of MP40 'Schmeisser' sub-machine guns was joined by the terrifying buzz-whirr of an MG42 light machine gun – 'Hitler's buzzsaw'.

Turning on their heels, Walker-Brown, Leng and their guide ran for their lives, making for the shadows of the trees from where they had emerged just minutes before. Even as they sprinted for that cover, bullets whipped past their heads and ricocheted off the ground. Hurling themselves into the embrace of the woodland, they hit the deck, as bursts of fire thwacked into the trees, ripping off bark and spraying splinters in all directions. With the yells of enemy soldiers ringing in their ears, the three men knew for sure they had to keep moving. On their feet again, they dashed further into the woodland, breaking free on the far side. With barely a pause they pelted up the mountainside, as gradually the sounds of pursuit faded away behind.

Somehow, all three had escaped injury. Ambushed by several rapid-firing weapons from no more than two-dozen yards away, not one of them had suffered so much as a scratch. The gunners on that MG42 alone had unleashed a full belt of ammunition at them from very close range, plus those wielding the MP40s had blasted out magazines of ammo. And yet every single bullet had missed. It was as if the gods themselves had shielded them from harm.

A while later they arrived back at the ghost village, which was shrouded in darkness. The whole of the next day they lay low in the ruins of Nola, for no one fancied braving a repeat of the kind of murderous ambush of the night before. This time, if they went courting danger again, the gods might not be so benevolent.

The following morning Walker-Brown received welcome news. Reports were that the enemy were moving out in force. All signs were that the *rastrellamento* was petering out. On the one hand, this was a fabulous development. It was as if their prayers had been answered. On the other, it was an unfortunate turn of events, for it meant the *raison d'être* of Operation Galia was being frustrated.

If the enemy were in truth withdrawing, only one option lay open to Walker-Brown and his men: they would have to kick the hornet's nest once again, and kick it hard. The SAS commander gave the order to move out. They were heading back to the Rossano Valley. There Walker-Brown hoped to meet up with any others from his scattered unit who might have escaped and survived the purge.

The return to the Rossano Valley proved a bittersweet experience. While there were no confirmed reports of any SAS casualties, the partisans and the Italian villagers had suffered terribly. In addition to commander Siligato and those killed with him at Codolo village, many more partisan groups had taken casualties. But the worst were the purges against the civilians. Scores had been butchered by the Nazis and Fascists, and their houses torched in so-called 'reprisals'.

Hitler had vowed that for every German soldier killed by the partisans, ten Italians would be executed. Across Italy, General Kesselring was doing his utmost to make that edict a bloody reality. The reprisals were indiscriminate. Men, women, children, village priests – all were fair game; if a town or hamlet were so much as suspected of supporting partisan efforts, they were earmarked for the slaughter. It was worse still in this region, where locals stood accused of aiding and abetting the activities of the 'British parachutists', who seemed to strike at will and then disappear like ghosts.

Their return to Rossano was bolstered by the appearance of Lieutenant Riccomini, Walker-Brown's standout deputy, who had split from the main party in the aftermath of the Pontremoli raid. SOE Major Lett and his men were also there. And what tales Riccomini and Lett had to tell.

Having split from Walker-Brown and the main SAS group, Riccomini and his two companions had tried to execute their getaway, even as the German ski troops had closed in. Shortly, the young SAS lieutenant was unable to walk, due to the pain from his injured ankle. It was then that his partisan guide, Falco Montefiori, had stepped in. Hefting Riccomini onto his shoulders, they'd pressed on. They were making for a bridge over the nearby river, which, if they could slip across it, would speed their getaway. But to get there they would have to pass through a field full of German soldiers sleeping in bivouacs, for there was no other way. The three fugitives decided to brazen it out. After all, who else but German troops would likely pass through a massive encampment of German troops?

With Riccomini hobbling beside Montefiori, and an SAS trooper called Sumpter bringing up the rear, the three figures moved ahead, making little effort to hide. In the darkness of that massive encampment, the bluff seemed to hold good, for they slipped through unchallenged. Ahead lay the bridge, a good thirty feet from end to end. They reached it and began to cross, when, at the halfway point, they spied a squad of German soldiers approaching from the far side. With the bridge being so narrow, it was going to be impossible to pass by each other at anything other than close quarters. Their hearts pounding, the three men pressed ahead as if they had every right to be there. Somehow, they pulled it off – the Germans simply failed to notice anything untoward or to issue any challenge.

The immediate danger over, Montefiori scooped up Riccomini once more, for the SAS lieutenant was finding it almost impossible to walk. After a while they stumbled across a small hut. It was there that they found shelter, with Montefiori massaging Riccomini's ankle from time to time, to aid its recovery. Finally, the lack of food drove them out. Montefiori was able to lead them to a mill house, where the family fed and sheltered the three fugitives, at great risk to themselves. When finally Riccomini seemed well enough to walk once more, they struck out for the Rossano Valley.

SOE Major Lett's evasion from the *rastrellamento* had been equally daring, and again he'd escaped the enemy's clutches due to a large dash of good fortune. Shortly after Walker-Brown and his party had departed for the big attack on Pontremoli – the hunted hitting the hunters – German troops had descended upon Lett's redoubt in strength. The SOE agent and his men had been forced to flee across a snow-covered hillside, under intense fire from a German machine gun that had been sited next to the local church. With bullets chasing their heels, they'd made it into the shelter of a copse of trees on the far side. From there they'd made a dash for 'the relatively safe heights of Monte Picchiara' – a 3,800-foot peak that dominated the landscape.

As with Walker-Brown, Lett had reasoned that only by taking to the most challenging and inhospitable terrain possible might he slip the enemy trap. Others seemed to have been of a similar mind: en route, he'd run into several men from Walker-Brown's SAS squadron, whose numbers had been scattered to the four corners of the wind as the hunt intensified. At one point they had gazed down from the snow-bound heights, only to see Chiesa, the burned-out village into which the SAS had originally para-chuted, crawling with enemy troops.

Incredibly, one of the SAS men that Lett had linked up with was still doggedly clinging to his mortar tube, and others were still carrying rounds. That man, Trooper Lofty Rose, argued that he should open fire. Chiesa was a hugely tempting target. Enemy troops lay thick about its ruins, as they tried to pick up clues as to where the elusive 'British parachutists' might have got to. But on balance Lett reasoned that lobbing down a few mortar rounds was a bad idea. It might kill a few of the enemy, but it was bound to give away their position, at which point they would have a far superior enemy force on their tail.

Over the next few days Lett and his party played a deadly game of cat and mouse with the enemy. Due to his intimate knowledge of the area (aided by his partisan friends), Lett was able to evade capture. But it had been touch and go. One night, when hiding in a remote hut, they'd seen a pair of German soldiers approaching through the darkness. After challenging them in Italian, the enemy troops had opted to retreat. Quickly, Lett had alerted all. Gathering their gear, they'd sloped off into the thickest of the shadows. Just moments after they had made it into the nearest cover, the enemy had attacked in force, raking the hut they'd vacated with machine-gun fire and volleys of grenades.

Had Lett not been so alert, they would all have been killed or captured. A few days later, while sheltering in a village, they were again surrounded by the enemy. Making a break for it, they'd dashed across an open field, but were spotted. Taking fire from two machine guns, they'd flung themselves flat in the snow. But with the weather being so severe and visibility so bad, the enemy couldn't see properly, and were forced to fire at random. Realising this, Lett and the others again slipped away. In the process, Trooper Rose and his fellow SAS man, Trooper Gargan, seized a pair of German soldiers on the edge of a nearby woodland and took them prisoner.

With those two German prisoners in tow, Lett kept the men moving fast. Finally, having given the enemy the slip, they paused for a breather. Lett ordered one of the younger partisans to watch over the two Germans. Misunderstanding the SOE agent's shout to keep his eye on the prisoners, the young man raised his weapon and shot the nearest German, killing him instantly. It had been an instinctive reaction born out of shock and confusion. A misunderstanding leading to a tragic accident. All Major Lett was able to do was apologise to the second prisoner for what had occurred. The young partisan was devastated, once he realised his mistake, and appalled at what he had just done.

Yet in the village they'd just slipped away from, far worse was about to occur. This would be no accident. Realising how narrowly they had missed their prey – the 'British parachutists' – German troops visited their rage on the locals, shooting up houses and murdering their inhabitants. On learning this, all felt less guilty somehow about the accidental killing of one of the German captives. The following afternoon Lett's group had arrived back in the Rossano Valley, where he was reunited with Walker-Brown.

*

While the losses suffered by the SAS and SOE to the *rastrella-mento* appeared to be minimal, Walker-Brown felt he had scores to settle, especially after the murder of so many Italian villagers. But his desire to go on the offensive was overshadowed by their problems. Many of the supplies that they had cached in the Rossano Valley had been found. Worse still, communications back to headquarters had broken down completely, as the SAS and SOE agents alike had been forced into the snowbound hills. For seven days and seven nights, Major Roy Farran, at SFHQ in Bari, had had not a whisper of a message from his men in the field. He was deeply concerned.

Dispatching a signal in the vague hope that it might somehow get picked up, he expressed in coded terms the extent of his disquiet: 'To Bob, from Roy. My hair is going grey and I really am beginning to think you might have become a wooden soldier . . . If yours is sick try to find another blower round about. If you have stopped a fast one, I assume Julia is a little girl. Till I hear I will occasionally look at Huntsville, Brighton, Leeds and Richmond.' A 'wooden soldier' was code for being killed; 'another blower' meant another radio set, one that was working; 'Julia is a little girl' was code for 'endex' – the end of Operation Galia and all it had sought to achieve. If Walker-Brown was dead, the mission would die with him.

'Looking at Huntsville etc.' signified that Farran would ask for reconnaissance flights to be made over those drop zones, to check for any sign of an SAS presence on the ground. On 26 January one such recce flight had been made, but nothing had been seen. In desperation, Farran decided to send out a search party, one charged to discover the fate of Walker-Brown and his men. Codenamed Operation Brake Two, the team was to be led by Sergeant Sidney Guscott. It was to head into the area on foot, and sneak past the enemy by what was believed to be a small gap in the Gothic Line. Travelling with them would be an Italian partisan known only as 'Tullio', who was to act as their guide.

In truth, Tullio was renowned among Major Lett and his partisans, for he had been banished from the area some time back due to criminality. Somehow he had managed to cross the lines and curry favour with SFHQ, who had recruited him as a guide. Now he was poised to head back into an area he knew well, leading a small party of SAS on what was basically a proof-of-life mission. If Tullio could slip Guscott and his party through the Gothic Line, they were to seek out any traces of the missing SAS squadron, and their SOE comrades in arms.

Back in the Rossano Valley, Walker-Brown was oblivious to all of this. More to the point, he had no intention of letting 'Julia' become 'a little girl'. Calling a halt to Operation Galia was the last thing on his mind. As far as he was concerned, the mission had been a standout success, the *rastrellamento* of the past week proving it. The proof was in the proverbial pudding. Moreover, as far as he knew, all of his men had survived the round-up and they remained keen as mustard to fight, which meant he was determined to continue. And that meant it was crucial that he secured a resupply drop, somehow, by whatever means.

There was a spare radio set secreted at a hidden location. He sent a party to fetch it. Once that was safely in his hands, he tried to contact SFHQ. There was no joy, but he dispatched a message 'blind' anyway – one that he just had to hope would get picked up by Major Farran in Bari. He requested an urgent resupply drop, and asked for the Huntsville DZ to be used, for at the time it remained the only one which was not menaced by the enemy.

As Walker-Brown would later report, 'a German patrol . . . was forty minutes march from DZ "Brighton", and the Rossano area was the only comparatively safe base in the area. Signals were put out on DZ "Huntsville".'

Though Walker-Brown couldn't know it, his radio message did make it through. Farran could hear him. It was just radio traffic going back the other way – from Bari to the Rossano Valley – that seemed to be down. Regardless, Farran now knew that, somehow, Walker-Brown and his men had weathered the *rastrellamento*. Equally remarkably, they seemed raring to go – Julia was definitely not about to become a little girl. Tellingly, Walker-Brown's chief request was for more Vickers machine guns plus oodles of ammunition, to replace those they had been forced to abandon after the daring attack on Pontremoli.

But as the Italian winter bit hard, all Allied aircraft were grounded. It wasn't until 2 February 1945 that the vaguest hint of a weather window opened. As luck would have it, the American unit originally tasked to carry out resupply drops to Operation Galia, the US 62 Troop Carrier Group (TCG), had been replaced. The incoming outfit, the US 64 TCG, was commanded by a legendary figure, Colonel John Cerney. The long-serving and highly-decorated colonel would prove to have a far more bullish attitude than his predecessor. Typically, he'd shifted his aircraft and aircrews from the tiny Malignano Airfield (today's Siena-Ampugnano Airport) to a much larger airbase, located at Rosignano, which lay just a short hop over the mountains from Operation Galia's base of operations.

Appreciating the challenges of operating over the Rossano Valley, and aware of the recent crash with the loss of all crew, Colonel Cerney decided to fly the aircraft that was to attempt the drop himself. What followed would be described by the SOE's Major Lett as the 'most brilliant piloting ever seen'. Walker-Brown reached a similar conclusion in his own report on Colonel Cerney's heroics: 'The aircraft flew round for ninety minutes before seeing our signals. Weather conditions were terrible, with thick low clouds lying halfway down the mountains . . . Despite this . . . the pilot succeeded in recognising the DZ and making a number of exceedingly accurate runs in. The aircraft flew around no fewer than six times inside a high ring of mountains with tops completely obscured, and with little or no safety margin . . . About two hours later the same aircraft returned and repeated the same performance.'

Colonel Cerney's incredible courage and flying skills paid off, resulting in the successful drop of those much-needed supplies. Along with the rations, weaponry and ammo, he had also released one human parachutist – Captain Milne, of the Royal Army Medical Corps (RAMC). With cases of frostbite and serious illness spiralling among the SAS, Milne had been sent in to carry out medical assessments. Walker-Brown and his men had spent five weeks behind the lines under constant pressure, often in freezing, blizzard-like conditions, lacking in proper cold-weather kit and mostly deprived of good sustenance and rest. A doctor was exactly what was required.

Once the supplies had been sorted and the men's various ailments treated, Walker-Brown took stock. They had three brand new Vickers machine guns to hand, with ample ammo. The majority of his men remained fighting fit. Now was the time to formulate his plan of attack and to select targets, he decided. As he and Lett mulled their options for offensive action, they realized things would have to be done a little differently in the aftermath of the *rastrellamento*. The enemy commanders must have realised they had come away empty handed. As far as they were concerned, not a single 'British parachutist' had been captured or killed. As a result, in many areas significant German garrisons had been left behind, which had to signify that the hunt had only been put on hold, as opposed to being called off completely. It appeared to be *rastrellamento* paused, as opposed to abandoned.

In light of this, Lett figured that Walker-Brown would be better off shifting his base of operations. On the far side of the Alta Via – that ancient high-altitude Roman pathway – at Borseda, a remote hamlet, lay a partisan stronghold. The partisan commander, Dany Bucchioni, was a man that Lett trusted implicitly. More to the point, Borseda was ensnared by high mountains, making it all but immune to enemy predations, and especially in the depths of a snowbound winter the likes of which they were experiencing now. To Walker-Brown, Lett's suggestion seemed like a wise move. And so, on 5 February 1945, he and the whole of his SAS Squadron, barring a handful who were too sick to walk, began the trek to Borseda.

Upon reaching their new base of operations, the SAS commander decided to go out seeking targets that very night. Twenty kilometres to the south of Borseda lay the town of Padivarma, complete with its enemy garrison. On the night of 6 February, Walker-Brown executed a recce of the place, to assess if it might be deserving of a mortar attack. But having studied the town, he demurred. He was after a far juicier target. Ideally, it should be one that they had hit repeatedly already – and long before the *rastrellamento* had started to bite. A target that would demonstrate powerfully just how badly the *rastrellamento* had failed.

In short, Walker-Brown was seeking the ultimate provocation.

Inevitably, perhaps, that would take him and his men back to where it had all begun. Walker-Brown fell back upon the obvious choice of targets – the one they knew best. They'd return to Borghetto, the German garrison town that they had hit time after time, the one at which the P-47 Thunderbolts had played such a signature role, as the American pilots had swooped to attack, adding airborne impetus to the SAS's actions on the ground.

As Walker-Brown fully appreciated, Borghetto's defences had been seriously beefed up. A second German garrison had been established at nearby Brugnato, so those troops could race to the defence of their neighbours. But to Walker-Brown's way of thinking, that was all to the good. With so many enemy soldiers based in the area, the last thing they would ever expect was for the elusive 'British parachutists' to mount a strike against such a heavily garrisoned target. With that in mind, on the night of 7 February, Walker-Brown and his men set forth into the stiffening wind and snow, moving on what soon became a very familiar trail, for they had walked this way before.

This would have to be a 'smash-and-grab' raid. With so many enemy troops billeted thereabouts, they could not afford to linger. The objective – to make their presence felt painfully; to show that the *rastrellamento* had come to nothing – had to be achieved quickly and decisively. With that in mind, Walker-Brown got his men – and the Vickers – into position overlooking the road leading into Borghetto, an all-too-familiar stalking ground. Shortly, the telltale, shifting fingers of light pierced the darkness. A convoy was inbound.

The leading vehicles approached. Just as soon as they were within range, Walker-Brown gave the order to open fire. As one, their weapons burst into full-throated action, and the results of the ambush proved devastating. Within seconds the leading two trucks were riddled with fire, the combined bursts from the Vickers and the Brens tearing into them. The cabs were ripped open, the stricken vehicles grinding to a halt, and in seconds they had burst into flames. Behind them a third truck was put out of action, even as the driver frantically tried to avoid the same fate as suffered by his comrades up ahead.

By then the road had been transformed into a mass of burning, fiery wreckage. Accordingly, Walker-Brown gave the order to pack up and ship out. With that, his men loaded up their heavy weaponry and slipped back into the sanctuary of the hills, disappearing just as swiftly as they had materialised. Even as the sound of their gunfire had faded away, and the smell of cordite and burning vehicles drifted through the cold winter air, so another of Walker-Brown's patrols had been busy on their own hit-and-run operation.

Walker-Brown's veteran saboteur, Sergeant Rookes, had staked out the road leading north-east out of La Spezia – more familiar terrain for the SAS. He and his team had taken with them one of the freshly delivered Vickers machine guns, plus three Brens. They'd selected an audacious ambush point, directly above where a large body of German troops were bivouacking at the side of the road. Columns of trucks were shunting into position for the night, and mules were standing docilely near by. Once in position, Rookes gave the order to open fire.

Caught by total surprise, even as they were setting camp and bedding down in the darkness, the enemy troops were thrown into total disarray. Powerful blasts from the Vickers took out truck after truck. One by one they began to burn, hungry flames licking through the fuel spilled from ruptured tanks and throwing a blazing light across the scene. As the fire from the SAS's well-sited machine guns continued to hammer down, figures began to panic. As they tried to run and hide, they were caught in the glare of the burning vehicles, and everywhere they were chased by angry blasts of fire. A few desultory bursts of rifle fire came back the other way, but none of the shots were on target or caused Rookes and his men the barest concern.

Finally, with ammo running low and with few targets left to hit, Rookes gave the order to pull out. As the men trudged up the hillside, they left behind them a scene of fiery devastation. Rookes would later report that they had 'destroyed eight enemy vehicles and inflicted a large number of casualties'. As he and his men hurried into the hills, setting a course for their new base, a powerful message had been sent. In the course of one night, two daring raids by the elusive 'British parachutists' had caused carnage and devastation on both flanks of La Spezia, a sizeable city. In a humiliating reversal of its intended outcome, the weeklong *rastrellamento* had simply served to embolden those that it had been designed to kill and capture.

In short, the SAS had not been stopped and they were on the hunt once more.

Sadly, those 7 February raids did not go without repercussions, and once again it was the innocent and the vulnerable who bore the brunt of the enemy's ire. In the direct aftermath, German troops 'burnt down two houses at Stadano and one house at Manzile', targeting two villages that just happened to be near the sites where the SAS had struck from out of the darkness.

Now that word was out – that the *rastrellamento* had failed – anywhere was fair game, as far as Walker-Brown was concerned.

He sought more targets, alighting upon Padivarma, the nearest town to their new base of operations; the one that he had rec-ce'd just a few nights before. But Dany Bucchioni, the local partisan leader, argued against any such attack. Things had changed dramatically, Bucchioni argued, and especially since the enemy now knew the full extent of their failings, and that the British raiders were still at large. From his sources, Bucchioni had learned that after the SAS's most recent attacks, German troops were moving out of their billets. Instead, they were demanding to be accommodated in the houses of Italian civilians.

In effect, they were using the locals as human shields.

Walker-Brown was aware of what a delicate – some would argue impossible – position that landed him and his men in. He con-cluded in his mission report that 'any attack on Padivarma would undoubtedly cause casualties to civilians, which, in Bucchioni's opinion would damage Allied popularity.' If the Italian villagers turned against the SAS, their kind of operations would be ren-dered all but impossible. In light of this he was forced to call off the attack he was planning, and to halt operations as they reassessed.

For two days Walker-Brown kicked his heels at their Bordesa base, wondering what to do next. On the morning of 10 February an aircraft hove into view, dropping 'operational money and comforts'. Little did the SAS commander or his men know, but this was to be Operation Galia's final air drop. Back at SAS headquarters, Colonel Franks – the man who had recruited Walker-Brown into the unit in the first place – was arguing that Galia had achieved all its objectives, and it was time to pull the men out. That very day, 10 February, Walker-Brown was advised to start the exfiltration of his troops, moving on foot back to Allied lines.

At first he declined. But upon reflection he began to see the sense in what Colonel Franks was suggesting. By now, many of his men were unwell. It was hardly surprising. They'd been on the go for the best part of six weeks, operating in the harshest of conditions with never enough rest. They were heavily fatigued. Even so, they had done all that Walker-Brown had asked of them, and more. After talking it through with his doctor, Captain Milne, Walker-Brown realised that to continue with the mission would be courting disaster.

There was another factor that compelled Walker-Brown to pull out – the increasing brutality with which the Germans, and the Italian Fascists, were treating the locals. Horrific reprisals were being carried out. As Walker-Brown recalled later, in a chilling account: 'I saw with my own eyes, sixteen young men and girls, all under twenty, lined up against the wall of a church and machine-gunned by the German Field Police. And also, six senior citizens who were strung up by meat hooks to lamp posts . . .' Walker-Brown cited these terrible experiences as one of his key reasons to withdraw. 'I signalled the SAS base and suggested we withdrew to be redeployed.'

And so, finally, it was decided that 'Julia' would indeed become 'a little girl'.

It was time to go.

For the exfiltration, Walker-Brown split his squadron into two. He was to lead the first group out himself. With him would be his own stick (HQ Troop), Sergeant Rookes's No. 3 stick and Lieutenant Gibbon's No. 4 stick. Captain Milne, the medic, would accompany him, along with a small group of partisans, commanded by Pippo Siboldi, who had done such sterling work on some of their earliest raids. Lieutenant Riccomini, whose ankle was now sufficiently healed, would follow twenty-four hours later, with his own No. 2 stick and Sergeant Wright's No. 1 stick.

They would be forced to leave behind one man. Parachutist Lofty Rose, of HQ Troop, would have to stay with Gordon Lett, for he was simply too sick to travel. Rose was instructed to make his own way back to Allied lines when he was fit enough to do so.

The route out leading across the Gothic Line was well-known. Over the past twelve months Lett and his partisans had used it repeatedly, spiriting escaped POWs back to Allied lines. For the first part, Walker-Brown and his party would be led by guides supplied by Dany Bucchioni, with others taking over along the way. But typically, Walker-Brown didn't want to fade out quietly. On the contrary, he was determined to go out with a bang. As Major Farran would report, on 10 February: 'Bob now pulling out, ambushing en route.' Walker-Brown was determined to give the enemy one or two parting shots.

At 1530 hours on 10 February, he and his party set out. Riccomini had been left with orders to carry out his own ambushes and sabotage work, as his party was to follow after a day's delay. Seeking to move light and fast, Walker-Brown decided to leave the heavy Vickers machine-guns for the partisans to make use of. The first leg of his and his party's journey snaked south-east some thirteen kilometres, to the tiny village of Bruscarolo. Fortunately the weather had turned mild, at least compared to what had gone before, and the SAS made good progress.

The following night they pressed on, linking arms in a human chain to cross the wide and fast-flowing Magra river. Beyond that lay the road leading into La Spezia – the very stretch of highway that Sergeant Rookes and his men had targeted just a few days earlier. Back then, they'd shot up that roadside enemy encampment in spectacular fashion. Right now, Walker-Brown was keen to leave his parting gift to the enemy along the same stretch of highway. He'd received intelligence that a German unit patrolled this route every night, and he set his men into ambush positions to await their arrival. But no one showed.

Walker-Brown was torn. Did he seek another target, or continue with the move south to Allied lines? Finally, he decided upon the latter course of action, which he justified in his mission report in the following terms: 'It was inadvisable to attack a road at a point on the escape route as it might interfere with . . . the second [SAS] party who were to come on later. It was not possible to attack the road to the north as there were enemy patrols reported . . . It was not possible to attack the road to the south because the partisans had blown a bridge . . . and there was a very large scale enemy reprisal in progress with artillery, mortars and MGs.'

Captain Milne, the medical officer, also added a voice of reason, advising that 'the men were exceedingly tired' and that long detours and delays could cost them dear. As Milne pointed out, 'the men carried two days rations only in the shape of bully,' short for Bully Beef – tins of corned beef with a small amount of added gelatine, a staple ration for British troops. In other words, they didn't have the reserves of food nor the energy to risk haring off after new targets, with all that might follow.

After moving on, Walker-Brown finally called a rest stop. Their uniforms were soaked from crossing the Magra river, and one man, Corporal Johnson, decided to remove his trousers in an effort to dry them. Draping them over what he thought was a low wall, much to his dismay the garments slithered out of view. Glancing over the 'wall', Johnson realised what had happened. It was the side of a well, and his trousers had dropped into its shadowy depths many feet below. Unable to retrieve them, Johnson was forced to continue on his way trouser-less, much to the ridicule of his brothers-in-arms.

Early on 12 February they reached a point where they changed guides, in preparation for the next leg of their journey. Their route lay south over Monte Boscoletto, a peak in the Apennines just short of 2,000 feet high, and then on through two remote villages, Vinca and Forno. From there the final leg would entail scaling the 5,200-foot-high Monte Altissimo, using a narrow pass that snaked between where two German Army regiments were positioned. On the far side of Monte Altissimo they hoped to link up with the Allied forces that were encamped there. To help steer the way, Walker-Brown had with him a map, a gift from Dany Bucchioni, one that detailed all the known German positions.

Still, what lay before them was daunting in the extreme. During one of the worst winters on record, and woefully ill-equipped for such a punishing trek over snow-bound, mountainous terrain, they faced being hunted and harried every step of the way. After some six weeks operating behind enemy lines, they were also ailing, plagued by exhaustion and malnourishment, and dressed in uniforms that were torn, ripped and threadbare.

As they pressed on the going got decidedly tougher. The terrain here was very different from that of the Rossano Valley, the ground underfoot being so much harsher and more severe. As a result, men who were already close to finished were pushed to the very brink. Of course, there was no option but to fight through.

For the whole of 13 February they marched on towards Vinca, after which Forno beckoned, a village lying some six kilometres further south, over some of the most inhospitable terrain imaginable. Theirs was a long and desperate slog, entailing hour after hour of marching through appalling conditions.

By the time they reached Vinca village, the men were frozen stiff and plagued by exhaustion. It was now that Walker-Brown faced a difficult decision. They were moving into territory that would be crawling with the enemy, but if they continued to lug their heavier weapons, he didn't think they would make it. 'Owing to the physical condition of the men, it was not possible for them to carry much on the last stage of the march,' Walker-Brown would later report. There was no option but to dump their Bren guns – their most potent firepower – leaving them with the local partisans.

As they readied themselves for a final superhuman effort – the ascent of Monte Altissimo – it struck Walker-Brown that the atmosphere in Vinca was tense and strained. The locals there were far less relaxed and welcoming than those in the Rossano Valley. It turned out that they had good reason for their disquiet. The previous summer, when the Germans had begun building fortifications along the Gothic Line, there had been sporadic attacks by local partisans. The Germans had been quick to react, for nothing was to be allowed to frustrate the raising of those monumental defences. On 24 August 1944, Waffen-SS troops – the armed wing of the SS – had set fire to two villages at the base of the mountain, before commencing an operation focused on Vinca itself.

Backed by the Brigata Nera, the Waffen-SS ascended the hillside and surrounded Vinca. Nearly all the men of the village were either out working in the fields, or had slipped away to the mountains. Over the ensuing hours of bloody horror, over 150 villagers were slaughtered. The ages of the victims ranged from eighty-four to a baby just two days old. Not content with such savagery, the killers returned over the next forty-eight hours to mutilate the bodies, beheading some and impaling skulls and corpses on stakes. This was intended to serve as a heinous 'warning' to any who might think to join the partisans, or to attempt to frustrate the work along the Gothic Line.

That had been six months ago. As the surviving villagers were painfully aware, the presence of Walker-Brown and his SAS troops at Vinca could bring about similar reprisals. Understandably, they wanted the 'British parachutists' gone as quickly as possible. But even so, what shocked and surprised the SAS most was the extent of the welcome they were offered, in spite of the recent horrors visited on this place. Locals shared what little food they had, and offered their barns as shelter for the British troops. This in a village that the Nazis had tried to wipe off the face of the earth.

Just after dawn the following day, 14 February, the SAS party set out. Before them lay the long and impossible-seeming climb up Monte Altissimo, somewhere on the far side of which lay Allied lines. The steep slopes were cut by fast-flowing, icy rivers, and time and again the party had to link arms to forge a way across. The enemy frontline was close now, and Walker-Brown kept urging all to keep hyper-alert. They were very lightly armed, and if they stumbled into a German patrol they could put up only a limited fight. Their only chance lay in remaining hidden and then slipping through unnoticed.

After fording another river, their vigilance paid off. The sound of giggling and laughter was detected from a patch of bushes. Creeping ahead silently, Walker-Brown and his men discovered a German *hauptmann* – captain – in a very compromising position with a young woman. Realising he'd been caught in flagrante, and with the weapons of a number of wild-looking British soldiers levelled at him, the officer quickly pulled up his trousers and put his hands in the air.

As for the woman, she was red-faced with embarrassment and seemed scared out of her wits. Walker-Brown let her go, but there would be no such clemency for the loved-up German officer. Indeed, after learning of the fate of the villagers of Vinca, sympathy for the enemy was in precious short supply right then. Walker-Brown figured that officer might come in useful. Marched ahead at gunpoint, he could be forced to converse with any German patrols they might encounter, for by far the most risk-laden part of the journey lay before them.

Seizing the moment, Corporal Johnson approached Walker-Brown and asked if he might possibly have the *hauptmann*'s trousers, his own having tumbled down the well. Tickled pink at the suggestion, Walker-Brown considered it for a moment. Finally, he refused Johnson's entirely reasonable request, for he argued that surely a German officer without his trousers would arouse more suspicion than one who was fully clothed. A trouserless *hauptmann* was hardly very likely to be able to talk them through enemy lines.

Late that afternoon, the fugitives arrived at Forno village, with their German prisoner in tow. Just as with Vinca, this place had also suffered at the hands of the forces of Nazi Germany. On 13 June 1944 the village had been attacked by enemy troops.

Lining up some sixty men along a river gorge, all were machine-gunned, their bullet-riddled bodies tumbling down the slope behind. Some of the dead of Forno had been only in their teens.

At Forno, they discovered four American airmen who were also trying to make it across the Gothic Line. Walker-Brown invited them to tag along. He decided they should push on under cover of the gathering night. If they did, then it was possible they could reach Allied lines by morning. He gave orders for the men to dump their rucksacks and everything else that might weigh them down. They'd press ahead taking only their trusty M1 carbines and spare ammunition.

As they prepared to set out, the guides who had steered them thus far proved reluctant to continue. Ahead, the terrain was thick with enemy. As Walker-Brown would note, the guides had heard reports of German troops reconnoitring the 'escape route on the western side of Monte Altissimo' – the very one that Walker-Brown and his men were about to attempt. To add to their worries, 'an enemy patrol was believed to have laid fresh minefields.'

After much cajoling, the guides were persuaded to carry on, but they suggested a change of direction. The well-worn track that stretched ahead was very possibly mined, yet higher up the hillside ran an ancient shepherd's path. It was likely that the enemy didn't even know of its existence. They should take to that immediately, the guides suggested, even as the light began to fade and the huge expanse of Monte Altissimo reared before them, dark and forbidding.

Walker-Brown agreed. They set out, the going arduous in the extreme. Up near-vertical slopes they trudged, battling through thick snow and ice, all the while the German *hauptmann* being

312

forced ahead, and with Walker-Brown's pistol aimed squarely at his back. For two thousand feet the men ascended. Although desperately tired and fatigued, they forced leaden legs to propel them ever upwards. The prize of the Allied frontline drew them on, for it lay over the far side of the mountain. There they could finally allow themselves to rest in warmth and comfort, after six weeks in near-Arctic conditions.

An hour before midnight, in the pitch darkness, they reached the top of Monte Altissimo. Thankfully it should be all downhill from there. Just as they prepared for the descent, the crump of exploding mortars echoed through the night. A German mortar crew were blasting rounds onto the track that snaked between the two enemy positions. Whether they were doing so to deter any would-be escapees, or were specifically targeting someone moving along that route, it was impossible to say. Either way, taking to this high shepherd's track had turned out to be a wise move indeed.

Moving like wraiths, the men began to descend, taking great care to maintain a foothold on the ice-covered rocks. Thirty minutes after moving off, something was spotted up ahead. Figures were moving up-slope, shrouded in the darkness. Unslinging their carbines, the SAS prepared for action. If they needed to fight their way through, then so be it. They had not come this far to fall at the final hurdle. As eyes strained to cut through the dark, the distant figures took shape and form – it was a patrol of four enemy soldiers.

No sooner had they spied the SAS up ahead, guns at the ready, than the German troops decided that discretion was very much the better part of valour. As one, they dashed off the path, making their escape 'into a gully', as Walker-Brown would report.

The SAS party moved off, their senses on high alert. By now it was now 0300 hours on 15 February. To the east, the first hint of dawn was lightening the horizon. That underlined the urgency of keeping on the move. Once the sun was up, they would stand far less chance of making it through, for obvious reasons.

Pushing onwards, all of a sudden the *hauptmann* at the front stumbled to a halt. An instant later, there was a detonation and something fiery went rocketing into the night. Up above it burst like a blinding mini-sun – a burning light hanging suspended in the dark heavens. The German officer must have triggered a tripwire which in turn had unleashed 'a white phosphorous flare', lighting up the area all around. Instantly, the fugitives dived for cover, bracing themselves to be hit by an enemy bombardment. But as the flare drifted down to earth and the light fizzled out, no enemy fire came their way. Somehow, they seemed to have remained undetected.

After that horrendous scare, Walker-Brown got them moving again. They pushed on for an hour, inching ahead and trying to scan the route for any further tripwires. Ahead, a series of stark, blocky silhouettes melted out of the darkness. A barn. An open shelter. Houses. A village lay before them – whether deserted or occupied, there was no way of knowing. With their senses on maximum alert, they crept towards the nearest buildings. Getting one section to cover the first house, Walker-Brown led a small body of men silently forward.

He paused, then grabbed a handful of stones. Once he was within range, he chucked first one and then another at the nearest window. If anyone was within, surely they would come to investigate. A moment later the window was swung wide. A face gazed out at them. It had the unmistakable features of one of the Buffalo Soldiers – a black American GI. Misunderstanding who was outside, and thinking Walker-Brown and his men were Germans, a minute later the front door opened and 'out came a whole platoon . . .'

The mix-up was quickly dealt with, as Walker-Brown explained that they were British soldiers who had just exfiltrated through enemy lines. That understanding being reached, he was informed that he and his men had reached the American military's most forward position along this stretch of the frontline. They had made it. They had done it. After nearly seven weeks operating behind enemy lines, Bob Walker-Brown and the first group from Operation Galia had made it through to Allied lines.

Their escape had crowned what had been a spectacularly successful mission.

Some days later Lieutenant Riccomini would also cross over the Gothic Line, leading the remaining Operation Galia SAS force to safety. In a striking irony, just as Walker-Brown and Riccomini and their men had made it back, so Sergeant Guscott and the men of Operation Break Two had reached the Rossano Valley – those men dispatched by Major Farran weeks earlier, to try to discover the fate of Walker-Brown and his force. Guscott would be ordered to remain in the area to give SOE Major Lett whatever assistance he might require. He would exfiltrate later, when Lett and his team finally moved out.

The diversion of thousands of German troops away from the Gothic Line near the city of La Spezia, to deal with the repeated sabotage operations of the SAS, had given the Allies the vital time they required to stiffen their defences. Two brigades of the 8th Indian Infantry Division had been moved across the

Apennines, to reinforce the US 92nd Division, the focus of the German counter-attack. Although some ground had been lost, the arrival of those reinforcements had prevented the enemy from pushing any further south.

Following the outstanding success of Operation Galia, Walker-Brown was immediately promoted to major and awarded the Distinguished Service Order (DSO) for the part he had played commanding the mission. His recommendation for the DSO was written up by Major Farran, and it stands as a fitting testament to Walker-Brown's courage and the achievements of those men he commanded.

On 27th December 1944 Captain Walker-Brown and thirty all ranks were dropped by parachute in the Apennines about a hundred and sixty kilometres behind the enemy lines . . . Immediately he began offensive activities against enemy lines of communication . . . Although handicapped by deep snow and very rugged terrain, he marched his men over the mountains, attacking enemy transport columns, mortaring enemy held villages, mining roads and ambushing marching columns, until the enemy was compelled to reply with a total of ten thousand troops . . . Captain Walker-Brown succeeded in avoiding the enemy net and preserving his force intact by a display of unparalleled guerrilla skill and personal courage. After the enemy drive was over, he renewed his attacks with undiminished vigour.

In addition to being responsible for the whole of the operation, on 30 Dec '44 whilst commanding an ambush on enemy vehicles travelling along the Genoa–Spezia road, he personally accounted for four of the enemy. On 4 Jan '45, despite enemy patrols on the same road, he successfully laid a mine on which a truck was destroyed, 12 Germans killed and 8 wounded. In attacks personally led by him a total of 60 Germans were killed or wounded.

During the months behind the lines, Walker-Brown's force destroyed twenty-three enemy vehicles, carried out . . . mortar attacks on enemy billets and machine-gunned at short range two large columns of marching troops. This magnificent record would not have been possible in the mountains in winter if Walker-Brown had not led his men with such vigour, enterprise, and complete disregard for personal safety.

When ordered to withdraw, Walker-Brown successfully exfiltrated his party intact through the enemy lines to safety. It is considered that his activities were perfect examples of how guerrilla operations of this sort should be carried out.

As Farran would subsequently write, when telling his own wartime story, in *Winged Dagger*, Operation Galia was a standout achievement with which few wartime missions could compare. 'Walker-Brown was dropped into the area,' Farran remarked, 'where he fought outstanding guerrilla actions for three months, in spite of the severe Arctic conditions, lack of supplies, and the fact that the enemy swept the area with over six thousand troops.' Coming from a figure of Farran's stature, that was fine praise indeed.

Already a recipient of the MBE, for previous missions behind enemy lines, including a daring escape from the enemy in September 1943, Lieutenant James Riccomini was to receive the

Military Cross for his participation in Operation Galia. The citation praised his personal skill, outstanding bravery and fortitude in the face of enemy fire, not to mention his role as a standout leader and inspiration to those he commanded. His actions were summed up as being exceptional, and far beyond the call of duty.

Following Operation Galia, Lieutenant Riccomini was soon in action once more. Less than two months after returning from the Rossano Valley, he formed part of a fifty-man SAS squadron, commanded by Major Roy Farran, which attacked a German military headquarters located in two villas in Botteghe d'Albinea, in the hills above Reggio Emilia in northern Italy. This daring mission was known as Operation Tombola. On 27 March 1945, while leading the assault on one of the villas, Riccomini was killed by machine-gun fire. He was twenty-seven years old.

Falco Montefiori, the partisan who had carried Lieutenant Riccomini on his back through German positions during the *rastrellamento*, did not receive any award from the Allies for his bravery, despite Major Lett's recommendations. Partisan commander Pippo Siboldi, who had fought alongside the SAS and exfiltrated with Walker-Brown and his party, volunteered to join Major Farran's Operation Tombola team. However, having had no parachute training, he broke his collar bone on landing and took no part in the action that ensued.

Immediately after the war, partisan commander Dany Bucchioni worked for a while with the British, before rejoining the Italian Army and rising to the rank of major general. He was also recommended for an award by Major Lett, for his work on Operation Blundell Violet. Bucchioni's citation concluded that as a result of his sterling efforts large numbers of escaped Allied

POWs had regained their freedom. The award of the King's Medal was confirmed by the Allied Screening Commission, but Bucchioni was not to receive it until 2001. He was also awarded an OBE in 2005 for his wartime service and his kindred spirit towards Britain ever since.

Of the thirty-three SAS men who parachuted into the Rossano Valley on 27 December 1944, twenty-seven made it back safely across the Gothic Line. For the six men of Lieutenant Shaughnessy's No. 5 stick, taken captive in the earliest days of Operation Galia, their story didn't end there, of course. After being taken to the prison at La Spezia, they were beaten regularly as their Fascist and German captors tried to extract as much information as possible. However, not a man among them was to reveal the slightest scrap of intelligence that would jeopardise the mission. When asked how many British parachutists had landed, Shaughnessy told his captors, defiantly, that thousands had already been dropped, with a similar number still to follow.

Shaughnessy kept up that pretence, warning his captors that the war would soon be over and that if any harm should be done to his men, those responsible would be hunted down and put to death, especially since the local partisans knew exactly who they were and would pass their names on to Allied forces. Fearing the truth of the SAS lieutenant's threats, none of the captives were handed over to the SS, whose methods would have been far more extreme and very likely terminal.

After two months the captives were forced to move. They joined a large body of POWs being marched through horrendous conditions north towards Germany. With little food and with many suffering from frostbite, those who fell behind were simply shot where they lay. All the way, Shaughnessy kept up his men's spirits. They were SAS, trained for trials such as this, he reminded them, and they would endure. Endure they did, finally reaching a POW camp in Germany in March 1945. After a month in captivity, they were liberated by American forces in April 1945.

Despite being captured, Lieutenant Shaughnessy and his men had shown great courage and tenacity. Shaughnessy's leadership and spirit had kept them going and had endeared him to his men greatly. Of course, the fact that none had broken, even under violent interrogation, had meant that Walker-Brown and the rest of the SAS Squadron were able to continue with their mission so successfully.

Once the Allies were ready for their big push through the Gothic Line, Major Gordon Lett had been recalled to SOE headquarters in Florence. Along with his SOE comrade Lieutenant Chris Leng, and the by then fully recovered SAS Sergeant Lofty Rose, he finally exfiltrated through the Gothic Line on 22 March 1945. Lett was awarded the DSO for his Operation Blundell Violet mission, the final part of the citation reading: 'Throughout the past eighteen months, Major Lett has shown conspicuous gallantry and devotion to duty. His work with the partisan forces is of the highest order and his courage and leadership are amply testified . . . He is most strongly recommended for the award of the immediate DSO.'

Lett was also awarded the Silver Medal for Military Valour by the Italian government. The Blundell Violet mission was responsible for assisting hundreds of POWs back to Allied lines, in the aftermath of the Italian Armistice. Lett remained in Italy until 1950, serving first as the Allied Military Governor in Pontremoli, and then in the British Consulate in the northern city of Bologna. The legacy of his time in the Rossano Valley was to plague his health, causing him to suffer a stroke in 1972. Learning of this, Walker-Brown wrote to him, revealing how saddened he was to hear of Lett's ill-health, and praising his bravery and resolve, which was almost without equal. Walker-Brown also acknowledged the enormous debt the SAS owed to Lett, from the war years. Fine sentiments indeed.

Gordon Lett died in 1989 at the age of seventy-nine. Bob Walker-Brown was to write his obituary in the SAS regimental magazine, *Mars and Minerva*.

After the war, and following the disbandment of the SAS, Bob Walker-Brown rejoined the Highland Light Infantry, and would go on to play a central role in British Special Forces, something that reflected his outstanding wartime service. Disbanded in October 1945, the SAS was reformed in the early 1950s and Walker-Brown duly signed up with 21 SAS (the territorial unit), as a 'training major', before being appointed to '22 SAS as second in command' and going on to command 23 SAS (the second territorial SAS regiment). Finally, he served with the Defence Intelligence Staff before 'retiring from the Army in 1964'. He settled in Wiltshire and died on 16 August 2009 at the age of ninety.

Walker-Brown left an enduring legacy, nowhere more typified than in his courageous and bold actions in and around the Rossano Valley, and on escaping from the enemy's clutches and bringing his men safely back to Allied lines. Although his route into the SAS had been somewhat unorthodox, it was clear that Colonel Franks had seen in the young captain all the attributes required to be an officer in Britain's elite forces – strength of will, fearlessness, fortitude, imagination and empathy, plus an undying determination to get the job done.

His leadership of Operation Galia, and the epic escape that followed, proved he had those vital qualities in abundance. He was a commander who typified what made the Special Air Service so very special. In leading his men to safety, Walker-Brown had made history in pulling off one of the most incredible escape and evasions in the annals of the SAS.

Acknowledgements

First and foremost, thank you to my esteemed readers. You go out and buy my books, in the hope that each will deliver an enjoyable, rewarding, illuminating read; another work that brings a story to life in vivid detail. I am most grateful and I hope I have managed to deliver that kind of reading experience in this book. Without you, there could be no author such as myself. You enable individuals like me to make a living from writing. You deserve the very first mention.

A huge thank you to all the family members of those depicted in these pages, without whose assistance and support I could not have written this book. Especially forthcoming and helpful were the Cary-Elwes family, principally Cate, who invited me into her Oxford home to peruse her father's wartime memorabilia and papers, after which we shared such a rich correspondence and many 'eureka moments' concerning his wartime activities.

Major Oswald Cary-Elwes' grandchildren also deserve special mention, including Richard, Gerald and Thomas. Thank you to all of you for the time we spent together discussing your grandfather's extraordinary wartime exploits. Huge thanks are also due to the late Clare Vining (née Cary-Elwes), who translated from the original French the book *I Chose The Storm*, by French resistance heroine Marie Chamming's.

I extend enormous thanks also to Gerald Hough, the son of Anthony Hough, who corresponded with me generously over his father's wartime service, and who read and commented so graciously on early drafts of that chapter in this book. Thank you.

Thank you Fiona Ferguson (née Mayne) and her husband, Norman, for inviting me into your family home, so that I might delve into Captain Robert Blair Mayne's war chest and wartime memorabilia, and to discuss with you his wartime and post-war story. I have gained invaluable insight in the process. I am most grateful.

Thank you to Scott Hackney, for sharing with me the private family archive of Charlie Hackney, including his unpublished account of the war years, and associated materials from the Hackney family archives, and for your correspondence over the same.

Thank you to David Farran, son of SAS commander Roy Farran, for sharing with me the materials you were able, and for your kind permission to quote from your father's excellent writings, and for our correspondence over the years regarding his standout wartime service. I am most grateful.

Thanks to Eric Lecomte, for corresponding with me over various aspects of the SAS service in France, as covered in this book. Special thanks to Thomas Liaudet and all at the AFPSAS, for your kind and tireless help in my research into the French aspects of the story told in these pages. Thanks also to Anthony Watrin, for your correspondence and insight into SAS operations in France.

A very special thank you to the late, great Pierre-Jean Cabut, for all of the help and guidance you were able to provide to me from your home in France. 'P-J', as he was known to all, sadly passed away just as this book was nearing completion, so he will never get to read a final copy. You were a champion of the cause of the SAS in France, doing so much to commemorate their operations and to keep the memory alive. Thank you and rest in peace.

Thank you to Will Ward, of CART Dorset, for providing the various insights and the press cutting for the Operation Colossus chapter – these all proved invaluable. Thank you also for introducing me to Joanna Burri-Weaver, the daughter of SAS Major Peter Weaver MC, and for enabling me to read the unpublished manuscript of her father's wartime service.

Thank you to Joanna Burri-Weaver for inviting me into your Purbeck home and for the long discussions we held about your father's wartime service, and for allowing me to peruse his wartime memorabilia and records, and especially for showing me the SAS's magnificent wartime flag.

Thank you also to Noelle McElhatton for introducing yourself to me at the Chartwell Literary Festival, and for sharing with me your sources and insights into the wartime service of SAS commander Colonel Blair 'Paddy' Mayne, DSO.

I have benefited greatly in the research for this book from the resources that the British, French and other governments, and related institutions, have invested into preserving for posterity the archives from the Second World War era. The preservation and cataloguing of a mountain of papers – official reports, personal correspondence, telegrams, etc. – plus photographic, film and sound archives is vital to authors such as myself, without which books of this nature could not be written. Devoting resources to the preservation of this historical record, and to making it accessible to the public, is something for which these governments and other institutions deserve high praise.

I extend a special thank you to the Imperial War Museum (IWM), whose archives are a treasure trove of some wonderful oral histories and the collections of private papers, without which I would not have been able to render the chapters told in this book as I have. The IWM archivists, likewise, deserve special mention, for reaching out to the families of those whose archives they hold, to secure the kind permission that I sought to quote from their private papers.

Thanks as ever to Julie Davies, ace researcher and translator, for your fine translations that I relied upon to tell some of these tales, and your astute and pertinent observations, assessment and guidance regarding same; but most of all for your heartfelt enthusiasm that these stories deserved to be told. Thanks also to Paul McKay and Ged Basson for offering a reader's view on early drafts.

Finally, I extent a massive thank you to fellow historian and author John McKay, whose contributions to the chapters as related in these pages were invaluable, and whose support, encouragement, insight and inspiration proved an invaluable support.

All at my publishers deserve the very best of praise for their committed, enthusiastic and visionary support of this project from the get-go. In the UK, Richard Milner, my long-standing editor, provided seminal guidance and feedback. The wider Quercus team also deserve the highest praise, and especially Hannah Robinson,

Dave Murphy and Jon Butler. Thank you also to Sophie Ransom, of Ransom PR, for your huge enthusiasm for this story from the very outset, and for working your special magic. In the USA the publishing team at Kensington Books were superlative, as always.

I need to extend my heartfelt thanks to my oldest daughter, Teän, for her sterling efforts and immense skills as applied to the Great Escapes series – you were there at the very start, and enabled me to bring what was then only a concept and a dream to a published reality. For that I am immensely grateful. And of course, I'd crave your indulgence and understanding for a father who spent far too many years away in the world's most obscure places and war zones, when you were growing up. I owe much to your love and forbearance.

Finally, I need to extend my deep thanks and heartfelt gratitude to my wife, Eva, and to David, Damien Jr and Sianna, who once again had to put up with 'Pappa' spending far too long locked in his study trying to do justice to this story. That I have – if I have – I owe to you all; to your love and support and kindness, and for putting up with me through it all.

This is a special story for the Lewis family, if for no other reason than my wife has played a very hands-on role in the research, archiving and transcribing the revisions of this book, not to mention overseeing the administration side of things. You stayed the course over the long months that it has taken to come to fruition, for which I am hugely grateful.

Acknowledgements on Sources

I am indebted to the following authors (and/or estates), who have covered some of the aspects of the story I have dealt with in *SAS Great Escapes Three* in their own writing. I extend my gratitude to those who kindly granted me permission to quote from their material. For readers whose interest has been piqued by this book, these authors and their titles would reward further reading (full details in the Bibliography that follows):

John Parker, whose father, Sapper Alfred Parker's memoir of his escape from PG78 (Sulmona) assisted greatly with the first chapter, and is contained in The Pegasus Archive.

Harold Tanky Challenor, whose book, *SAS and the Met*, tells of the time he spent during the Second World War soldiering (mostly) with the SAS, and of his incredible escapes.

Gerald Hough, whose biography of his father, Major Anthony Hough, entitled *Desert Raids with The SAS*, is an excellent account of his full wartime history.

Marie Chamming's, whose wartime biography, *I Chose the Storm* (translated from the French by Clare Vining), reveals much about the escape story of Major Oswald Cary-Elwes and his SAS party.

Monty Halls' book, *Escaping Hitler*, furnishes a fine account of the mission led by Bob Walker-Brown, and of particular note is Halls' retracing of the SAS party's escape route.

Brian Lett, whose books featuring the wartime story of his father, SOE Major Gordon Lett, and the Italian partisans and others, are *The SAS in Tuscany 1943–1945* and *An Extraordinary Italian Imprisonment*.

Malcolm Tudor, whose book *SAS In Italy 1943–1945*, covers Operation Galia in some detail.

Robert Hann, whose book featuring his father, Stanley Hann, *SAS Operation Galia*, tells the story of that mission.

Blair 'Paddy' Mayne, whose wartime compilation/diary/scrapbook, *The Paddy Mayne Diary (SAS War Diary 1941–45)*, constitutes a fine record of that regiment's wartime history.

Sources

Material quoted from the UK archive files listed below, is by kind courtesy of the UK National Archives. This book contains public-sector information licensed under the Open Government Licence v3.0.

Material quoted from the French archive files, and other sources listed herein, is by kind courtesy of the Service Historique de la Défense/Ministère des Armées (France).

Imperial War Museum

IWM 337 – Private Papers of Captain M. J. Pleydell MC
IWM 16909 Handscombe, Albert Edward (Oral History)
IWM 20604 Walker-Brown, Robert John (Oral History)

The National Archives

WO 208/3316 A Parker E & E report
DEFE 2/152 Final Report
DEFE 2/153 Planning

PREM 3/100 WSC

AIR 2/7450 Early Plans

CAB 106/8 Witness

CAB 79/9/13

WO 373/95/454

WO 373/95 – Escapes from Campo 21, Italy, Recommendations for Awards

WO 208/5399 – Capt. ER MacDermott escape report

WO 208/3316 – Lt RC Rickett escape report

DEFE 2/357 – Operation Marigold

WO 218/177 – Operation Speedwell

WO 373/63/129 – Escapes from Campo 102

WO 208/3319 – Debrief

WO 373/96/358 – Citation

WO 373/186

WO 205/211 – Operation Galia Preliminary Report

HS 6/830 – Operation Blundell Violet

WO 204/220 – SAS Operation Order Number 1 Operation Galia

AIR 20/8843 – SAS Signals

CAB 103/586 – Loan of Field Marshal Rommel's war diaries to the Enemy Documents Section (EDS)

PREM 3/330/9 – Combined Operations

WO 218/102 – Signals

WO 373/46 – Citations

WO 373/185/19 – Citations

HS 9/976/9 – SOE

WO 373/26/79 – Citations

WO 208/5402 – POW debriefs

WO 218/114 – HQ SAS Troops

WO 218/115 – HQ SAS Troops

WO 219/2342 – SAS summary

WO 219/2389 – SAS ops

Nat Archives WO 373/12/574 – DSO citation Capt Bob Walker-Brown

PREM 195/3 – WSC memo to FDR, 26 July 1943

Other Published Sources

'Obituary, Anthony Grenville-Bell', *The Times*, 28 March 2008

'Britain Adopts Paratroopers', *Western Morning News*, 17 February 1941

'Nazis Admit British Daring and Resolution', *Evening Despatch*, 17 February 1941

'British 'Chutists Scare Duce People', *Waco Times Herald*, 14 February 1941

'British Hint Paratroopers May Be At Work', *Detroit Evening Times*, 15 February 1941

'Prison for British Paratroops', *Daily Record and Mail*, 17 February 1941

'Second World War blunder that doomed 50,000 British POWs', Tom Carver, *The Observer*, 1 November 2009

'Oswald Cary-Elwes Obituary', Charles Cary-Elwes, *Old Amplefordian News*, 1994

Untitled article, *Peterborough Telegraph*, 29 October 1969

'Lieutenant Bob Walker-Brown', Obituary, *Daily Telegraph*, 17 September 2009

'The Little Corporal Who Doesn't Drink Milk', Air Forces Escape and Evasion Society, Winter 1987 Edition

Other Non-published Sources

Looking Back to the French SAS in Brittany 1944, Oswald Cary-Elwes

SAS Brigade Operational Instruction No. 9 – Operation Overlord 4 French Para Bn

SAS Brigade Operational Instruction No. 24 – HQ SAS Tps/TSB/5/G

Eric Mills, Operation Lost personal diary

Operation Lost report – Major O. A. Cary-Elwes

HQ SAS Tps TSB/6/2 – Pat Smith report

conscript-heroes.com/Art44-Brittany-Shelburne.html

ww2escapelines.co.uk/article/la-maison-dalphonse-house-alphonse

pegasusarchive.org/colossus/frames.htm

Charles Hackney, *A Soldier's Life*, unpublished manuscript and notes, Hackney family collection, undated

Selected Bibliography

Anon., *The SAS War Diary*, London: Extraordinary Editions, 2011

Tom Carver, *Where the Hell Have You Been?*, Short Books, 2009

Tanky Challenor and Alfred Draper, *SAS and the Met*, Barnsley: Leo Cooper, 1990

Marie Chamming's, *I Chose the Storm*, Victory Books, 2022

Johnny Cooper, *One of The Originals*, London: Pan Books, 1991

Virginia Cowles, *The Phantom Major*, Barnsley: Pen & Sword, 2010

Roy Farran, *Winged Dagger*, Weidenfeld Military, 1986

Monty Halls, *Escaping Hitler*, Sidgwick & Jackson (Pan Macmillan), 2017

Robert Hann, *SAS Operation Galia*, Exeter: Impress Books, 2009

Stephen Hastings, *The Drums of Memory*, Barnsley: Pen & Sword, 1994

Gerald Hough, *Desert Raids with the SAS*, Barnsley: Pen & Sword, 2021

Malcolm James (Pleydell), *Born of the Desert*, Barnsley: Frontline Books, 2015

Nicholas Jellicoe, *George Jellicoe*, Barnsley: Pen & Sword, 2021

W. B. Kennedy Shaw, *Long Range Desert Group*, Barnsley: Frontline Books, 2015

Brian Lett, *The SAS in Tuscany 1943–1945*, Barnsley: Pen & Sword, 2011

——, *An Extraordinary Italian Imprisonment*, Barnsley: Pen & Sword, 2014

Gordon Lett, *Rossano – A Valley In Flames*, Frontline Books, 2011

Damien Lewis, *SAS Ghost Patrol*, London: Quercus, 2018

——, *Shadow Raiders*, London: Quercus, 2019

——, *SAS Band of Brothers*, London: Quercus, 2020

——, *SAS Great Escapes*, London: Quercus, 2020

——, *SAS Brothers in Arms*, London: Quercus, 2022

B. H. Liddell Hart, *The Rommel Papers*, New York: Harcourt Brace & Company, 1953

David Lloyd Owen, *The Desert My Dwelling Place*, London: Cassell & Company, 1957

——, *The Long Range Desert Group*, Barnsley: Leo Cooper, 2001

Carol Mather, *When the Grass Stops Growing*, Barnsley: Pen & Sword, 1997

Gavin Mortimer, *2 SAS*, Osprey, 2023

Lawrence Paterson, *Operation Colossus,* Greenhill Books, 2020

Tom Petch, *Speed, Aggression, Surprise*, WH Allen, 2022

Malcolm Tudor, *SAS in Italy 1943–1945*, Fonthill, 2018

A. P. Wavell, *Other Men's Flowers*, London: Jonathan Cape, 1968

Ex-Lance-Corporal X, QGM, *The SAS & LRDG Roll of Honour 1941–47*, SAS-LRDG-ROH, 2016

Index

Who Dares Cares supports our Armed Forces, Emergency Services and Veterans including their families who are suffering from Post-Traumatic Stress Disorder (PTSD). They provide weekend retreat facilities where individuals and families can spend a weekend away from the daily grind and relax in fun activities, Walk, Talk and Brew Groups where they have teams of volunteers across the United Kingdom meeting with groups of people who maybe just want to clear their head and have the support of charity volunteers through participating in some gentle exercise or attending a PTSD awareness group or individual session to help provide a better understanding of what the signs and symptoms of PTSD are, how to manage symptoms and ways that families can better support in a way that is helpful to the individual. The charity recognises the importance of exercise as part of recovery and they work to encourage this and make this accessible for those who are struggling with PTSD and anxiety related issues.

The charity was founded in Hamilton, Scotland in 2016 by two former serving soldiers, Calum MacLeod (King's Own Scottish Borderers) and Colin Maclachlan (Royal Scots and Special Air Service). After Calum and Colin met, sharing their own stories, and becoming friends, bound by their own experiences, they both realised they could help so many other people, who were left 'alone' to deal with their experiences, thoughts and traumas.

They decided to build a platform that would provide help and support to individuals and their families, all in the way of Who Dares Cares.

There are a number of volunteers that support the charity, all with varying skills, from military backgrounds to nurses, who offer help and support to all of their followers in many different ways. The volunteers are just that, volunteers. They are dedicated to the charity and give up their own time and effort to support other people in so many different ways. Without them, Who Dares Cares wouldn't be able to provide the dedicated support that they can.

Anyone with a service record and a history of PTSD should apply for support, even if you're not sure you meet the criteria, each application is assessed on an individual basis. For more details please email the Who Dares Cares Support Team Mailbox on wdc@who-dares-cares.com and if you wish to learn more about this amazing charity and how you can support its vital work, please visit www.who-dares-cares.com.

It is not about suffering from PTSD,
it is about learning to live with PTSD!

AFPSAS
WHO DARES WINS

The AFPSAS (Association des familles des parachutistes S.A.S. de la France Libre), includes the Free French SAS from 3rd and 4th SAS (Special Air Service) regiments and their families.

The 'French SAS Squadron' traces its origins to 1940 when the 1ère compagnie d'infanterie de l'air (1ère CIA) was formed by Capitaine Georges Bergé. Initially operating in North-Africa, its men joined David Stirling upon the creation of the Special Air Service (SAS). They would return to the UK in 1943 and form the 3rd and the 4th SAS squadron. They would operate across Nazi-occupied territories and in particular in France. Along with the men of 1st and 2nd SAS, they would be the first forces to land on French soil on D-Day, parachuting during the night of 5/6 June 1944. The regiment would continue to operate throughout the war, undertaking daring missions in occupied territories, harassing enemy troops by organising sabotage and ambushes as well as training the local resistance. The French SAS squadrons would complete their final missions helping to liberate Holland.

The AFPSAS promotes the social well-being of the veterans from those units, as well as supporting their families. It also aims at commemorating the history and esprit de corps of the SAS regiment and passing that on to younger generations. It works with the media, researchers, historians and writers focused on the history of the SAS regiment during the Second

World War. It also supports specialised re-enacting teams and relevant museums.

The association operates out of France with a local liaison in the UK and also works in partnership with the Belgian and Dutch associations. It supports commemorative events across those countries. In November 2022, it co-sponsored the unveiling of a commemorative plaque dedicated to the 3rd and 4th SAS regiments, in London. In recent years, the AFPSAS has set-up the first freely accessible, online memorial listing of the men of the 3rd and 4th SAS regiments. It can be viewed here: https://memorial.afpsas.fr

The AFPSAS is affiliated to the *Souvenir Français au Royaume-Uni* aka the *French War Graves Commission in the UK*, a registered Charity in England and Wales, charity number 1185088.

It can be contacted at the following address: getintouch@afpsas.fr

Rebuilding lives after sight loss

Blind Veterans UK helps vision-impaired ex-Servicemen and women to rebuild their lives after sight loss. They provide rehabilitation, training, practical advice and emotional support to veterans regardless of how or when they lost their sight.

The charity was founded in London in 1915 by publisher and newspaper owner Sir Arthur Pearson. Sir Arthur, who was blind himself, recognised that the substantial numbers of veterans losing their sight during the First World War needed help. Originally called the Blinded Soldiers and Sailors Care Committee, the charity soon became known as St Dunstan's, which was the name of the first headquarters in Regent's Park, London.

Drawing on his own experience of sight loss, Sir Arthur's aim was to help veterans acquire new skills to adapt to their sight loss and live a fulfilling, independent life.

Blind Veterans UK has supported those blinded in subsequent wars and military engagements, including the Second World War and, more recently, the conflicts in the Falklands, Iraq and Afghanistan. They have two specially designed veterans' centres – in North Wales and on the South Coast of England – where beneficiaries can receive rehabilitation, respite, training and care.

In 1952 Her Majesty The Queen became Patron of St Dunstan's, after the death of their previous Patron, her father, King George VI. HM The Queen remained as Patron until December 2016 whereupon HRH The Countess of Wessex became Patron.

In 2018 HRH The Countess of Wessex unveiled a statue to commemorate the achievements of blind veterans supported since the First World War. The statue, entitled Victory Over Blindness, depicts seven blinded First World War soldiers leading one another away from the battlefield with their hand on the shoulder of the man in front. It stands proudly outside Manchester Piccadilly station as the only permanent memorial to the injured of that conflict.

In 2022 Blind Veterans UK updated their Articles of Association to be able to provide their specialist vision-rehabilitation support to those affected by war-like activity, including terrorist activities. As a consequence, they are now able to support the people of Ukraine by offering their expertise to those who have sustained blindness through war-like activity.

Anyone with a service record and a vision impairment should apply for support, even if you're not sure you meet the criteria, each application is assessed on an individual basis. For more details please call the support team on 0800 389 7979 and if you wish to learn more about this amazing charity and how you can support its vital work, please visit www.blindveterans.org.uk